The Societal Codification
of Korean English

Bloomsbury Advances in World Englishes

Series Editor:
Alexander Onysko, University of Klagenfurt, Austria

Advisory Board:
Umberto Ansaldo (Curtin University, Australia) C. Suzanne Hilgendorf (Simon Fraser University, Canada)
Allan James (University of Klagenfurt, Austria)
Andrew Kirkpatrick (Griffith University, Australia)
Lisa Lim (Curtin University, Australia)
Christiane Meierkord (University of Bochum, Germany)
Salikoko Mufwene (University of Chicago, USA)
Alastair Pennycook (University of Technology Sydney, Australia)
Mario Saraceni (University of Portsmouth, UK)
Philip Seargeant (The Open University, UK)
Peter Siemund (University of Hamburg, Germany)
Bertus van Rooy (University of Amsterdam, The Netherlands)
Lionel Wee (National University of Singapore, Singapore)

Capturing the intense interest in research on Englishes worldwide, Bloomsbury Advances in World Englishes promotes approaches to the complexities of world Englishes from a multitude of linguistic perspectives. Responding to recent trends in socio-cognitive, critical sociolinguistic, contact linguistic and communication-based research, books in this series investigate the interactions of Englishes with other languages and add new theoretical, methodological and applied perspectives to the field.

Bloomsbury Advances in World Englishes adopts an inclusive understanding of world Englishes and their interactions, which considers all dialects of English, Englishes in multilingual constellations, English-based pidgins and creoles, learner Englishes and the global spread of English as significant manifestations of Englishes in the world. Encouraging methodological and theoretical pluralism, encompassing sociolinguistics, cognitive and psycholinguistics, anthropological linguistics, historical linguistics, pragmatics, literary-linguistics and discourse analysis, this series offers an innovative insight into the manifold instantiations and usages of Englishes in the world.

Titles in the Series:
Research Developments in World Englishes (inaugural volume)
Edited by Alexander Onysko

Metaphor in Language and Culture Across World Englishes
Edited by Marcus Callies and Marta Degani

The Societal Codification of Korean English
Alex Baratta

The Societal Codification of Korean English

Alex Baratta

BLOOMSBURY ACADEMIC
LONDON • NEW YORK • OXFORD • NEW DELHI • SYDNEY

BLOOMSBURY ACADEMIC
Bloomsbury Publishing Plc
50 Bedford Square, London, WC1B 3DP, UK
1385 Broadway, New York, NY 10018, USA
29 Earlsfort Terrace, Dublin 2, Ireland

BLOOMSBURY, BLOOMSBURY ACADEMIC and the Diana logo are trademarks
of Bloomsbury Publishing Plc

First published in Great Britain 2022
This paperback edition published 2023

Copyright © Alex Baratta, 2022

Alex Baratta has asserted his right under the Copyright, Designs and
Patents Act, 1988, to be identified as Author of this work.

For legal purposes the Acknowledgements on p. vii constitute an extension
of this copyright page.

Series design by Rebecca Heselton

All rights reserved. No part of this publication may be reproduced or transmitted
in any form or by any means, electronic or mechanical, including photocopying,
recording, or any information storage or retrieval system, without prior
permission in writing from the publishers.

Bloomsbury Publishing Plc does not have any control over, or responsibility for, any
third-party websites referred to or in this book. All internet addresses given in this
book were correct at the time of going to press. The author and publisher regret any
inconvenience caused if addresses have changed or sites have ceased to exist,
but can accept no responsibility for any such changes.

A catalogue record for this book is available from the British Library.

Library of Congress Cataloging-in-Publication Data

Names: Baratta, Alex, author.
Title: The societal codification of Korean English / Alex Baratta.
Description: London; New York: Bloomsbury Academic, 2021. |
Series: Bloomsbury advances in world Englishes |
Includes bibliographical references and index. |
Identifiers: LCCN 2021025491 (print) | LCCN 2021025492 (ebook) |
ISBN 9781350188556 (hardback) | ISBN 9781350188563 (ebook) |
ISBN 9781350188570 (epub)
Subjects: LCSH: English language–Korea (South) | English
language–Dialects–Korea (South) | English language–Foreign elements–Korean.
Classification: LCC PE3502.K6 B37 2021 (print) |
LCC PE3502.K6 (ebook) | DDC 427/.9519–dc23/eng/20210930
LC record available at https://lccn.loc.gov/2021025491
LC ebook record available at https://lccn.loc.gov/2021025492

ISBN: HB: 978-1-3501-8855-6
PB: 978-1-3501-8908-9
ePDF: 978-1-3501-8856-3
eBook: 978-1-3501-8857-0

Series: Bloomsbury Advances in World Englishes

Typeset by Deanta Global Publishing Services, Chennai, India

To find out more about our authors and books visit www.bloomsbury.com and
sign up for our newsletters.

Contents

List of Illustrations — vi

1 Introduction — 1
2 A discussion of four key topics — 23
3 Societal codification — 55
4 The lexical and grammatical aspects of Korean English — 83
5 Media English in Korea — 155
6 Korean English in the EFL classroom — 177
Conclusion — 191

References — 195
Index — 215

Illustrations

Figures

1	A previous model being applied here to the discussion of societal codification	70
2	Poster as part of societal codification of Korean English	71
3	Societal codification via a mass-produced soft drink	74
4	Societal codification via a public sign at an amusement park	103

Tables

1	Choi's Table of Konglish	131
2	Choi's List of Common Konglish Expressions	132
3	Priz Website on Konglish	144
4	Priz Examples of Fabricated Phrases	145
5	Priz Examples of Abbreviated Expressions	145
6	Priz Samples of Vocabulary	146
7	Sydney to Seoul: Examples of Vocabulary	149
8	How to Study Korean Samples of Vocabulary	152

1

Introduction

Type the word 'Englishes' into a Word document, as I have just done, and it is still, stubbornly, coming up as an error. For many reading this book, we already know that this word is anything but an error. Rather, it is a wholly appropriate term that captures the diversity of the English language in all its forms around the world. This is something that a singular reference alone can never do. In fact, such a reference might even suggest a one-size-fits-all approach to a language that will never be one size for all. Indeed, English as we know it has expanded its influence to the point that its international spread – from Hollywood movies to CNN to bilingual road signs in Tokyo – is largely taken for granted. Perhaps we expect to see and/or hear English in some form, whether on holiday in Spain or at a business conference in Nairobi. I do not seek to present a detailed picture regarding the influence and spread of the English language, however, as this has been well documented already (Kachru, 1982; Crystal, 2008; Mesthrie and Bhatt, 2008). Instead, I use this linguistic spread as the springboard from which to then delve into a full discussion of the variety of English as used in Korea. This allows for a spotlight on one particular variety of English, while also functioning as a stand-in for other varieties of English which do not always get the respect and recognition they deserve. This chapter thus presents an overview of the relevant topics in Chapters 2 and 3, which serve to set the scene for the later discussion of Korean English in Chapter 4.

Specifically, Chapter 2 discusses the following topics: the terms used to refer to Englishes within the expanding circle, often involving blended nomenclatures such as Chinglish; errors versus innovations; and the distinctions made in terms of native versus non-native speakers of English. Chapter 3 discusses a way to conceptualize linguistic codification beyond more 'traditional' means, such as government-backed grammar books and dictionaries, thus providing an in-depth focus centred on this important topic, and how it ultimately relates to the discussions in Chapters 4 and 5, concerning the ways in which Korean

English needs to be understood as established and ultimately reinforced by its speakers.

The purpose of covering these topics that are understood already to an audience who are knowledgeable regarding World Englishes, such as educators and linguists, is as follows. First, the audience is not assumed to be exclusively made up of those with a background knowledge of the relevant topics, such as World Englishes, let alone having research backgrounds in this area. Therefore, some broad background on the relevant topics which pertain to the overall focus on Korean English is necessary, and is presented systematically in Chapter 2. Ideally, it is hoped that some of the audience may well include those with an interest in Korean culture, or even English teachers in Korea who may be familiar with Koreans' use of English, but are otherwise unaware of the theoretical discussion behind this.

Second, the topics covered in Chapter 2 combine to provide a thorough grounding to help inform and locate the overall purpose for this book's content: to argue that Korean English, not only like other expanding circle Englishes but also as with language overall, is legitimate, established and in everyday use, but largely without the need for such establishment to be provided by more 'traditional' means. That is, the people who use this variety of English are responsible for perpetuating its use within society, and in turn establishing it as a recognized variety of English. As I will explain, expanding circle Englishes, which Korean English clearly is, do not necessarily receive their due recognition, despite their use in society. As such, it is time to address this, both as a gap in knowledge regarding these varieties' role in society and to address what for some is a perceived lack of legitimacy (Kachru, 2006; Ahn, 2014; Galloway and Rose, 2015; Rüdiger, 2019).

What's in a name? Korean English versus Konglish

Chapter 2 will take up the discussion in more detail than the summaries presented here, but it is very important to begin with an unpacking of the most relevant term of all for this book: *Korean English*. Some may disagree with this term in fact, being more familiar with the term *Konglish* instead, which, I concede, is indeed commonly used to describe the variety of English associated with Korea (Kent, 1999; Song, 2016; Rüdiger, 2018). However, I object to the latter term for two reasons.

First, blended nomenclatures arguably do not lead to language varieties being taken particularly seriously. Pinkham's (2000) use of the term *Chinglish*, used to describe translation errors from Mandarin to English on public signs in China, has now become somewhat synonymous with errors in general. From my experience of teaching large numbers of Chinese graduate students, their conceptualization of the term goes far beyond English mistranslations on Chinese public signs and extends to their own English, notably errors made within their academic writing in English. While anecdotal, the negative perceptions of the term *Chinglish* are not merely based on my own assertions. He and Li (2009: 71) refer to the term as reflecting a 'social stigma' and argue instead for an established variety of English in China – China English – which serves as the counterpart for Korean English. Given the stigma attached to the term *Chinglish*, I believe that the terms used to refer to English varieties should avoid blended nomenclatures which incorporate *-ish*. This is not a suffix as such, but instead forms part of the word *English*, of course. Nonetheless, it is conceivable that blended terms might suggest the use of *-ish* as a suffix per se, with the semantic implications for this informal suffix essentially reflecting 'to some extent' (*He's tallish, let's meet at 3ish*, and so on). Thus, Konglish, for some, refers to a variety of English which is not quite one or the other perhaps, not somehow 'fully formed'. But such an assertion would fly in the face of a variety of English which is otherwise used by Koreans – and non-Koreans – with a fully functioning use of vocabulary and grammar – Korean English. To thus demote it to a blended term is not accurate, given the connotations of such terms. This is not about political correctness but *linguistic* correctness.

Second, the term *Korean English* connotes a more established variety of English. This is agreed with by Ahn (2014), who in fact refers to Konglish as reflecting changes in Korean due to contact with English, and Korean English as instead reflecting a nativization of the English language (Shim, 1999; Seong and Lee, 2008). I do not suggest, of course, that those who use the term *Konglish* do so scornfully, regarding it as a variety of English which is 'defective' in some way. I do in fact acknowledge that the term can be used by those who otherwise regard this variety with complete respect, seeing Konglish as an appropriate term for a legitimate variety of English. Korean English, however, goes further in terms of acknowledging linguistic legitimacy and as such, it will be the term used throughout this book, with references to Konglish only made based on reflecting other individuals' use of this word.

Another concession concerns the work of Song (2016), who argues against the label of 'X English' unless a variety is indeed a New English. Song argues that Korean English, as a *Learner English*, is thus not qualified to be given this title and, instead, should be referred to as 'English in Korea'. Schneider (2007) concurs, arguing for a need to distinguish between the two types of English. Song takes on the evidence that has been presented for the existence of Korean English, the same evidence that will be presented in this book. For example, evidence of Korean English in terms of grammatical constructions codified in Korean high school EFL textbooks (Shim, 1999) is claimed to be an insufficient benchmark for the existence of Korean English. Bruthiaux (2003: 171) agrees, arguing against declaring a variety of English to be a new variety simply on the basis of it being 'taught extensively as a foreign language but spoken by a small minority and rarely or never for purposes of internal communication'.

A corpus-based study by Hadikin (2014) is also held up as insufficient evidence for Korean English, in that his sample of seventy Korean-English bilinguals, largely university students perhaps, is not deemed to be sufficient in reflecting a broader societal use of English in Korea. Song's response overall to these studies, and perhaps others, is that a more representative sample is needed of speakers from all walks of life – and education levels – in order to truly appreciate the ways in which Koreans use English, and also how it is used in different contexts of communication.

In response to what is clearly a robust argument against the existence of Korean English, I make the following points. First, within the expanding circle in particular, there is evidence of disagreement as to the establishment, or not, of English varieties. Thus, while authors agree that China English is indeed a New English (He and Li, 2009), there are those who do not (Fang, 2020). Other authors indeed argue that English has become nativized within Eastern cultures, such as Japan (McKenzie, 2008) and Korea (Ahn, 2014). Song (2016), however, rejects the work of Ahn regarding Korean English as a New English, largely on the basis of her use of the term without, once again, it having been established as a new variety; indeed, most of her participants only know of the term *Konglish*. As Rüdiger (2019) makes clear, however, Song's view excludes the outer-circle countries from ownership of the English language. Moreover, we might also consider current movements, notably the ways in which 'the world Englishes paradigm has pushed to decolonize the academic study of the English language' (Westphal, 2021: 1). This does not mean that we should automatically assign the label of 'Korean English' to the variety used by Koreans. Instead, we need to address perceptions of expanding circle Englishes as somehow not fully fledged varieties, and recognize them as varieties in their own right based on evidence for their widespread use and codification of such within society. The book will indeed present evidence for both.

However, amid such disagreement, perhaps largely reflective of the criteria Song (2016) puts forward, it is important to address two points. First, even outside of a large-scale study on a country's use of a foreign language, valuable though that would be, we cannot ignore the ways in which a language – here, English – has developed into a distinct form. To put it another way, are there features of English as used by Koreans that are predictable, in terms of grammar and vocabulary? There clearly are, and much will be said of this in Chapter 4. This might not be sufficient for some to characterize a variety of English as a New English; however, it also means that the language has developed to a point that it is distinctive enough to no longer be a carbon copy of an inner-circle variety; it is used by sufficient numbers of people in society that its distinctions are predictable; its features are not random; and overall, and as I will discuss in Chapter 3, we need to consider linguistic codification as ultimately being in the hands of the people, and not necessarily governments and publishing houses. While Song (2016) therefore feels that it is simply too premature to label English in Korea as Korean English, we should also consider Schneider's (2014: 227) comment, that it is ideal to 'detect and trace . . . structural innovations as early as possible', and not do so retrospectively once codification has taken place. On the other hand, and as I will argue, codification of Korean English has taken place, and continues to do so, via the people who use it and the extensive use of various media in Korea – Chapter 3 will develop this argument in detail.

I therefore argue that the English language has developed in Korea to the extent that we can reveal solid examples as to how Koreans do indeed use this variety and, as such, using the nomenclature of Korean English is not felt to be a premature judgement. While the use of a large-scale sociolinguistic study as Song (2016) argues for would indeed generate much useful data and insights, we should not ignore the fact that Koreans use English and have made it their own. Though this does not apply to Korea as a whole perhaps, and the older generation more so might be less proficient in English (Baratta, 2019a), English is indeed used in Korea on a wider scale than the small sample within Hadikin's study would suggest.

The thrust of my argument is that we need to reconceptualize codification from a more societal perspective. First, people's use of a language is the first step towards codification (see Chapter 3 for a further discussion). This would include not merely conversations using the English language in Korea, but also uses of English beyond this. In Chapter 5, for example, I discuss the use of English within Korean media, such as TV and print ads. Song (1998) argues against this use of English, however, as evidence of a New English per se, in that media use of English is, as with previous examples, insufficient; instead, we need evidence of English use in home, school and work. Haarmann (1986) refers to such media use as an example of 'impersonal bilingualism', referring to the use of English 'for appealing to the public's positive feelings, not for practical communication' (Song, 2016: 60).

Nonetheless, Lee (2020: 600) points out that given the spread of English in Korea, there is in fact evidence for more everyday use of this language, notably in school settings. Lee references prestigious high schools in particular, 'which are supposed to produce the "cream of the crop" in Korea'. One such example is the Korean Minjok Leadership Academy (KMLA), which adopts an 'English-Only' policy. KMLA requires students to speak only English from the beginning to the end of each school day from Monday to Saturday, with teachers also following this directive. While standard inner-circle English is perhaps the variety focused on, it is likely that students will not always default to this variety within all their communication, perhaps – unintentional though it might be – following patterns associated with Korean English instead. Korean English is perhaps more likely to be used for the casual conversations that students engage in at this school, for which English is once again the expected language, not Korean.

This book will develop my arguments against Song's claims, in part by suggesting that we need to reconsider the concept of Korean English as not a monolithic variety in the first instance, but as a series of varieties which would include both English conversation and media use, for example. Both of these categories can be subdivided further, with 'conversation' involving a Korean using English to give directions to a tourist, and using the language to communicate to another Korean. Though anecdotal, my experience teaching English at an English summer camp in Korea enabled me to get a window into this latter use. I had noticed that of the ten students I taught, their parents would write to them while they were at the camp, using English as the language of communication. I did not read their letters of course, so cannot know if they featured specific aspects of one English or another. Perhaps the parents were attempting to use standard (American) English. Nonetheless, this offers a glimpse into how Koreans can use English with each other, and while the context here is rather obvious (i.e. a parent wants to reinforce with his/her child the language that the child is studying at a summer camp), it still represents what might be a societal usage that takes place on a wider scale.

In summary, my brief defence here regarding my use of the term *Korean English*, which will be expanded upon of course, will be to some readers unconvincing, perhaps even naïve. However, I respond to this with the main point of the book, which is to provide a focus on the myriad ways that English is being used in Korea by Koreans, which suggests that English is more widespread in Korea than some of the previous studies (e.g. Hadikin, 2014) suggest. From here, I discuss the ways in which Korean English has been codified, in a manner that requires us, partly at least, to reconceptualize this key term.

The three circles of English

Korean English belongs to the expanding circle of English, one of three circles proposed by Kachru (1985). Here, Kachru argues for the inner circle as reflecting Englishes which are the native and dominant languages of specific countries – the United Kingdom, the United States, Canada, Ireland, Australia and New Zealand. The outer circle represents countries in which English may also be dominant, and even have official language status (e.g. India), but countries in which English is dominant due to a colonial past. Beyond India, other examples would include Nigerian English, Singaporean English and Pakistani English. The expanding circle includes Englishes which are used in countries which do not otherwise have a colonial history of English as the outer circle does, but countries in which English has a prominent presence and role, such as Japan, China and, of course, Korea.

It is notable that it is often the expanding circle of Englishes that are referred to with blended names, such as Chinglish, Konglish, Japlish. There is some crossover, of course, in that the outer-circle variety in Singapore is referred to as Singlish, though it does have a more official title – Colloquial Singaporean English (Alsagoff and Ho, 1998). Likewise, Indian English is sometimes perhaps (mis)understood with the term *Hinglish*, though it could be argued that this latter term is more reflective of code-mixing between English and Hindi (Chand, 2016), whereas Indian English – like Korean English – would involve a more systematic use of language, one that is less random than the immediate context of individuals' use of code-mixing. Nonetheless, to use blended terms largely for the expanding circle suggests that these varieties are somehow not quite 'there' yet, have yet to sort themselves out and, indeed, are not established. This offers another rationale to change the terms used and, in doing so, make a small, yet important step in the right direction.

A further point to make regarding the use of blended nomenclatures for outer-circle Englishes, such as Hinglish and Singlish, is that these terms might nonetheless connote a degree more respect, or less negativity, solely on the basis that they are used in countries in which English has a longer history and is understood to be more established. Such establishment is seen with these varieties of English being used in education, media and government (Song, 2016). Thus, while I argue that a nomenclature that involves 'a country name plus English' allows for more recognition, status and legitimacy, outer-circle varieties, as compared with the expanding circle, already have such status comparatively-speaking. However, the focus on Korean English can ideally help to reconsider ideas regarding its status, or lack thereof, and instead approach it as a recognized variety.

The terminology used to describe Englishes around the world

There are many terms already in use to describe the global spread of the English language, such as *Glocal English, English as a Lingua Franca, International English, International Englishes* and *New Englishes*, among several others. Each term has its merits, based on differing conceptualizations of Englishes, such as the use of an English that can be understood internationally when often the individuals using it are not native speakers, hence *English as a Lingua Franca*. Likewise, Glocal English addresses the international function of English both across borders and in various contexts of communication, while also addressing its important function for the speakers when using it *intra*nationally. I have, however, argued for the use of an otherwise already existing term, World Englishes (Baratta, 2019a: 11), and this is the term I use throughout this book. My rationale for this term as used here, and in my previous book, is based on the following two points.

First, by using the term inclusively, it means that inner-circle Englishes are not, implicitly at least, being held up as the linguistic standard from which all others deviate and must try to emulate, with deviations being understood as deficit. Kachru's (1991) work within 'liberation linguistics' has arguably led to the outer-circle Englishes being placed on a par with the inner-circle varieties. However, public attitudes towards non-inner-circle Englishes (NICE) can sometimes still regard them in low esteem, with inner-circle standard regarded as *the* standard. An example of this is reflected with Singapore's Speak Good English campaign, which essentially means avoiding Singlish in favour of Standard Singaporean English (itself modelled on British English), a position also supported by the National University of Singapore which promotes the use of 'correct' English, part of the Promotion of Standard English (PROSE). Wee (2002) regards the government's position on this as prejudicial; and while it would be wrong to ignore the power afforded to standard inner-circle English as a means to pass IELTS/TOEFL exams, as well as university entrance exams and its role in academic writing, it would also be wrong to downgrade a variety of English that serves its speakers quite well in, broadly speaking, non-academic/professional contexts.

Second, by using the term *World Englishes* in this more inclusive manner, it also addresses the simple fact that each variety of English is indeed 'worldly' – either used internationally per se for myriad communicative purposes and/or used among smaller communities in more local settings. The unifying factor, however, is that by definition, each and every variety is being used in a different setting at any given moment, which can include a café in downtown Accra, an international linguistics conference in Durban, university students chatting in Singapore and so on – I'm sure many readers can provide their own examples. Seen in this manner, each variety of English, given its spread across the world, *is* a world English. Turner (1984) in fact suggested such an approach some time ago, arguing for Australian English to be treated as a world language. The implication of this is that inner-circle varieties should be incorporated into the world paradigm on equal footing along with all others, as opposed to being the starting point.

Linguistic errors versus innovations

One of the main points of discussion regarding World Englishes is the need to make a clear distinction between an error and an innovation. Often, standard inner-circle English is seen as the linguistic blueprint, certainly in educational contexts, and any uses of English that do not reflect the inner circle are sometimes regarded as 'wrong' (Bamgbose, 1998; Görlach, 2002; Huddart, 2014; Jee, 2016; Meriläinen, 2017). Indeed, 'Standard American English' is the intended referent in advertisements for American English teaching (Strother, 2015). However, even if a feature of an English variety begins life as a pure error (as I use the term), once its usage gets a foothold in society and it starts to be used more and more, then at this point its origins need not matter – it has become part of a speech community's language. Gut (2011) discusses 'transfer errors' and 'learner errors' (page 102) as the cause for what will eventually become innovations, fixed forms of language. Gut explains how cross-linguistic influence (CLI) can manifest itself, involving direct borrowings or loans, mixed structures and hypercorrection, among other examples. van Rooy (2011) further explains how features which may have originated as errors have become systematic and accepted within Black South African English, with systematicity and acceptance seen as factors crucial to the status of 'innovation'. van Rooy also discusses how the process from error to innovation might be largely the same in both Learner and New Englishes, but with the latter variety, the suggested use of English on a regular basis ensures innovation, in that the new features 'become entrenched in the communicative repertoires of those communities' (page 205). While the use of English in Korea does not necessarily follow the use within, say, India, I will show, as mentioned, how it is nonetheless used by Koreans to the extent that English – vocabulary and grammar – has become 'Koreanized'. Of note also is the fact that innovations are often recognized as innovations after the fact, with the bridge between 'new use of English' and 'established use of English' often lost to time.

Any negative attitudes towards NICE, specifically in terms of declaring their usage as involving errors, can also be found in the inner circle. Recently, a school in the West Midlands in England banned the use of non-standard British English which reflected the local dialect, if not a sociolect used by the students. Some of the banned expressions included *they was* for *they were*; *I day* instead of *I didn't*; and *I cor do that* instead of *I can't do that*. These expressions, and others, were displayed in the school on a poster, as an example of how not to use language in school-based work. The banned uses of English are not wrong of course, but to be fair, the poster did acknowledge a time and place for such non-standard uses. The phrases and use of grammar that were targeted represent, as do all non-standard varieties, a systematic and predictable use of language, but use that merely differs from the standard. Indeed, if such uses were based on an otherwise haphazard and random use of language among students, then how could their language even be tabulated in the first instance? Nonetheless, systematicity is no match sometimes for public attitudes. Snell (2013) has covered this in detail regarding inner-circle dialects of school children, notably in the Teeside area of England in the Northeast. Constructions such as *give it us*, for *give it to me*, are common, but so is the children's ability to code-switch, using the latter construction for classroom talk with teachers present, and the former with their friends on the playground.

From this very brief look at issues tied to inner-circle dialects, it is clear that they can be seen as both a marker of solidarity and yet a marker of 'bad English', or certainly negative public attitudes (Milroy and Milroy, 1999). A better approach would be to treat the standard and the non-standard alike as equal, which, linguistically speaking, they already are. This is, therefore, an issue within the inner circle also and not just beyond it. There is a need to educate children that different contexts simply require different uses of the English language (or any language for that matter), so they can come away with an increased awareness and appreciation for both their home language and the standard. It is possible that some of the children from the West Midlands school, and potentially their parents, use the banned phrases at home, as part of their home language. If so, then this can help explain why the suggestion that such language is inappropriate for educational contexts can cause offence, as it did based on some of the parents' responses who were interviewed in a BBC news report.

Anecdotally, I have also heard from two Pakistani individuals the expression *sorry to cut you*, meaning *sorry to cut you off* (i.e. *sorry to interrupt you*). Two speakers' use of a given expression cannot of course even begin to speak for an entire nation, but it is a start in initiating a conversation as to whether the 'missing' preposition in the previous expression reflects a pure error or indeed, represents a standard aspect of a particular variety of English. Likewise, my Chinese students without exception use the term *researches* (e.g. *there have been many researches*), when (standard) inner-circle English would collectively treat this word as a non-count noun (e.g. *there has been much research*). However, linguistic 'strength in numbers' can help to equate to innovations and from here, establishment (Bamgbose, 1998; van der Walt and van Rooy, 2002; Honna, 2008). While it is premature to declare *researches* a feature of China English, I certainly don't feel qualified to write it off as an error either.

On a final note, if we revisit the word *Englishes*, we can see how innovations sometimes come to be. The more pertinent aspect is that this word is widely used, if not exclusively used, within the field of Linguistics and TEFL. I don't personally know of anyone within such pedagogic areas who would consider the term *Englishes* 'wrong', 'bad grammar' or the like, and who would flag its usage within an academic paper. As long as the word is being used to refer to the varieties of the English language in the world then its use is legitimate, even if it's a somewhat esoteric use tied mainly to education and research contexts, and not the public at large. The fact that spell and grammar check does not recognize *Englishes* helps to illustrate the larger discussion within this book on codification. Most of us perhaps rely on spell and grammar check to ensure our language is accurate, and yet, some of the directives offered are *not* accurate (e.g. spell check's insistence on flagging use of passive voice, when this is otherwise grammatically well-constructed). Simply put, who decides what is or is not an error?

As I will argue, codification is largely in the hands of society (Bamgbose, 1998; Milroy and Milroy, 1999; Seidlhofer, 2001; Mauranen, 2012; Baratta, 2019a), and not in the hands of a relative (but often powerful) minority who prescribe grammatical standards for the masses. Kruger and van Rooy (2017) cite the example of published written texts which can act as a vehicle for innovations becoming conventionalized; this has relevance for my later discussion on the use of English by Korean authors in English-language newspapers and within English-medium academic journals. This is not to suggest that standards are not needed, far from it. Rather, the point is that there is a time and a place for all varieties of a given language. This is one of the bedrocks of this book and a means to argue that standard British English has a time and place, but so does Korean English – and all varieties in between. And with regard to the word *Englishes*, it might well be that its usage is largely tied to Linguistics and thus, it could be considered as reflecting a technical register. That the word might not be used in widespread society, however, does not mean linguists have got it wrong. Moreover, if a given word and/or grammatical feature is used within society on a larger scale, then we must also see this as legitimate. Do we need to wait for trusted sources to give society the go-ahead to use a language that is already in use? We do not.

Native and non-native speakers

There is active debate about what constitutes a native speaker of a language (Trudgill, 1995; Medgyes, 2001; Seidlhofer, 2001; Higgins, 2003; Cook, 2005). While this will be covered in greater detail in Chapter 2, one of the main points to make is that being considered a native speaker of English (for now, someone whose first language is an inner-circle variety) should not necessarily give such an individual the status of 'final arbiter' of the language (Phillipson, 1992: 194). Kachru (1998) also discusses functional nativeness, which refers to the various contexts in which a language functions within a societal setting. In the case of English in a non-inner-circle country, its functions may indeed be very widespread, and tied to media, government and the economy. The implication of this is that the speakers have made English their own and in concurrence with Bamgbose (1998) the standards for determining the 'correctness' of the features should not be based on external (e.g. native speaker) criteria, but internal assessment from those who have appropriated English for their own use.

With regard to teaching English, there is a responsibility for the teacher, whether native or non-native, to teach the variety that is deemed most appropriate for the students; this might in fact be decided already by the school's administration, if not the country's government, and propagated by the textbooks used (a link to codification, albeit more in a 'traditional' sense). However, it is important that teachers, regardless of their national origin and first language, do not give students the impression that English is singular and, instead, adopt a pedagogic approach that incorporates NICE (Alptekin, 2002; Kirkpatrick, 2006; He and Zhang, 2010; Mahboob, 2014; Ates, Eslami and Wright, 2015; Dinh, 2017; Hino, 2017). At Chukyo University in Japan, the School of World Englishes seeks to prepare students for their future use of English, for example, with one of its goals indeed focused on cross-cultural understanding, which is inherent in the use of a global language.

Many students already understand the plurality of English perhaps, especially if they use a NICE at home. But they need to know that their English is a linguistic equal to standard inner circle (Baratta, 2019a). Again, this is not to deny the power that standard inner-circle English has, and it serves an important function (Prodromou, 2006), but we must be clear that the power it has is not inherent. Rather, it is societies, having decided what the standard will be, who then bequeath power to such varieties of language, with subsequent power to pass IELTS exams, which then determines if students are accepted to university, which can have a knock-on effect of whether or not they get their prized career. The linguistic reality is far different – there is nothing inherent in language, be it accent, grammatical structure or word usage. The linguistic reality is admittedly no match for societal reality at times, but it needs to be discussed in an English class which is, after all, linguistics-based. This suggested societal reality pertains to the attitudes, values and judgements that are placed on various forms of language and in turn the speaker. This can include judgements made of regional accents in the UK, such as the Liverpool and Glasgow varieties (see Coupland and Bishop, 2007), non-standard inner-circle English, such as Ebonics (Haddix, 2012); or more relevant to this discussion, non-inner-circle Englishes.

Quirk (1990) took the view that to promote such varieties of English would weaken the need for standards, in this case standard inner circle. Quirk explained that 'the mass of ordinary native-English speakers have never lost their respect for Standard English, and it needs to be understood abroad too . . . that Standard English is alive and well, its existence and its value alike clearly recognized' (page 10). Quirk goes on to address Kachru's (1991) view, which holds that attempting to promote a standard within all three circles ignores the need for the sociolinguistic realities outside inner-circle countries. This suggested linguistic relativism is addressed by Quirk as subsequently leading to situations in which a non-inner-circle variety of English would not fare well in certain contexts, such as the workplace, and presumably within the inner circle itself. Quirk (1990: 10) points to the 'harsher but more realistic judgement of those with authority to employ or promote them' (i.e. the non-native speaker). The workplace is indeed a relevant context in which speaking the 'wrong language' can have implications, such as teaching (Archangeli et al., 2010; Garner, 2013; Baratta, 2017), finance (Moore et al., 2016) and library work (Lippi-Green, 1997).

However, this does not mean that the linguistic reality involving varieties of English spoken by millions of people around the world can be ignored. Indeed, there is a time when standard inner-circle English is the preferred model, and times when it might not be. The key point is that students need to be taught the importance of context – and EFL teachers need to make them aware of this – in order to determine what 'correct' English might involve at a given moment. Wholesale advocation for one variety or the other is impractical, but an understanding of different varieties of English is a more realistic approach. Moreover, we cannot assume a native speaker model as the starting point when native speakers themselves may well reside outside their country of origin. In cases such as this, should native speakers assume that a standard variety is sufficient, or might they find that learning a few words of a different variety of English, such as Ghanaian English, would be entirely necessary – necessary for better communication, but also a way to truly engage with the locals.

A final point to make is that for speakers of NICE, are they not native speakers? I speak fluent American English, but as I live in England I can also get by in British English. Thus, I shop for *aubergine*, not *eggplant*, and fill the car with *petrol*, not *gas*. Is knowing the British words and occasional grammatical differences (e.g. *write to me*, not *write me*) enough to declare myself 'fluent'? I don't speak with an English accent, so this might be held against me. But if I am otherwise fluent in terms of the vocabulary and occasional grammatical differences, would this not be sufficient? It is sufficient for everyday life, but it seems that inner-circle speakers might be granted the automatic status of fluent speaker of *any* inner-circle variety solely on the basis that they speak an inner-circle variety in the first instance, albeit the standard form more so. In other words, the (standard) inner-circle varieties in toto have been regarded as the standard for some time (Meriläinen, 2017), but this does not change the fact that a speaker of, say, Indian English, is nonetheless a native speaker of that variety; I myself am not.

Nelson (2008) discusses intelligibility among English speakers, offering examples ranging from Prince Charles's disdain for American English influence, to momentary misunderstandings involving American and Australian English.

Where such 'difference' exists, at least in the second example in which the Australian word for a food item was not understood (*capsicum* for US *bell pepper*), there might be a degree of playful banter. Again, once the English in question pertains to outside the inner circle, there is the potential for its difference from inner-circle varieties to be met more negatively. Nelson (2008) in fact suggests that when a national inner-circle standard is used, more so in professional contexts, communication is perhaps largely guaranteed among two different inner-circle speakers. But outside of this context, involving, say, dialect, 'deviations abound' (page 303), and this would apply to non-inner-circle Englishes. However, for the speakers of a given variety of English, who use this variety among themselves, there should be little cause for communication difficulties – in this case, the vocabulary, for example, associated with Korean English.

And once again, rather than assume a scenario involving Koreans having to adjust to native speakers, why can't the opposite be the case? In the times I have visited Korea since 1995 when I first arrived, I have indeed noticed a shift in terms of how I am expected to communicate with Koreans. The expectation, judging by the sheer number of Koreans who will speak to me in Korean (e.g. a stranger asking me for directions, or the price of a toy my daughter was playing with) suggests that their attitude is 'if you are here, perhaps you might speak Korean'. Korean is not Korean English of course, but the larger issue is that when visiting Korea, it is not unreasonable to expect that Korean English (if not Korean on occasion) might be deployed by the speakers of this variety. It's their turf.

Seen from this more egalitarian perspective, a speaker who is indeed fluent in a NICE is, by definition, a native speaker. This is not to suggest that I could not learn Indian English even though I am not Indian, and an Indian could equally learn standard American English (and even some non-standard varieties, such as Ebonics). But however we conceptualize 'native speaker' of English, my argument is that inner-circle English speakers should not be seen as the overall caretakers of English. There is, in fact, evidence that inner-circle English speakers are having to learn NICE.

In 2012, Eddie Wrenn writing for the Daily Mail reported on British diplomats learning more local forms of Indian English, here referred to as Hinglish. As the article states, and as I mentioned earlier, Hinglish is referring to the mixing of English and Hindi, but in the process, British diplomats are having to go beyond English as this is not seen as sufficient for conducting business transactions when posted to India. By extension, learning Indian English and its use of grammar (e.g. *I am having a house* – see van Rooy, 2014) and vocabulary (e.g. *prepone*) is perhaps even more essential, due to the predictable nature of established varieties of language which should, theoretically, be easier to acquire (and perhaps prove easier for British diplomats to learn than Hindi or Gujarati). Communities and countries around the world have made English their own, infusing it with elements of pre-existing languages in their country in terms of grammar and vocabulary, as well of course as exporting their languages to inner-circle Englishes in the first instance (e.g. the Hindi origins of the word *pyjamas*, as but one of many more examples).

Why focus on Korean English?

There are several reasons why I have chosen to focus on the variety of English as used in, and associated with, the Republic of Korea (to clarify, the focus is indeed on South Korea, as I have no specific information on the use of English in North Korea).

First, on a personal level, I lived in Korea from 1995 to 1998, first while serving in the US Army and upon my discharge, working as an English teacher in the Seoul area (in the city of Gwacheon). I had begun teaching English to Korean children and businessmen while in the army and after my military discharge, I was employed as an English teacher at an English academy (known as a *hagwon*). I had started to learn Korean before returning there as a civilian teacher, and in time I was able to improve my speaking skills (but nowhere near the level of fluency). It was during my time in Korea that not only did I pick up my Korean skills, learning Korean that went beyond the textbook, but I also acquired quite a few words of what was introduced to me as *Konglish*. Interestingly, some of the vocabulary used is not English-based at all, such as Koreans' use of the word *arbeit*, in German, this means 'work', but in Korea it refers to a part-time job.

I recall my first introduction to 'Konglish' when I came across the expression *grand open* (for *grand opening*). I saw this expression on everything from menus for recently opened restaurants to huge tapestry-like banners draped over new department stores. I can honestly say that my immediate reaction was not one of shock, involving a mental question of 'why did they make a mistake?'; rather, it elicited a pleasant surprise and an understanding that this was merely the Korean version of an otherwise English expression. A love for language and culture perhaps explains my reaction, and fuelled my interest to learn more. In addition, my teaching of English was not tied solely to the textbooks, which focused on standard American English, though allowing for various stylistic registers (everything from *how do you do?* to *how's it goin'?*). Instead, I also focused on the uses of English that reflected a more realistic approach to the English language, so that the Korean students, especially in advanced classes, could ideally sound more like a 'native' and less like a textbook. The bigger picture is of course tied to recognizing that regardless of the language used, we need to deploy different varieties of the same language, sometimes in a given day, in order to communicate effectively.

From this personal experience and background, I have also chosen to focus on Korean English as the recent Korean wave of culture spreading across the world (or *hallyu*, as the Koreans say) has ensured that many people have become more familiar with Korea (Ahn, 2019; 2021). While much of this familiarity is tied to K-POP and Korean drama of course, I believe it should, and does, extend to other aspects, such as the Korean language, Korean cuisine and even a recent book explaining the Korean concept of *nunchi* (*The Power of Nunchi: The Korean Secret to Happiness and Success* by Euny Hong, 2019). This expansion of Korean pop culture in particular has been referred to as *Hallyuwood* (Farrar, 2010), and as Ahn (2019: 1) says, has 'familiarized English speakers with Korean words'. This has led to an Englishization of such words, to be discussed further in Chapter 3. For now, however, this is linguistic evidence of the power and influence of this Korean cultural wave and I feel that a focus on the Korean use of English is a worthy, and relevant, aspect of *hallyu*, investigating Korea from a linguistic perspective, which itself is tied to Korean culture. Moreover, K-POP fans, from France to Brazil, have started to learn Korean to some extent, judging by their Korean expressions written on banners for the K-POP band members to see when they arrive at the airport. Blommaert (2010) references the 'bits of language' that make up a person's communicative repertoire; and in this case, this could be applied to learning Korean to the extent it reflects a specific focus aligned with K-POP. I will take this discussion up later in the book, focusing specifically on the use of Korean English vocabulary to the extent it relates to K-POP fandom and, as such, identifies K-POP fans from around the world to each other and perhaps membership in the community of K-POP fans.

Finally, the larger linguistic picture is clearly focused on Englishes within the expanding circle, an area that has arguably not received the attention it needs. In this way, Korean English, while not Japanese English or China English, for example, shares aspects in common, in terms of being in a group which has been regarded as less established, and not receiving much attention in the literature compared with inner- and outer-circle varieties (Jenkins, 2000; Kachru, 2006; Ahn, 2014; Galloway and Rose, 2015; Rüdiger, 2019). As Rüdiger (2019: 3) explains, 'it is unclear . . . why Expanding Circle Englishes . . . should not be allowed to partake in the ownership of English.' In keeping with her position, one suggested by similar points made by Kachru (1982) regarding the labelling of 'deficient' to such varieties of English, we need more focus on this area. Having said this, there is evidence of some investigation into this particular circle, helping to bring attention to areas such as South America (e.g. Friedrich and Berns, 2003) and, indeed, Asia and its use of English; the latter is covered a great deal in the journal *Asian Englishes*.

The fact that we have a particular variety of English to write about in the first instance is but one way to determine its establishment, as just one aspect of codification that will be discussed, and shining a linguistic spotlight on Korea can allow for more knowledge about language change in general: the spread of the English language, a more modern way in which languages are codified, and the specific ways in which Koreans have made English their own.

Societal codification

The discussion of codification is the overall basis of my book, yet embedded in this focus are several others. These include the need to approach all languages and varieties within with objectivity and, above all, respect; the need to problematize the otherwise traditional notions of linguistic codification; the idea that society is the ultimate judge of what language they will use; and, finally, the implications for teaching EFL in Korea, or beyond, with Korean English being an effective means (as are all NICE) to teach inner-circle English. To begin this section, and end Chapter 1, I now point out the discussion points around my approach to linguistic codification.

Codification refers to the practice of selecting, developing and, overall, establishing a particular language use in, and for, society. It is important to first distinguish conventionalization and legitimization as part of this discussion, however. Kruger and van Rooy (2017), for example, investigate features of Black South African English (BSAfE) within the context of written texts, focusing on the ways in which grammatical features are perpetuated (e.g. the construction *can be able to*). Conventionalization is described as the use of innovations that occur gradually within a use of a language, here English, based on how the language is adapted by speakers across various contexts of communication. Legitimization is seen as the ways in which approval is tacitly given to such features. Such approval, as I argue, is already bestowed upon a language variety by virtue of the speakers themselves, whose use of innovations becomes widespread and certainly frequent enough to then become established in their language. The legitimization that Kruger and van Rooy (2017) speak of, however, is that provided by editors of publications (e.g. newspapers), fulfilling the role of linguistic gatekeepers regarding the features of BSAfE that occur. Bamgbose (1998) concurs that written works can be a means to spread features, as part of publishing houses and the media, 'even in the absence of overt codification of the variety in question' (Kruger and van Rooy, 2017: 21). As I will discuss, the Korean media indeed plays a part in this, with media including K-POP, drama and advertisements, to also include more broad applications in terms of the way English is propagated throughout Korean society.

However, I argue again that it is the speakers who ultimately approve of a language variety, reflecting a lack of overt codification but instead a more societal level of codification, one initiated with the development of innovations, which become conventions of the community's use of English and, in turn, are legitimized by the community itself and not outsiders. This legitimization is based on the reinforcement of the features in question, which is its own codification. From here, the next step is indeed codification in a more understood sense (e.g. dictionaries), but nowadays this often proceeds through less 'traditional' means (e.g. online dictionaries produced by individuals with an interest in the language variety in question). Beyond this, however, are further examples of societal codification, using additional non-traditional means (e.g. blogs, public signage, TV shows and so on), with 'traditional' again understood as dictionaries, grammar books and school-based textbooks, and then such resources often seen as legitimate if deriving from authoritative sources, such as prestigious publishing houses or backed by the government itself. As I argue, codification need not be limited to such a narrow interpretation.

Obvious though it might be, it is somewhat overlooked that a language must already be established in order to be written about in the first instance. In other words, without a predictable use of grammar and vocabulary, there would be little to write about, whether the focus is Korean English or Ghanaian English. There are many textbooks and journal articles that discuss a wide variety of World Englishes and again, this points to such varieties – including Korean English – as being predictable and systematic. To put it another way, we cannot wait, nor do we need to, for Korean English to be 'officially' codified by means of dictionaries and textbooks in the usual understanding of such (again, school-based textbooks and dictionaries such as the *Oxford English Dictionary*). There may of course be evidence of Korean English words making their way into the

Oxford English Dictionary and there is also evidence of high school English textbooks – the latter a more traditional means of codification – having been used in Korea (Chang et al., 1989; Shim, 1999), whose features do not reflect inner-circle norms (e.g. the use of *day by day*, meaning 'daily'). Nonetheless, in the overall absence of international mass production of dictionaries and grammar books dedicated partly, if not solely, to Korean English, this variety has already been established to the extent that it is alive and well; and thus, we are enabled to have a concrete discussion of it in terms of identifying its features.

Second, and as I have mentioned, society uses the language for itself, having chosen the language for itself. Even in extreme cases where certain languages are discouraged by the government, if not effectively banned, such as the case in Franco's Spain where only Spanish was supported, individuals will still make up their own minds. Even if this means going 'underground', certain languages will be heard – the people decide. Thus, society is responsible for codifying a language and, in turn, reinforcing it (Milroy and Milroy, 1999; Baratta, 2019a). We needn't turn necessarily to the subject of 'how' and 'when', valuable though that can be, with regard to establishment. Instead, a language has to be established in order for its speakers to have something to talk about at all; from here, as mentioned earlier, its repeated use in society ensures that it becomes more embedded, hence reinforced. I will discuss, however, how establishment does not always have to equate to predictability regarding language use, as part of my later discussion of contextual codification.

Third, we can see the ways in which a given society uses English beyond the grass roots level of the speakers themselves. In this case, societal codification also refers to the way businesses and companies use English and, in doing so, once again reinforce specific vocabulary, expressions and grammar. The aforementioned usage of *grand open* throughout Korean society – on menus, billboards, posters, shop windows and flyers, for example – ensures that this particular expression, among others, is sealed in Koreans' minds.

Furthermore, social media is another way in which society is reinforcing a language, thus helping to codify it further. This can include emails and texts, for example, and thus refers more to written English in Korea than spoken, and broadly can involve computer-mediated conversation. Warshauer, Black and Chou (2010: 490) explain that 'an estimated 55 billion emails are sent every day' using English, which can lead to NICE being spread online. Seargeant and Tagg (2011) also discuss the influence of computer-mediated conversation (CMC) on the spread of language, though they point towards what can otherwise be an unstable use in terms of the variability, suggesting a lack of reinforcement of established features. Nonetheless, it stands to reason that over time, the continued use of English within such a context by those who are not native speakers can lead to features being established, whether lexical, grammatical or both. Meriläinen (2017: 762) uses the term *propagation*, referring to the spread and 'entrenchment' of new features in a community which can be driven by 'social factors', which would include a great many contexts of communication, with CMC one of them.

Kachru and Smith (2008: 3) explain this best: 'codification is not a prerequisite for legitimizing a language. For instance, Australians spoke Australian English for years before a dictionary of Australian English – the Macquarie Dictionary – was compiled and a grammatical description of Australian English (Collins and Blair, 1989) appeared.' The reference to codification here, however, is arguably focused on a more 'traditional' means of such, pertaining to dictionaries, grammar guides and textbooks. But language is in the hands of society, who establish the language that they use and in doing so, codify – and reinforce – it in the process. I close this paragraph with a telling quote from Milroy and Milroy (1999: 45), who argue that 'ultimately, language is the property of the communities that use it. . . . It is not the exclusive property of governments, educators or prescriptive grammarians, and it is arrogant to believe that it is.'

A final point to consider is that sometimes the aforementioned traditional means of linguistic codification do not always get it right. In the Indian context, Chelliah (2001) discusses the use of Common Errors in English (CEIE) guidebooks, which prepare Indians for post-graduate examinations designed to help them access government-level positions. Ostensibly, such guidebooks promote inner-circle English, not Indian English, and yet, some of the errors identified in the guidebooks are anything but. Hashem (2015: 422) offers the example of *the children enjoyed playing in the water* which is marked as an error on the grounds that there is a need for a reflexive verb (*the children enjoyed themselves playing in the water*); both varieties are indeed correct. Chelliah (2001) further points out that some of the authors of these books are not always sufficiently aware of either inner-circle English or Indian English, but the publishers of the CEIE guidebooks have 'ultimate control over what becomes available to the public . . . (and) take advantage of the examination-oriented reading clientele' (page 172).

Chapter 2 now follows which provides a more in-depth look at the various topics which inform this focus on Korean English: the rationale for using the term *Korean English*; a discussion of the error-innovation distinction; and a final focus on native versus non-native speakers.

2

A discussion of four key topics

This chapter serves to expand on the summaries provided in Chapter 1 to better inform a discussion on World Englishes, in general, and Korean English, specifically. The focus will be on the terms used to refer to expanding circle Englishes, errors versus innovations and native versus non-native speakers. The central theme in my book is one of linguistic equality and legitimacy, and by discussing the three topics it helps to address this. First, the topics are discussed with an eye cast not merely on Korean English but the expanding circle overall. Clearly, however, the principles of linguistic equality would apply to all languages. Within the three topics are inherent issues tied to privilege, such as native speakers being often seen as the ideal and innovations in non-inner-circle Englishes sometimes regarded as deficiencies, no matter how long they have been in use, given standard inner-circle English being championed as the ideal (Quirk, 1990). Thus, by discussing these issues, which could be applied to Korean English, it can help to better set the scene for the later focus on this variety. Thus, I do not focus on these topics for the benefit of a readership which already has extensive knowledge in this area, and presumably would largely agree with the need to respect all language varieties. But again, it is necessary to unpack topics and concepts which may indeed be familiar to many readers as a means to then reveal the significance of these topics within the context of the English which is the focus of my book – Korean English.

Terms used to refer to expanding circle Englishes

As I have pointed out, it seems to be the case that Englishes within the expanding circle are generally referred to with the blended nomenclature of the country name plus the (implied) suffix *-ish*. Whether or not this was inspired by the coining of the term *Chinglish* I don't know, but I have argued that blended terms are an inappropriate way to refer to such Englishes. This is based on the associations with such terms. Pinkham (2000) used the term *Chinglish* to refer to translation errors between Chinese languages and English. This is most prominently reflected in the written context of bilingual public signs in China, where translations from, say, Mandarin to English involve mistranslations (Lyu, 2011; Wang and Zhang, 2016; Xu and Tian, 2018). This might involve grammatical accuracy, but unintended meaning, or sometimes a meaning which makes no sense. Indeed, Eaves (2011: 65) defines Chinglish as 'a nonsensical, problematic form of English that is the result of poor translation, misspelling, and errors'. This is reflected on some of the public signs in use within China, consisting of translations such as *slip carefully, deformed person exclusive use, please vomiting here, racist park* and *fuck vegetables*.

For some, the mere mention of Chinglish can elicit laughter – certainly the case with my many Chinese students when we raise the subject of Chinglish in class. He and Li (2009: 71), citing Confucius, point out that 'without a legitimate name, then without authority to the words'. I believe that this is reflective of the term *Konglish* equally so; and it is unlikely that speakers would wish their language to be laughed at. When I mention China English, however, the laughter ceases. This of course is, again, purely anecdotal, and it is perhaps the case that many individuals have not come across the term *China English*, including Chinese people themselves. However, the familiarity with terms such as *Chinglish* and *Konglish* is problematic, in my view. The terms per se are not the issue but, rather, the connotations that have come to attach themselves to blended nomenclatures are. If such terms are reflective of a language variety which is not regarded as a 'complete' language, 'bad' English or, as is usually the case with Chinglish in particular, translation errors, then it can never really expect to be taken seriously. I will expand on this discussion in Chapter 4 in relation to the term *Konglish* by defining it against Korean English and more so, unpacking the various reasons why Konglish may, unlike Chinglish, be recognized more as a specific – and predictable – use of English in Korea, perhaps reflecting its more recognized vocabulary. While this would suggest a more positive overall perception, as opposed to it automatically being seen as translation errors, blended terms are still best avoided. Park (2017: 60), in fact, refers to the term *Konglish* as a 'pejorative label', rendering Koreans 'as incompetent speakers', with Hadikin (2014) also suggesting avoidance of the term due to its ambiguity. McPhail (2018) further implies that the term *Konglish* is indicative of a lack of prestige and respect, which, McPhail argues, are attributes that this language variety should otherwise enjoy by its speakers.

From my previous work on World Englishes (2019a: 230), a British participant had this to say regarding blended terms:

> I don't think they are proper English. They are not correct English, if they were they'd be called English, not 'AnotherLanguage + English'. They are variations of English, and are influenced by another language.

This is telling, albeit coming from the only participant in a group of thirty-six individuals (who represented all three circles of English) who felt that NICE, expanding circle more so perhaps, were not 'proper' English. The earlier reference to expanding circle Englishes being variations of English influenced by another language is, broadly speaking, entirely correct and hardly controversial. Many languages are influenced by others, and English itself is no exception. If we look at British English, then this itself has been historically influenced by Celtic languages followed by Latin, before Germanic influence from the Angles, Saxons and Jutes came into play, followed by influence from Old Norse and French. As James Nicoll (1990) bluntly puts it: 'The problem with defending the purity of the English language is that English is about as pure as a cribhouse whore. We don't just borrow words; on occasion, English has pursued other languages down alleyways to beat them unconscious and rifle their pockets for new vocabulary.'

Arguably, the influence of other languages on a given variety is less of an issue to some when its origins stretch farther back in time. English, for example, has its 'Old English' period going back hundreds of years; Korean English does not. Nonetheless, the influence of other languages which leads to new varieties can be seen with all varieties of English, including *sub*-varieties, such as British dialects. It seems, however, that the participant's comment is regarding linguistic variation and influence as connoting a deficit in the sense that she is regarding blended terms as not reflective of an 'official' language. This might in turn imply that such varieties are not really varieties at all, but merely involve borrowings from English and this, as such, does not pertain to an established variety of the English language in her mind.

From this, it suggests again that terminologies can play a role in this kind of thinking, as the individual indeed references the use of blended terms as a negative issue, certainly in terms of what she believes such terms reflect. I do not suggest, of course, that a change of term is going to subsequently change negative attitudes towards NICE, more so those in the expanding circle. I further concede once again that for some, terms such as *Konglish* connote anything but negativity and are instead reflective of national pride for some Koreans, in having made English their own (and indeed, many non-Koreans may feel this way). However, if expanding circle varieties wish to be taken more seriously, and subsequently the speakers of such varieties, then there is a need to change the terms used as this is arguably a step, albeit just one, in the right direction. While some might wholeheartedly agree, they may subsequently argue that it is premature to 'upgrade' an English variety's designation to something more linguistically established, which a name change might imply – this will be discussed more in Chapter 3 but briefly now in the following paragraphs.

Moving to the relevant literature regarding Chinglish, He and Li (2009) dismiss the term *Chinglish* for reasons I have mentioned, largely based on the negative perceptions this term has (Kirkpatrick and Xu, 2002). As He and Li rightfully point out, 'the course of a localized variety of English would be difficult to advance without a sound and informed name for that variety' (page 71). Much of their article's introduction takes time to delve into the different names used for the Chinese variety of English, thus providing a sound rationale for their ultimate choice of China English as a term. In doing so, they also reject alternate names such as Chinese English, in alignment with Jiang (2002), on the grounds that this has come to reflect problems with mastery of the English language and, as such, suggests learning errors perhaps. Using an adjective to precede a variety of English, one that refers to the country where the variety is spoken (e.g. American English, Indian English and so on) in turn reflects an institutionalized variety – this strongly suggests some kind of official status or at least a variety which has both intra- and international usage (Mufwene, 1994). However, for performance varieties such as that used in China and used largely for international purposes with non-Chinese speakers, then He and Li (2009) argue for China English as a fitting term.

However, asserting that so-called performance varieties – those tied to China, Korea and Japan – do not necessarily involve communication intranationally as do varieties such as Indian English is perhaps somewhat uninformed. Kachru (1992c: 5) argues that English has 'penetrated deep into the Japanese language and culture' and there is in fact support for a nativized variety of English in Japan (Kachru, 1992a; Morrow, 2004; Stanlaw, 2004; McKenzie, 2008), which would suggest that despite its youth when compared with outer-circle varieties, Japanese English, as with Korean English and China English, involves perhaps a more embedded status and is used among Japanese individuals. Moreover, Ahn (2017: 33) declares in fact that Konglish 'is being used by virtually all Koreans'. As an illustration, many of the children I taught English to in Korea would routinely point to classmates who were cheating in class and shout out *cunning*. In Korean English, this means *cheating* and is clearly based on the semantic implications of the English word *cunning*. Another example heard by my students was *hotchkiss*, meaning *stapler* (and deriving from a brand name of stapler in the United States).

While China English has been used in different ways by researchers, He and Li (2009: 83) define it as having standard English (i.e. inner circle) as its root, but 'colored with characteristic features of Chinese phonology, lexis, syntax and discourse pragmatics'. Such features, as I will argue, clearly suggest predictability in the language. Examples include expressions such as *paper tiger*, *One China Policy* and *beggar chicken*. In terms of syntax, there are pro-drop tendencies (e.g. *miss you a lot*), among other features such as placing subordinate clauses before the main clause (e.g. *Because I was sick, I couldn't attend the meeting*). That some features derive from the direct influence of Mandarin, while perhaps unsurprising, is not the most pertinent issue. Rather, the fact that such features have reached a stage that we can refer to them as reflecting China English is more important. Hu (2004: 28) in fact argues that China English should be used 'as a standard', on equal terms with British, American and the other 'World Englishes'.

I have referred to China English as a starting point for several reasons. First, it relates to the broader focus on expanding circle Englishes, though as I will discuss in Chapter 4, English has had different journeys in expanding circle countries which can be very different from one another. Nonetheless, the debate around expanding circle Englishes and whether or not they are 'official' or 'established' is applicable to Korean English and China English alike, and expanding circle Englishes are the bedrock of the focus on Korean English per se. Second, the paper of He and Li is very informative and detailed regarding the issues with blended nomenclatures, given its initial discussion of such. It is clearly by no means the only publication on the subject (see also Hu, 2004; Eaves, 2011; Hsu, 2019; Fang, 2020), but this again shows evidence of recognition for this particular English variety and the inherent issues within, such as the appropriate term to use. Third, it offers an insight into the ways in which expanding circle varieties can be recognized on a more official level, given the features that comprise China English. In this case, 'official' does not necessarily translate into government recognition, but certainly *societal* recognition, which refers to a recognition of the various features – syntactic, lexical and phonological – that members of society use, perhaps without giving them much thought, which would suggest a degree of acquisition. Finally, while He and Li (2009) acknowledge the fact that China English has been interpreted differently by various researchers, the term is arguably the best at capturing this particular variety, thus avoiding what appears to be general agreement in the literature that Chinglish has negative connotations (Kirkpatrick and Xu, 2002; Hu, 2004; Eaves, 2011; Baratta, 2019a);

as I argue, blended terms in toto can have negative connotations and this would apply to the expanding circle overall.

As acknowledged, some have argued that it might be premature to suggest certain features of emergent Englishes as being fully established (Siqi and Sewell, 2014; Song, 2016). By 'established', I am referring specifically, as does Song, to the extent to which the features are used throughout society. Song argues that to confer the status of New English on a variety, we would expect to see it used throughout society, in many contexts of communication (e.g. education, government) and by people from all walks of life (e.g. professional and non-professional alike). More than simply asserting that a given word and/or use of grammar has been codified by its speakers, we thus need to ascertain *who* is doing the speaking, *how many* of them and *how often*. These are indeed valid points raised by Song (2016), but I emphasize again that as long as there is evidence (which I will present) of a form of English that is being used predictably and regularly, and in different contexts within society, then this should be considered, even if it is not widespread throughout society. Indeed, not all Indians speak Indian English or other varieties of English for that matter, in a country in which English is well established and even has a longer history than English in Australia, an inner-circle country. Even if Song were to be persuaded by some of my later examples regarding the ways Koreans have made English their own, he would still refer to it as 'English in Korea'. Nonetheless, I still discuss this topic in favour of a Korean English approach, with the chapters to follow explaining why.

Furthermore, at what point do we declare linguistic establishment? I will discuss this further in Chapter 3, but if we're waiting for school-based textbooks, grammar guides, government approval or the publication of a dictionary on the subject of an expanding circle English by a prestigious company, then we're perhaps in for a long wait. If the Singaporean government had encouraged the use of Singlish as opposed to deriding it (as part of its Speak Good English campaign) then it stands to reason that government approval could only be regarded positively by many. On the other hand, people are going to use Singlish anyway as society has decided, by already putting their stamp on the English language and as with inner-circle dialects perhaps, the speakers simply get on with it without needing grammar books to teach them a variety that they already use. While Kachru (1992a) has argued that the inclusion of teaching materials can be a step to an English variety becoming recognized (and there is evidence for this in fact in Korea – see Shim, 1999), another factor mentioned is *attitude*. This lies entirely with the speakers and/or the inhabitants of a country regarding a particular English variety.

Fang (2020) argues that China English does not necessarily enjoy the respect of Chinese society given its need for further recognition, with Chinese educators defaulting to inner-circle English (Hu, 2005), despite otherwise promoting the idea of China English as its own variety. Eaves (2011: 70) argues that China English is on its way to becoming an established variety of English, which would suggest it's not quite 'there' yet, with Fang (2020) confirming as much, though others (e.g. Hu, 2004; Ma and Xu, 2017; Hsu, 2019) believe that China English has already arrived. However, an earlier paper by Fang (2017: 22) explains that China English needs to be codified 'if it is to be placed within the large family of WE' further describing this as 'a long process'. This comment could also be directed towards expanding circle varieties in general, perhaps.

My argument in all this lies in a reconceptualization of what it means for a language to be 'official', 'recognized' and 'established'; again, this will be covered in greater depth in Chapter 3, but a chief point that I will again make is that a language is established once it is used throughout society, or at least a sizeable portion of it (e.g. that is tied to a certain region). It is thus recognized by its speakers precisely because it is used by them. In summary, language use and establishment are in the hands of the speakers, not grammarians, educators, the government or even mom and dad (e.g. *don't drop your g's!*). People will use the language they wish and deploy it.

Thus, to insist on the production of school-based textbooks, governmental approval or some kind of 'recognition' that is backed up by those in power, all as a means to declare a language variety as 'official', goes against the reality on the ground. This is also seen, as I touched on briefly, with non-standard English within the inner circle. For example, while grammar books historically, and even today, teach the standard form, dialectal speakers have nonetheless been able to use their own variety, even without the 'guidance' of dialectal textbooks. The grammar books I refer to collectively are those used to teach native speakers of English (or other languages), for example, how to use their first language in terms of the 'correct' grammar. In the context of EFL textbooks, they very often reference standard inner-circle English also, though coverage of more informal registers is often included too. To put it another way, is there evidence of grammar books, historically at least, teaching non-standard forms? While all this might suggest an internalized understanding of dialectal grammar (e.g. *I were cold, he be happy, give it us*), as opposed to conscious knowledge of the rules, it nonetheless makes it clear that speakers know their way around their language, without books to guide them. It is time to reconceptualize linguistic codification, otherwise we will be left waiting for it to happen by means of textbooks, for example, that might not be on their way anytime soon.

Thus, outer-circle Englishes, by means of the terms used to refer to them, such as Indian English and Ghanaian English, arguably enjoy a bit more respect, as such terms can help to connote 'linguistic arrival', as it were. Blended terms, however, do not connote such; and therefore, we need to use terms which include the full name of the country (e.g. China, Korean), as opposed to reducing them (e.g. *Chin-, Kon-*). I do not seek to present myself as a rebel, offering a blanket argument against 'the establishment', whether comprising people (e.g. education ministers), companies (e.g. university presses) or organizations (e.g. The British Council). I give them all their due respect and recognition. I simply wish to place language back in the hands of the people who use it, where it does in fact already reside, and as such, a language is not in need of more traditional means of establishment when it is, in fact, already established on the ground level. The argument that emanates from this is that, once again, society does not need to wait for the production of more traditional means of codification once a language is used by individuals in society in predictable ways. This argument does not in turn ignore the importance of such traditional means of codification. Indeed, if a future textbook that is mass-produced on the subject of Korean English is made available for students as part of university TESOL courses, then this is clearly a positive development. But in the meantime, Koreans are getting on with the job of using their variety of English.

Thus, I argue against opposing views which would insist on traditional codification methods as not merely being a way to grant a language variety official status, but would also be seen as confirming that the variety is widespread in society and understood by a sufficient number of people. But again, is it not already the case for those who speak the variety that it is established; for this reason, it is deployed by them for communicative purposes. Also, let us consider how certain sociolects are not always understood by certain groups in society, even members of the same household. In England, for example, the ways that the younger generation use English might be confusing to their parents; I don't know of mass codification, however, that would help teach the older generation 'youth speak' (for lack of a better word). Likewise, the speakers don't require such, as they already know what they're doing (e.g. I have learned that *that is well sick* equates to *that is really good*).

To give a more specific example, let us consider Multicultural London English (MLE). Undoubtedly, it would now be very easy to find multiple examples of its features, from phonology to lexis, from online resources once again to more academic-based work such as that found in journals, with Kerswill (2014) having contributed a great deal to this particular variety of British English. However, the speakers of this variety have created the language among themselves without the aid of such resources, which came after the language. The more relevant factor here is that the speakers of MLE do not represent the kind of widespread usage that is otherwise expected of a New English (i.e. a new variety outside of the inner circle). There are British people who neither speak nor understand MLE. This would include parents; and the potential for not understanding key aspects of their children's conversations if MLE is being used (Bindel, 2013; Harding, 2013). Some would argue that we need to compare (linguistic) 'like with like', which an inner-circle sociolect and an expanding circle English, are not. But the larger principle is comparable: there are some varieties of English used in any part of the world which are neither codified nor equate to a widespread use – but they are used and understood by their speakers.

This does not mean that textbooks on the subject of China/Korean/Japanese English for US diplomats would not be a positive development; I would welcome this. Likewise, the more that expanding circle Englishes can have their vocabulary incorporated into the *Oxford English Dictionary*, the better. Indeed, I am anything but against the more 'traditional' means of establishment – I just seek recognition for the speakers themselves. Thus, to wait for such traditional methods as the means to then declare China English to have officially moved into the establishment, and as such, *China English* is now declared to be the unanimously agreed upon term that is now ready for launch is not a realistic way to approach language. I also understand that as expanding circle Englishes continue to develop, and perhaps additional corpora can be produced regarding their specific features as based on public usage, then we can be that bit more confident to confirm the findings that are coming in now regarding expanding circle Englishes and their grammatical and lexical make-up.

Errors versus innovations

I start by focusing on two potential constructions, which have caused me a degree of confusion in my role as a teacher. The confusion has been based on whether or not the constructions constitute errors and, subsequently, do I flag them as such in my students' essays? I should also point out that by 'students', I refer to native and non-native speakers of English alike:

To get a student to work well, you must motivate them.
If this was the case, we could proceed.

The first sentence uses a plural pronoun to refer to an individual, and when I was at school, the use of subjunctive mood was signalled through the past-tense form (e.g. *If this were the case . . .*). Nonetheless, the examples provided are commonly seen in my students' essays, and certainly heard a great deal in everyday speech. The use of 'they' to refer to someone whose sex is unknown serves partly to avoid sexist language. Its usage is quite common however throughout society, and as such, this is the starting point for what might have been considered an error previously to now be an innovation. Increasing use of this pronoun for singular referents is subsequently legitimized by its use not only in conversation but also in writing – such as essays – and even on the level of celebrities preferring to be referred to as 'they'. But the starting point is again the speakers of a language variety, which is perhaps undisputed. However, I reiterate that they can also function as the end point, before updates and innovations to a language are provided courtesy of dictionaries and textbooks. Herein lies a clue as to how to distinguish between what I have referred to as 'pure errors' (Baratta, 2019a) and innovations, the latter representing grammar and lexis which has essentially caught on within a community of speakers to the extent that it is widespread, predictable and essentially, not questioned by the speakers for the most part, at least not while they're using the particular form in communication. Even if a new form started life as an error in one English (or any language), its widespread and stable usage makes it an innovation in another (Li, 2010; Rosen, 2016) – whether we like it or not.

I would never tell my students not to split their infinitives, not to end sentences with prepositions and it's fine with me if they write *compared to* instead of *compared with*. However, I will point out comma splices, missing apostrophes and confusion with 'its' versus 'it's'; this is because at this stage in the development of inner-circle standard English (across all varieties, as far as I know), the following sentences would be deemed incorrect:

The training started yesterday, he was ready to begin.
The countrys leaders are meeting next week.
The cat hurt it's paw.

These three sentences are incorrect from an orthographic point of view, but not grammatical per se. Nonetheless, they would be judged as incorrect as, respectively, English does not allow for commas to divide two complete sentences (at least not in formal academic writing); an apostrophe is needed to show possessive function; and the cat did *not* hurt 'it is' paw. Interestingly, spell check only picks up on the word *countrys*, but otherwise allows for the comma splice and the misuse of *it's*. Complicating matters, some readers may even disagree, at least with my judgement of the splice. I admit to seeing comma splices and sentence fragments in literary writing or newspapers, for example, suggesting that punctuation rules can sometimes be flouted for rhetorical effect. So does this mean a comma splice, as but one example, is not necessarily 'wrong' if used in the right context?

An inner-circle example of what was at one point in time an innovation, certainly heard within the north of England, involves the use of an object pronoun followed by a plural referent, such as *them kids*. This usage is so widespread now, certainly in everyday conversations, that I am confident to label this as an innovation and, hence, it is correct. With regard to the many instances of conversations I have had with non-native English speakers from all over the world who represent many language backgrounds, another example is provided here: *He suggested me to go*. The grammatical rule being obeyed here concerns *suggest* + indirect object + *to*-infinitive when suggesting some course of action to an individual. However, inner-circle standard would require a *that*-complement instead: *He suggested that I go*. The former example, though incorrect in inner-circle standard, is not incorrect if it can be demonstrated that its usage is now an innovative feature of NICE, though which particular variety(ies) of English I can't say. Moreover, from my EFL students' writing, notably Chinese, I have also come across the following grammatical constructions, with the inner-circle standard provided to the right:

> *I am difficult to learn English* – *It is difficult for me to learn English.*
> *I am lack of confidence* – *I lack confidence.*

Given the frequency and even predictability of these expressions, I now question whether these are indeed features that are on their way to becoming part of a NICE. To put it another way, if we 'correct' the grammatical usage shown earlier, and individuals still default to the original forms, then their resistance to learn the 'correct' form might suggest something else entirely, such as a form that has now become acceptable in their own English, even if the form is tied to fossilization from a language acquisition perspective. Again, it can be difficult to distinguish pure errors from innovations, or certainly innovations in progress, but it is precisely for this reason that we must be cautious on both sides: neither too hasty to correct differences nor too hasty to declare them an innovation. Errors require correction, but differences might simply require a polite note that they are not wrong, but merely used in the wrong context (i.e. a context, such as academic writing, which would generally require standard inner circle). On the other hand, I am more confident to declare the following as China English, *ABC* and *BBC*, based on my students' own assertion of such – referring to American-born Chinese and British-born Chinese, respectively. As Kachru (1983: 45) states, 'a deviation, as opposed to a mistake, is systematic within a variety and not idiosyncratic.'

But as the two initial examples at the start of this section illustrate, determining what is or is not an error can be problematic even with inner-circle English among inner-circle speakers. I also recall a British individual who is against what he perceives to be the American usage of *can I get a coffee?* The issue is not a request for a cup of coffee, but the manner in which it is delivered. In this individual's mind, we don't ask if we can get something when in the communicative context of a café, restaurant or the like; instead, we ask if we can *have* it (or something similar, such as *may I have* or even *I would like*). The problem with this logic is that the request of *can I get*, American or not, is not likely to be taken literally. If I ask *can I get a coffee/sandwich/Big Mac*, I am clearly not asking for permission to go behind the counter and help myself, no more than double negatives would be interpreted as positives (e.g. if I can't get *no* satisfaction, then this means that I must get *some* satisfaction – right? Wrong). The issue for the individual concerned here is one tied to pragmatic awareness, but the sentence is otherwise grammatically correct (assuming standard English grammar is the target). The sentence is also semantically clear, as a reflection of how meaning is made within specific contexts, here requests.

I am also reminded of what is clearly an American expression – *have you been menued?* This is asked of customers at restaurants sometimes and while some might argue that *menu* isn't a verb, well it is now. This kind of linguistic usage is in fact quite common – linguistic conversion – in which nouns become verbs, and vice versa. The key factor once again is societal usage and subsequent reinforcement, much to the chagrin of those who insist on some kind of 'standard', to the extent that they are, in effect, denying the reality of language change. Entire books could be filled with a discussion just on the verbal sparring between Americans and British people alone regarding 'proper' English, whether grammatical as illustrated with the word *menu*, or lexical. For the latter category, Jones (2001) in fact cites a heated argument in which a British man, during an argument, screamed at his American wife that the 'correct' word was *football*, not *soccer*. Time, as will be discussed later, is a factor. The American usage of *menu* is relatively recent, but the past participle usage of *gotten*, as opposed to British

English *got*, has been around for longer and this might offer an important clue as to why such differences are seen as just that – differences, but not generally deficiencies.

I would hope that the potential for differences to be met with occasional negative attitudes and disapproval, even within the inner-circle speaking world of just two varieties of English, is sufficient to set the scene, though much more could of course be said, involving inner-circle dialects, accents and even standard forms. However, given that American and British English are inner circle and longer established than expanding circle varieties, and more so if we are dealing with standard forms for both, then this can be seen by some as the linguistic blueprint for all other varieties to follow, occasional disagreements notwithstanding. Thus, once we move into expanding circle, or even outer-circle, territory, differences from inner-circle (standard) English are sometimes met with disapproval (Kachru, 1982). As Meriläinen (2017: 762) states, 'deviations from "native-speaker" norms have traditionally been characterized as "errors" demonstrating incomplete mastery of English.'

Perhaps a more concrete manner to determine errors from innovations applies to spelling, as opposed to grammar and lexis. There are many examples of this to be found on public signs, and in the Korean context such examples consist of *baby back lips, bakely* and *clean blue crap*, as but three examples, respectively for *baby back ribs, bakery* and *clean blue crab*. It is easier to confidently declare these examples as pure errors, partly because common sense plays a part. That is, at a BBQ restaurant, it is understandable that we eat *ribs*, not *lips*, and the other references should speak for themselves. We can also determine that the origin of these spelling errors is based, partly at least, on Korean pronunciation and the issues this presents when speaking or translating to English. Furthermore, it is also highly likely that with a knowledge of the errors, more so *crap* for *crab*, it would be immediately corrected – if not on the sign itself, then certainly in the reader's mind. Another example of how one language's phonological inventory can sometimes lead to translation issues – themselves tied to pronunciation – can be seen/heard in the Korean pronunciation of *coffee*, realized more as *ko-pee*. This is because the Korean language lacks the voiceless labiodental fricative, /f/.

The final chapter will discuss the use of expanding circle English, notably Korean English of course, within the English classroom. For now, it is important to recognize all varieties of English as varieties, and not suggest that there is only one key variety in the world, even if that is the focus of the classroom. Deciding on which variety of English to use at a given moment means that standard inner circle may not serve speakers well and at other times, dialectal usage or informal conversation replete with taboo language might. This is true in the inner circle alone, where even English 'monolinguals' surely don't use the same variety of English all day, every day. Registers change, words change and even dialects change depending on the context. The contextual complexity is perhaps even more profound when in a NICE country where inner-circle individuals will be exposed to many other 'new' varieties. Thus, it is important that the error-innovation distinction is understood; and at this point, there are several further issues to consider as part of this distinction.

First, inner-circle standard norms, as suggested, cannot be viewed as the starting and end point for English-language proficiency, simply because when such linguistic norms are appropriate to be taught and mastered (e.g. for academic and career-based contexts), there are many other situations in which another variety of English will be needed. More than this, many inner-circle speakers themselves do not always use standard English in the first instance, and so EFL students need to be made aware of this – and exposed to such non-standard forms in the classroom – especially if planning to reside overseas. By maintaining the view that any use of English, more so NICE, that differs from the inner-circle standard is wrong, then this perpetuates a certain linguistic imperialism, even if intentions are otherwise for good and merely based on the view that standard inner-circle English is the most socially powerful language. As I discussed previously, there is no reason why individuals cannot be taught the standard inner-circle variety of English alongside other varieties and made aware of the importance of contextual factors in choosing which English to deploy. This is not to suggest that EFL students are unaware of the importance of context in terms of using the language variety that is most appropriate. Likewise, it is highly unlikely Quirk would disagree with my point. Quirk's argument was not against the use of non-inner-circle varieties, but on the possibility of not exposing students to the standard variety in the first instance. As Quirk (1990: 10) warns, speakers have 'been denied the command of standard English'.

Nonetheless, there is no reason to assume that the EFL classroom cannot accommodate more than one variety of English. This can range from teaching students inner-circle dialects to allowing them to understand standard English in terms of how it differs from their own variety of English. The final chapter offers suggestions for classroom activities in which such an approach can be used, reflective of more modern approaches (Matsuda, 2020). Thus, there is room for more than one variety and a need to help students understand the time and place for one variety (e.g. standard English for academic writing) versus another (e.g. a discussion of non-inner-circle Englishes for those planning overseas travel, say, to India).

As I mentioned earlier, this is not about political correctness but linguistic correctness. All languages, from Basque to Zulu, exhibit a predictable and systematic structure, understood by the speakers – there is nothing inherently more 'logical', 'better', 'prettier' and so on in one language's syntax, morphology and lexis than within that of another language (Baratta, 2021b, forthcoming). However, if NICE speakers are expecting to be taught an inner-circle standard as part of their ESF/EFL class, then that is what they should receive. The caution that must be applied, however, perhaps more so for inner-circle English teachers, is not to make students feel as if their country's variety of English is somehow inferior, even if the students themselves feel this way.

Second, there is a wholly practical need to expose people to the variety of Englishes around the word (Alptekin, 2002; Matsuda, 2017; Rose, 2017), given that what works in one country might not make sense in another, and considering those who work and travel overseas, this makes sense. For inner-circle English teachers, an education in NICE can help to develop more respect for such varieties and understand more about the way language works. There are in fact university courses which now focus on World Englishes, found in diverse locations such as the United States, Japan, South Africa and Germany, and this is important for those who plan to move overseas to teach English in a country in which a NICE is spoken. Likewise, to educate NICE speakers about the diversity of English – from inner-circle dialects to other NICE varieties – can mean that students can communicate with others better, realizing that inner-circle varieties, including the standard form, can only go so far. Clearly, linguistic overload in the form of exposure to too much diversity is not an ideal approach, but neither is presenting a singular focus of the English language in an increasingly globalized world. This is very important for the English classroom; and, as mentioned, coverage of Korean English in the English classroom will be presented later in the book, with NICE an accessible and innovative means to help teach a given variety of English set against the broader need to have sufficient knowledge of the variety of English for overall communicative success (Friedrich, 2002; He and Zhang, 2010; Bayyurt and Sifakis, 2017).

This raises the question, then, regarding how to distinguish pure errors in someone's use of English as opposed to features which have now become (or are becoming) innovations and are thus recognized as innovations at least by the speakers of a given variety of English. Because once specific features are established in a variety of English, they 'cannot be called learner errors – however far removed from a Standard variety of English they might be' (Gut, 2011: 121). My approach is not to focus on the origins necessarily of innovations, to include those expressions and grammatical features which may indeed have started life as errors in an inner-circle variety – once established, such features are established. To determine such linguistic establishment, which as I have argued need not be tied to official or more traditional means, can involve certain factors. Jenkins (2009) argues that to correctly determine an error from an innovation, we must consider systematicity, frequency, and communicative effectiveness. Implied in this is the number of speakers, especially given the link a language has to a community of speakers (e.g. a regional dialect), if not a country (e.g. Standard Australian English). Thus, a sufficient number of speakers who use and understand the features of a given language variety in society is an important factor in determining the extent to which said variety is viable.

Bamgbose (1998) concurs in large part, providing a systematic means to chart the progress from error to innovation, first explaining that the choices available in determining errors from innovations is to use the standard inner-circle variety as the benchmark, or determine correctness based on 'internal factors' (page 2). These factors are now presented in the form of questions themselves posed by Bamgbose (page 3):

- How many people use the innovation?
- How widely dispersed is it?
- Who uses it?
- Where is the usage sanctioned?
- What is the attitude of users and non-users to it?

Bullets one and two clearly suggest that there is (linguistic) strength in numbers, but if we combine bullets three and five, then we can obtain a picture regarding the associations made with the features in question. For example, Bamgbose (1998) explains that features of Nigerian English (e.g. *I cannot be able to go*) are likely to be labelled as non-standard, as their occurrence in acrolectal varieties is 'virtually nil' (ibid). This in turn suggests that those who desire to speak a prestige variety of English would avoid such features; though speculative, this in turn could imply that social class is a factor. However, this alone does not change the fact that features have indeed been identified as used in Nigerian English, even if some public attitudes are negative; the main point, then, is that such features are identified and used in society, which is the case. This is not to downplay the role of attitude; indeed, attitudes and judgements towards language forms is nothing new, whether regional accents in the UK (Coupland

and Bishop, 2007) or indeed, features of Nigerian English. The larger issue is indeed for individuals to agree that specific language features exist in the first instance; even if judgements can be negative, this does not prevent the language variety in question as being *recognized*. In other words, while acceptance of the variety is strengthened if tied to acrolectal use, this should not negate the fact that the variety is nonetheless already 'accepted' by those who use it, even if it is associated with a basilectal variety.

Bullet four ties in clearly with the extent to which a feature has been codified. In this instance, Bamgbose uses the term *codification* 'in the restricted sense of putting the innovation into a written form in a grammar, a lexical or pronouncing dictionary, course books or any other type of reference manual' (page 4). This is my definition of 'traditional codification'. While Bamgbose seems to suggest that such means of codification are not always ideal, in the sense that non-native Englishes are often held to native speaker norms and are unlikely to receive the status they deserve based on a lack of codification as outlined earlier, he nonetheless clearly acknowledges that it is the authority behind such means of codification that allow for non-native Englishes to gain full acceptance.

Bamgbose again claims that linguistic nativization can be difficult to accept, less so at the level of semantic and lexical innovations, but more so for grammatical innovations. This demonstrates, however, that innovations have become identified as such; what is missing is a larger acceptance across society, and with that, more prestige attached to such features. As I will argue in the next chapter, we cannot wait for codification, as defined earlier, to happen; regardless of the level of prestige that is afforded, or not, to certain varieties, that they are used and are recognized – have become legitimated by the speakers – is its own form of codification. Second, I will later demonstrate how features of Korean English are not merely reinforced by the speakers – some of whom might not be Korean at all, but reside there. This reinforcement can involve online dictionaries, personal blogs and media in society. Thus, my argument is that we need to consider codification as both societal legitimization of language features, while also accepting that the hallowed use of dictionaries and grammar guides need not be tied to publishing houses and school-based textbooks alone.

I again refer to opposing views, which would argue that the very fact a non-native variety is stigmatized means that there are implications for those who use it as their sole form of communication in the English language. To this, I would agree, and there would be, as Quirk (1990) points out, negative implications possibly for communicative contexts such as IELTS/TOEFL exams, job interviews and academic writing, what van Rooy (2011: 196) would refer to as 'high-stake communicative domains'. But my point is again that no one variety can be relied on all the time for communicative competence and success. The idea, though hardly controversial, is to teach a variety of English that indeed carries the prestige and acceptance needed to pass exams and help to secure employment. But let us also use other varieties – and promote them in the classroom – which may indeed reflect the students' 'home variety' of English, and even use such to help teach the standard inner-circle variety. More on this will be discussed in the final chapter.

Gut (2011) and van Rooy (2011) also provide further insight into the error-innovation distinction. Gut references nativization, referenced earlier by Bamgbose, the process by which a change takes place in a language variety to the extent that it represents an innovation. While such features may have arisen from initial errors, themselves based perhaps on negative transfer from a speaker's first language, they can in time become 'stable features' (page 102). However, as with Bamgbose (1998), Gut also acknowledges that the extent to which new features are labelled as innovations is dependent on the extent to which they are used throughout society and – once again – used by those who are deemed to be 'authoritative' (e.g. teachers, politicians) (page 120). Conversely, any feature that is not widely spread, held in low esteem and not codified (presumably on the basis of the 'traditional' definition of this word, as provided earlier) is more likely to be labelled as an error.

Beyond this, Gut (2011) further argues that the classification of errors and innovations can be determined at an even broader level, that which involves the government. Citing Malaysia as an example, in which British English is seen as the norm, then clearly, anything outside of this variety can be labelled as an 'error'. I would suggest instead that it is not an error if it is one of several features – whether lexical or grammatical – which has its recognition acknowledged and it is used throughout society. The key here is that 'error' can sometimes be societal shorthand for features that are stigmatized, but features that otherwise make up the everyday communicative repertoire of individuals in society. I state again that there is no discrepancy in using the required variety for tests and another for, say, home use, and any lack of esteem very often is not perpetuated by the speakers of the stigmatized variety, who may use it as part of covert prestige. And finally, the lack of codification is once again argued to not be an obstacle for a language variety which is otherwise in use in society, even if spoken only by a small community. Codification and even use of a stigmatized variety by 'authorities' would clearly change the variety's status quite quickly. But we cannot wait for this event to occur and must therefore recognize such varieties as they are, and consider how they have been codified in other ways (as explained in the following chapter). And the EFL classroom is a very relevant context in which to consider these factors (see Chapter 6).

van Rooy (2011) was discussed earlier in terms of linguistic innovation and conventionalization. The former is achieved, and thus separate from an error, when new forms are created, often unintentionally, as part of the overall process of communication, whether based on simplification, hypercorrection or other means. These represent innovations, but acceptance is not necessarily immediate. It is important, however, to first clarify 'acceptance'. As has been made clear, there are some individuals who will never accept anything other than a standard variety – more so inner circle – as *the* standard (whether based on genuine beliefs in its 'inherent' correctness or simply based on the communicative power, say in academia, of this variety). On the other hand, these individuals are not necessarily denying the existence of all other (non-prestige) varieties. Moreover, acceptance, as van Rooy uses the word, points towards societal factors, such as the use of the variety in contexts such as education, public media and courts, which can then lead to 'entrenching certain forms' (page 193). This keyword also extends to the features being accepted by native speakers, and acrolectal speakers, by virtue of the speakers of the New English being accepted into the speech community of native and acrolectal speakers.

van Rooy explains how features of Black South African English have gradually become more accepted, features such as *can/could be able to*. Again, the acceptance is based on this construction's acceptance, and subsequent approval, by teachers, as well as its use within English webpages on the .za domain and the websites of public corporations. If teachers approve it, then this can help to allow for a particular feature to be deemed 'correct' and thus, clearly not an error. This feature was actually rejected for correctness by more than half the teachers in Gough's (1996) study, but by 2010 it was already very widespread, seen with its use on South African English webpages (more than 10 million different sites). It is speculative as to how it spread, but if educational contexts approve it, then this can surely lead to more usage outside of this context, and, thus, it can appear with more frequency throughout society.

Once again, however, it seems to be a case of not just mere acceptance. Clearly, for those who use a certain feature in their English, they must surely accept it. The issue appears to lie with *who* does the accepting (or unaccepting, as the case may be). If we leave acceptance of a particular linguistic feature, or an entire variety, in the hands of authorities, such as educators, then this would lead to fairly rigid criteria for codification. If, however, we chart the use of a variety by its speakers, independent of who they are and what role they serve in society, then surely this is the starting point. I will also argue in Chapter 3 that this should also serve as the end point as far as the speakers are concerned. However, my approach to codification also involves a secondary process, involving both traditional means (e.g. dictionaries) in non-traditional formats (e.g. personal online sites), as well as a host of other public media.

My points thus far, in light of the content of the following chapter also, are presented as follows:

- More traditional and 'authoritative' means of codification should not be regarded as the most prestigious, or sole, means of codification.
- Instead, we need to look to the features as used by the speakers – Are they indeed used to such an extent that we can declare them to be innovations?
- If so, then I largely regard this – legitimization – as its own codification, as part of a societal approach to this process.
- Likewise, traditional means – such as dictionaries and grammar-based textbooks – need to be reinterpreted, to include online dictionaries and public media (e.g. signs used in society) as a more modern approach to a traditional means of codification.

To continue, the need for systematicity is perhaps a given in any language, in that for a language to function it must have rules which make its use predictable, from word order to typology and much more in between. Mandarin is a SVO language, whereas Korean is SOV, respectively realized as *I love you* and *I you love*. English speakers would say *I collapsed*; Basque speakers would say *me collapsed* instead. Football in Australia refers to Australian Rules Football, but in the United States and the United Kingdom the word refers to two other sports. Again, there are many more examples that could be given, and even found in just one language variety alone, whether English or Burushaski. In keeping with this view, we can understand 'rules' as conventions, grammatical and lexical features that occur with sufficient frequency as to warrant their usage as correct from the speakers' point of view. That is, the language deployed is understandable to its speakers because it is predictable. However, 'rules', as I use the term, does not equate to unchanging aspects which are fixed (along the lines of 'rules can't be broken'). Rather, as a given language changes, its varieties will reflect this by, over time, adopting new rules for usage. Of course, it is not enough for a language to be systematic per se – the implication is it must have the backing of a sizeable number of speakers, albeit for purely practical reasons tied to such numbers and thus allowing it to be more easily recognized than, say, an English variety spoken by a group of just ten speakers, if such a variety even exists (though as a boy, I created my own language which I called *Malanto* – this was just as 'real' to me even though I was the only speaker).

Frequency is also a key issue, as errors can be systematic also, another reason that distinguishing errors from true innovations can be difficult. But today's errors can of course become tomorrow's innovations. Quite often, it might be the case that innovations are only confidently labelled as such when their use in a language variety is irrefutable, with the process of going from error to innovation lost to time. I had pointed out in Chapter 1 that just two individual uses of the expression *sorry to cut you* was hardly sufficient to declare this a feature of a variety of English, but it is sufficient, in my view, to suggest it is not necessarily a coincidence, given the shared national background of the two speakers.

It may well be the case that individuals whose first language does not have articles may struggle with article usage in English. This would lead to errors, of course, which may be similar, even the same, across individuals' use of English who otherwise share the same L1. One suggested difference between errors and innovations in this case, however, is that errors may tend to be more random, thus less predictable. While we might predict difficulties with article usage among, for example, Korean EFL students, and based on our previous teaching experience, it might be the case that the errors per se are not uniform in terms of type. For example, some students might omit articles when they are otherwise required (*I went to see doctor*), add them when they're not required (*I like to do the yoga*) or use them in a way which, while not grammatically incorrect, sounds stylistically unusual (e.g. *Can I give you the advice?*, instead of *Can I give you some advice?*); collectively, this would point to a certain consistency, but not in the sense of the exact same types of error being discovered. Thus, 'article errors' may suggest consistency in a broad sense, but if the errors are not in themselves uniform with respect to what is otherwise correct article usage then this might not suggest an innovation in progress (at least not yet) (Kruger and van Rooy, 2017).

True innovations can arguably only reach that stage when they have otherwise demonstrated a more uniform consistency among language users, are not random, and, thus, innovations would be expected to demonstrate predictability. This is certainly not the case with translation errors, which would not necessarily (but could) reveal a uniform and consistent mistranslation. For example, a public sign in Seoul may involve a translation error which the same sign just two streets away does not. A sign which uses the directive of *head careful*, for example, is a mistranslation from the Korean 머리 조심, meaning *mind your head/watch out for your head*. I wouldn't expect *head careful*, however, to feature on all such relevant signs in Korea, or even most of them – this is one reason to classify this as a pure error. If *head careful*, however, becomes widespread in the future of Korean English, to the extent that it is seen and heard throughout the country, then this can safely be considered an innovation. At this point, however, how 'innovative' would it even be, as it would be regarded as merely Korean English at that point, used without much further consideration from the speakers. From this perspective, innovations are not really 'innovative' at all once they have taken hold in society and are therefore accepted as simply an everyday use of language which is otherwise not questioned by its speakers.

Another example stems from a sign in Korea which declares *drunken not allowed*. While this is clear in meaning of course, the grammar is incorrect. *Drunken* is an adjective and so a following noun that adjectives serve to modify (e.g. *drunken people*) should be present, but it is not. Again, if two such signs are seen, whether 100 miles away from each other or just one nightclub away from each other, we might assume a default position that *drunken not allowed* is not necessarily an error. This is somewhat presumptuous, in that two signs do not a language determine. But in the absence of conducting a nationwide, or at least a citywide, analysis of such public signs, the assumption, and it is an assumption, might be that something got lost in translation regarding *drunken not allowed* and, thus, we might expect other such public signs to use an inner-circle expression, such as *drunk persons not admitted*.

Following on from this, we should consider the simple fact that bilingual signs using both a country's official language(s) and English are designed for international communication. In other words, public signs in Korea which involve translations to English are using English to communicate not merely with inner-circle speakers but also with everyone else. This is a very relevant example of the use of English as a lingua franca. While Dutch, Nigerians, Mexicans and Indonesians, for example, may understand Korean, the assumption in using English within public signs is that non-native speakers of English will nonetheless understand English in the first instance more than Korean perhaps. The point here is that the use of English within public signs is deployed for international understanding, but not generally for *intranational* understanding. Even a Korean who is fluent in English would surely rely on his/her first language – Korean – as the main semantic guide, whether the sign is communicating *no entry*, *watch your step* or *toll booth ahead*. In trying to communicate with the world using an international language mistakes will happen.

Korean English, however, is used within Korean society as a whole (McPhail, 2018) and in ways Chapter 5 will explain; this strongly suggests that this expanding circle variety does have an intranational communicative function, despite McPhail acknowledging that for some Koreans, Konglish (the term he uses), has low status. Nonetheless, McPhail states that regarding this variety, 'the future is also bright' (page 50), citing a growing popularity in Korean society for not merely English, but the Korean variety. He offers examples of the use of this English variety within Korean society, including coffee shops, car dealers, fast food restaurants and hotels (examples of such public media are presented in Chapter 5). Granted, this use of English in Korean public media is perhaps not how some would characterize 'X English' (Song, 2016), but such usage should not be excluded from 'X English' either. Such use is nonetheless telling, as it shows how a country has made English its own, and this should not be tied solely to conversations or written documents in the English language.

Rüdiger (2019) in fact suggests that this is the case, with increasing numbers of Koreans using English to communicate with each other intranationally, such as couples and English-only clubs on university campuses in Korea. Her data is comprised of the SPOKE corpus which consists of transcripts and audio recordings of informal conversations between herself and 115 Koreans, who in this case were aged between 18 and 44. The participants were further made up of students and early professionals. The data consists of sixty hours of recorded materials and given that the conversations took place in a coffee shop, this arguably helped to make the resulting conversations more natural. The participants rated their English as either intermediate or advanced, but clearly sufficient to hold a conversation. But given that from these conversations Rüdiger was able to produce a list of grammatical features that united the participants' language, then this is an important step to suggest innovative features of Korean English given the frequency of usage among the participants.

Therefore, pure errors seen on public signs which use English are more reflective of an attempt to speak 'the world's English', but not perhaps a more domestic variety. There may of course be exceptions to this, however, in cases in which aspects of Korean English grammar – thus an established grammar and not based on translation errors – can be seen on public signs; more will be discussed on this in the next chapter.

The need for communicative effectiveness is tied to the speakers understanding each other, otherwise how could a variety of any language eventually ever get off the ground? However, as demonstrated by the examples of public signs, grammatical, lexical or orthographic errors do not necessarily impede communication. However, the understanding is that a variety of English needs to have consistency in its forms so that such predictability is a means to further prevent any misunderstandings. That some speakers do not always understand each other's use of language (even within the inner circle) does not change the fact, of course, that each speaker is obeying the established and systematic rules of his/her language, whether referring to a *mobile phone* (British English), *cell phone* (American English) or a *hand phone* (Korean English).

From classroom experiences with my Chinese students' systematic use of English, two expressions immediately come to mind: *researches* and *dumb English*. Initially, I used to flag *researches* as an error, as inner-circle standard treats *research* as a non-count noun. However, academic research shows that a tendency for NICE is to treat non-count nouns as countable (Lowenberg, 1993; Brown, 1995; Jenkins, 2009) and this might be a factor in the use of this particular word. In terms of *dumb English*, this is not so much a grammatical issue (e.g. *he uses dumb English* is not actually grammatically incorrect) but more of a semantic and/or stylistic one, as within academic writing, this expression comes across (to me) as too informal and a bit blunt. However, the deeper issue is that this represents a direct translation from a Chinese expression – 哑巴英语 – which translates as shown earlier in English.

The expression refers to the difficulties Chinese individuals sometimes have in speaking English due to lack of practice, even when they are otherwise competent in reading and overall understanding. Perhaps *mute English* is more appropriate, but it represents an expression which is not otherwise understood in inner-circle countries perhaps (at least not as intended). Li et al. (2007) in fact refer to mute English as a national phenomenon, addressing the fact that it is a term often used by parents and teachers in China. If said term is then used as a direct translation to English and, given enough time, catches on, then this is a factor in deciding it to be a feature of China English. For now, however, do we conceptualize this expression as Chinglish or as China English? If this expression is used with enough regularity among Chinese individuals, here graduate students, then this is a key factor in determining its status. While many of my students have used it in their essays and occasionally when talking with me in my office, we need to determine just how many is 'many' within Chinese society, however, notably when using certain English expressions. So while *dumb English* is a common expression in Mandarin, I can't say that it represents China English. But its somewhat common usage, at least in this one specific context, means I cannot simply write it off as an error either. Honna (2008) points to a feature which might be considered Japanese English, consisting of the use of *my-* as a prefix (e.g. *I have two my-cars*). As Honna states, this usage 'will be considered a Japanese neologism if resorted to by *a sizable number of speakers*' (page 123; emphasis mine); again, the link to numbers is a key component which is implicit in the need for frequency and systematicity in declaring a feature, whether grammatical or lexical, to be an innovation. Stanlaw (2004: 20) in fact uses the term *Japanese English*, not Japlish, to refer to the borrowings of English vocabulary in Japan, but given the 'home-grown' status of many English-based words and expressions, they should no longer be seen as merely borrowings and by implication, these are words used by 'a sizable number of speakers'. One example is the expression *paper driver*, referring to someone who has a licence, but doesn't necessarily drive.

Referring back to the classroom context, whether this involves an EFL class per se in London or merely lecturing in English for a law class at Harvard, I agree with Hamid and Baldauf (2013: 477) that 'nowhere is this distinction between errors and innovations more desirable than in L2 pedagogy'. Indeed, if teachers are unaware of the differences found in NICE, then this might have an influence on how they mark students' assessed work. Granted, the standard for academic essays and exams in inner-circle schools and universities is standard English of course. However, marking a student's use of features of NICE as wrong is itself an incorrect judgement. Instead, the teacher, aware of certain features of NICE, is thus better placed to mark such usage as merely inappropriate for the context of academic writing, but not, in itself, an error.

Granted, the final score for essays and exams might not reflect a high weighting for grammatical accuracy compared with analysis. Furthermore, we cannot realistically expect teachers, especially those outside Linguistics/EFL, to be immediately aware of NICE, either in terms of their grammatical differences from inner-circle standard or even as a concept. Complicating matters further, do the students necessarily know whether their use of English is an innovation or an error? In the case of expanding circle Englishes in particular, this may not be the case. A lack of awareness may also reflect, partly at least, the possibility that expanding circle speakers are automatically defaulting to a use of language because its use is widespread in their country. As such, there might not be any conscious knowledge of the features in question because they are so widespread. To put it another way, English grammar books, certainly historically, only explained the grammar of one variety – standard English. A lack of grammar books for dialects, however, never stopped speakers of dialects from using their language with precision and ease, as a lack of grammatical explanation of dialect was unnecessary in light of the fact dialectal speakers were already subconsciously aware of the rules, by repeated exposure to, and practice of, their home language – a point I had made earlier. Yano (2009: 247) points to this suggested 'feel' for one's language use, stating that L2 English speakers 'are becoming "functionally" native speakers ... (and) are acquiring native-speaker intuition on grammatical correctness and acceptability as well as generative ability in their varieties of English'.

Nonetheless, Hamid and Baldauf (2013: 478) state that 'teachers' judgements may become problematic because many features of L2 English are yet to be codified and disseminated in recognition of the claim to an L2 variety status'. This is a valid claim; and again, I stress that I am not against traditional methods of codification, which would, undoubtedly, make things more clear from an educational perspective perhaps. One suggestion would be to analyze students' written texts, such as academic essays, to see to what extent their use of grammar and lexis deviates from the standard form expected in, say, the United States or the United Kingdom. If such deviations occur with great frequency among many students, then this cannot automatically elevate it from an error to an innovation, but it certainly suggests that we might not want to label it a learner error either. From much experience of reading and marking essays from my Chinese students, words such as *mute English* and *major* (i.e. academic major) appear with great frequency, as does the word *researches* (e.g. *there have been many researches in this area*). This is a starting point at least to an investigation into China English, but not Chinglish. However, it is unclear how much time teachers would have to devote to the task of compiling a corpus, even for those employed as EFL teachers. As language is in the hands of its speakers, then perhaps the speakers can initiate the process of such codification themselves, and as Chapter 3 makes clear, this is already happening, albeit from a more modern perspective – the internet and social media.

There is no clear answer at times to the question of whether a feature is an error or an innovation. Given the difficulties in deciding between the two, I suggest that one way forward is to withhold judgement, especially in the classroom. That is to say, unless we can definitely categorize a feature as being a pure error (e.g. *He can swims*), then as EFL/linguistics teachers, we can ideally make time in our class for a discussion of NICE; to also include a discussion of grammars different from inner-circle English and then ask for students' views on the matter; and we can then explain that our duty is to promote standard English grammar in students' essays. Respectively, these three suggestions are not designed to initiate a tokenistic discussion that is not taken further, to burden students to provide definitive answers, or to suggest standard English is simply the best. Rather, these suggestions, and others like them, can collectively serve to explain that standard English is but one variety and we as educators are simply promoting it in its rightful context of usage. Moreover, we need to allow students to have their say, for those who might have something to say on the matter, as a means to include them in the class discussion. And if indeed the conversation identifies what are codified aspects of students' NICE, then we can treat them as such and avoid categorizing them as errors, as part of a joint meaning-making approach to education.

Native versus non-native speakers

I finish this chapter by focusing on native versus non-native speakers of English, in terms of the definition of such and the implications the term *native speaker* has with regard to NICE speakers. Clearly, conceptualizations of who a native speaker is applies to English in particular, given the widespread use of this language with so many speakers who are not natives.

First, it needs to be said that the number of speakers of English worldwide is approximately 2 billion (Crystal, 2008). Of this number, native speakers – the inner circle – make up about a fifth. Clearly, then, the majority of English speakers are not native speakers and, yet, they are using the English language in some way, perhaps on a daily basis. This can include what might be considered low levels of English competence to complete fluency with an inner-circle variety, including those who are proficient in a NICE as well.

Defining a native speaker of any language, there are varied opinions though with some overlap between them. These can include those who speak the language they learned first in childhood (Cook, 2005); the use of a language considered to be a speaker's L1/mother tongue (Medyes, 2001); and 'stakeholders of the language . . . they know what the language is . . . and what the language isn't' (Davis, 2003: 1). Cook (1999: 185) refers to native speakers as the 'rightful speakers', with Rajagopalan (2005: 285) declaring that such individuals have the status of 'unassailable authority and absolute infallibility'.

Taking this into overall consideration, native speaker status is based on one's first language, and thus for many who speak English outside the inner circle this would mean that they are not native speakers of English. On the other hand, are they not native speakers of their country's variety of English? This might be for some a broad interpretation, but I cannot, strictly speaking, consider myself a native speaker of a NICE. In this sense, I would need to learn from the 'natives' –

as I did while in Korea. This is a point I had made earlier, and one more consideration at this point is to ask to what extent does being an inner-circle English speaker bestow upon an individual 'absolute infallibility'? Can we be certain that native speakers of English aren't themselves making mistakes in their own use of English that go beyond legitimate uses of non-standard grammar? Does being a native speaker of English mean that the speaker is automatically qualified to *teach* English?

Notions of rightful speakers as being from the inner circle, who have claim to a language and are the experts, are implied earlier, but this is not absolute simply based on being an inner-circle speaker. As I have illustrated, even within the inner circle, there are disagreements as to what is correct, with inner-circle dialects in particular sometimes up against negative societal perceptions for deviating from standard norms (Haddix, 2012). Paikeday (1985) had in fact earlier described the view that native speaker teachers are superior to non-native speakers as being a linguistic mirage, with similar views including Kachru and Nelson (2006) who argue in terms of the native speaker myth, which includes the idea that NICE speakers, for example, are forever attempting to emulate inner-circle standards. Phillipson (1992) takes this further, using the term *linguicism* which refers to prejudice based on language use. As it has been argued (Frumkin, 2007; Baugh, 2017; Baratta, 2016, 2017, 2018a, 2018b, 2019a; Cantone et al, 2019), language is a proxy for the social categories which it represents, such as race, class and ethnicity, among others. If any of these categories is in some way stigmatized or Othered, then such negativity is passed on to the language and, subsequently, the speaker. This is hardly a unique argument, but it is still an ongoing societal issue.

Phillipson's (1992: 47) definition of linguicism reads thus: 'ideologies, structures, and practices which are used to legitimate, effectuate, and reproduce an unequal division of power and resources (both material and immaterial) between groups which is defined on the basis of language'. Holliday (2005: 55) argues that 'linguicism may be in operation simultaneously with sexism, racism, or classism, but linguicism refers exclusively to ideologies and structures where language is the means for effecting or maintaining an unequal allocation of power and resources'. This is important to mention here in that, notions of inherent linguistic superiority whether based on accent (Baratta, 2018a), dialect or indeed, the inner-circle of English, can lead to consequences for NICE speakers, certainly in terms of not recognizing the value of their varieties. Pennycook (2001: 60) further references 'language rights' and this is a relevant subject (Baratta, 2017) – the right to teach some kind of standard, while also having one's variety of English respected in the classroom.

An extreme example of linguicism was perhaps reflected in a Starbucks café in California in 2017, when two Koreans, who were speaking Korean, were then confronted by a customer (presumably an American) who objected to them not speaking English. Her response included 'I hate it' and 'everyone here speaks English'. Korean is not the issue per se; the larger problem is tied to issues reflecting nationalism and racism. Moving back to the discussion of native versus non-native speaker, the issue again lies mostly with rigid notions of correct English; and thus, for some, anything which falls outside this will be deemed incorrect (Görlach, 2002; Kachru, Kachru and Nelson, 2006). It may also be the case that English is often seen as being in the hands of those who 'had it first' (Brutt-Griffler, 2002; Jenkins, 2007). Strictly speaking, this would apply to British English (but not all British Englishes of course), but is extended towards the inner circle in general. Amid many differing attitudes and certainly negativity sometimes felt towards NICE, I refer to a statement by Widdowson (1994: 385):

> How English develops in the world is no business whatsoever of native speakers in England, the United States, or anywhere else. They have no say in the matter, no right to intervene or pass judgment. They are irrelevant. The very fact that English is an international language means that no nation can have custody over it. To grant such custody of the language is necessarily to arrest its development and so undermine its international status. It is a matter of considerable pride and satisfaction for native speakers of English that their language is an international means of communication. But the point is that it is only international to the extent that it is not their language. It is not a possession which they lease out to others, while retaining the freehold. Other people actually own it.

The foregoing statement captures the spirit of this book, based on the simple fact that English is in the hands of those who use it, speakers who will make it their own and bend it to their will and insert it with their cultural influence. The statement reflects the linguistic reality, but I concede again that linguistic reality is often no match for societal attitudes – in this case sometimes involving snap judgements based on a person's language use. In this case, language use not based on simply using inappropriate language in a given setting (e.g. surely taboo language would be off limits in a church), but based on not conforming to a designated standard of language that would in turn ignore variety. However, more egalitarian concepts of native speaker exist, such as the idea that native speaker is more of a social construction than a linguistic one (Higgins, 2003). This ties in with the previous comments made regarding essentially two realities –

the linguistic reality and the societal reality. If precision in English is required for teaching, then this does not require someone from the inner circle, but for some students, only an inner-circle speaker will do (Butler, 2007b; Hewings and Tagg, 2012; McKenzie, 2013). Again, societal perceptions, for good or bad, often trump linguistic realities.

Braine (1999a) explains that defining a native speaker in the modern era can be problematic, given the globalized world with more movement across borders. As people move, so does language. Even several decades ago, Kachru (1981) pointed out that it would be a mistake to label non-native speakers as such simply because they do not speak an inner-circle variety, with Trudgill (1995: 315) suggesting a less rigid dichotomy of 'either-or' with regard to native speakers, and instead suggesting a 'more or less' paradigm, with 'some people (being) more native speakers than others'. Canagarajah (2005) suggests a similar approach, in that he talks of novice and expert in relation to English ability, with Davis (2013: 26) applying 'native user' to 'a highly proficient speaker of a language'. The advantage here is that the key term of *user* does not automatically exclude anyone based on their circle of origin. This suggests that proficiency in English, regardless of which circle it derives from, is key, and proficiency is determined by the context. For those who nonetheless prefer to use the terms *native versus non-native speaker* (even if just for ease of reference, as I have done in this book), the sheer numbers of 'non-native' speakers of English means that they, as a majority, would not be aptly described as non-natives (Seidlhofer, 2001). But if we adopt an approach which takes proficiency into consideration, and not one's birthplace and/or first language, then this allows for a more realistic approach perhaps. To teach the kind of English that will pass exams and get into a prestigious university, standard inner circle is the relevant choice, but to understand how English might be used in everyday situations among the native speakers, outside of formal, academic contexts, then there is a need to understand such varieties. This can include more informal registers (though standard English can be used informally, of course), slang and even dialectal expressions (e.g. in the UK, consider the multiple words for *bread roll*, such as *bun, barm, bap, tea cake* and so on). Both communicative contexts require proficiency, and this can range from expletive-laden dialect in the United States, or indeed Korean English in Seoul.

This would tie in with the view put forward by Zoghbor (2018: 831), that English is not an exclusive 'property' which is owned by the inner circle, but is instead owned by all its speakers, who have found a way to make English their own. Perhaps, then, a better approach lies not with redefining native speaker and non-native speaker as such, but instead by focusing on one's English ability. Determining ability in English would then require determining what are the communicative standards and expectations for the use of English in a given context, as teaching a university course would have different expectations than conversing in more informal English. There is no reason, of course, that individuals cannot deploy more than one variety of English. This is another reason to teach more than one variety in the classroom, given the diversity within this language.

There is much more that could be covered in this section alone, but I would hope that the coverage within this chapter overall has provided a firm bedrock with which to approach the study of an expanding circle variety of English. In closing, then, this chapter has made the following points, which are wholly relevant to a discussion of Korean English and by extension, a focus on linguistic equality:

- Terms used to describe expanding circle Englishes need to reflect a degree of respect; even for those who argue that such Englishes have not been recognized to the extent that outer-circle Englishes have, there are more appropriate terms to use that don't involve blended nomenclatures.
- There is a need to understand the nature of language change and with this, to avoid setting inner-circle standard English as the standard in toto.
- Determining errors from mere differences from one variety of English to another is not always a straightforward task, but this should not lead to adopting an easy way out, to consider difference as deficit – notably in NICE students' academic English.
- However we define native versus non-native speakers of English, the reality is that there are many proficient speakers of English(es) in the world, and most of them are not from the inner circle; thus, we might approach English speakers based on their ability.
- However, ability in a language is also relative to the situation and may not always involve – or have to involve at all – proficiency in an inner-circle variety of English.

Chapter 3 presents a detailed picture of the ways in which linguistic codification has already taken place for Korean English, and how it can take place for language varieties in general. As such, codification needs to be recognized in ways that differ from more traditional notions.

3

Societal codification

In this chapter I expand on the points already made for societal codification as its own means to provide linguistic evidence that a variety of English is alive and well and, as such, is already established. Indeed, societal use of language acts as its own means of codification, with subsequent reinforcement and establishment. For this reason, traditional means of codification do not codify as such; they instead grant a language 'official' status, something that was already granted by the language's speakers in as much as it is already being used for communicative purposes, which is what language is for. 'Traditional codification', a definition of which was provided in the previous chapter by Bamgbose (1998), refers to the setting out of the grammatical rules and lexical features of a given language within authoritative texts, such as school-based textbooks and dictionaries – again, this is the definition of 'traditional codification' as I use the term here. There is, in fact, no argument from me in terms of such means of codification being a powerful means to grant a variety prestige and status, and to make it official. However, I explain my own argument to this, and other points, all of which combine to address my book's central argument regarding codification:

- A given language variety is codified at the level of conventionalization, to borrow the term, and definition of such, as provided by Kruger and van Rooy (2017); while they would not necessarily agree that this equates to codification, I argue otherwise.
- This is because once features of a language variety have indeed spread and are functional within a society, or part of it, then this means that not only are these features innovations, but that they are being used among the speakers to communicate; this in turn reinforces the language used. As Schneider (2014: 86) explains, 'every subsequent use deepens and intensifies the path for future uses along the same track, of the same kind'.
- As such, to expect that traditional codification is the final seal of approval for a variety, or legitimization (Kruger and van Rooy, 2017), without which

the variety is not completely recognized (or is recognized, but viewed with negativity) is an unrealistic view.
- To put it another way, can we genuinely argue that the only thing standing between a variety of English and societal 'legitimacy' and 'officialdom' are the means of codification as part of a traditional approach?
- Speakers decide for themselves how and when to deploy a given language variety, whether there are dictionaries, textbooks or even overall respect available for the variety; as such, innovations become conventionalized by virtue of their innovative status and the features are legitimized by repeated usage within speech communities.
- Going further, I argue that the tools of traditional codification, such as dictionaries, textbooks and grammar guides, are also available, albeit in a more modern format, such as online materials – all of which are written by people with skin in the game for the most part, and whose materials can also help to reinforce – codify – the very language that is already underway by its speakers.
- Thus, online sources represent a more modern way in which features can be legitimized, as well as several other means such as public media, TV, music and so on.

As an example of the kind of legitimacy that is afforded to a language once it makes its way into 'regular' dictionaries, Ahn (2021) reports that there are sixty-four Korean words in use within the *Oxford English Dictionary*, and thus we might be more 'confident' that these words are now essentially part of the English language. However, their use within non-Korean society pre-dated their publication in the *OED* (the words largely refer to various aspects of Korean culture, with examples including *chaebol, kimchi, taekwondo* and *ondol*, respectively referring to family-owned corporations, a famous Korean fermented dish, a martial art and the underground heating system used in Korean homes).

The main points are that Korean English, as well as other varieties in the expanding circle, have already been established in the first instance by the speakers who use them, with further evidence being seen in this book and many others like it – texts which report on grammatical and lexical features that pertain to a specific English. This would also include websites as a means of providing information on various Englishes as their own form of codification. From here, I will discuss the ways in which Englishes are used within society beyond the speakers themselves and seen, for example, within a vast range of contexts such as billboards, stores, magazines and essentially any public-facing outlet, to use a necessarily broad word. Finally, I will discuss the use of social media as a more current means of spreading and reinforcing a language variety, as well as perhaps influencing others. Together, this points towards languages already having been established in the first instance from which we can then expect to see, hear and read them in society, within a more modern approach to what I otherwise refer to as codification.

The people's use of language

I begin by stating the obvious – people do not need to have their language explained to them in dictionaries, grammar books or textbooks. As I have stressed, I am not against such an approach – reflective of the aforementioned traditional codification – and it can undoubtedly go a long way to giving a language prestige, credibility perhaps and officialdom. But such notions are societal, not linguistic. A language is a language because of a systematic use of grammar and lexis, put together in a comprehensible way for its speakers to understand each other. For this reason, the speakers of Korean English have essentially codified the language because of its use within society on multiple levels and this is the starting point for the discussion here. Again, by 'codification' at the level of actual language use, I am referring to conventionalization (Kruger and van Rooy, 2017), but by extension the resulting effect of legitimization, as described in the opening of this chapter. Mufwene (2001: 106) explains that 'it is those who speak a language on a regular basis – and in a manner they consider normal to themselves – who develop the norms for their communities'. I would go further, and include the word *use* alongside *speak a language*. This allows for a wider net to be cast when unpacking the ways in which a language functions in a given society, here Korea, with such usage also including, as I will demonstrate, public media.

But Mufwene's quote again points to the community of speakers – and language users – who set the norms by innovation, conventionalization through repeated use and, in turn, legitimization. The need for official means of codification, as some would argue, is still nonetheless a reality in Korea, but existing, partly at least, within media such as the internet, newspapers, product slogans and as we will see, a more traditional means after all – high school English textbooks (Shim, 1999). Another aspect of Mufwene's argument involves race, in which Englishes that are spoken by descendants of Europeans (e.g. Australian English) are referred to as 'legitimate offspring' (page 108); illegitimate varieties are those which are spoken by individuals not fully descended, or descended at all, from

Europeans. In the case of Korean English, the historical standard was American English of course. The Koreans have made it their own, but the implication of not having mastered 'proper' English may have racial undertones. This is pure speculation, but it ties in with notions of who 'owns' the language. If language is viewed in this way, then the 'owners' can get very possessive. As I argued (Baratta, 2019a), the imperative sometimes shouted at individuals of *speak English!* might be replaced more nowadays with *speak my/our (inner-circle) English!*

Some will assert that expanding circle Englishes are perhaps still in comparative infancy compared with the outer-circle and, thus, are still properly designated as 'English in X' (Song, 2016). While Song (2016), and others, would argue that the language needs to be widespread throughout society, which Korean English, he argues, is not, this is based on comparison with outer-circle (if not inner-circle) norms. Korea is not India, and English has been on a different trajectory in Korea – one not initiated with a colonial past. The fact that expanding circle Englishes are perhaps not used on an official level (e.g. government) might point to a reason why codification in the traditional sense has not yet become a reality. But this suggests somewhat of a rigid and even elitist view of codification, one that implies a language needs to be codified by official bodies in order to *become* official and recognized by those in power, who have said power to authorize school-based textbooks, in turn produced by reputable printing presses, as well as having dictionaries printed.

If Korean English were reflected in the *Oxford English Dictionary* on a wide scale (i.e. beyond the current inclusion of Korean borrowed words), as opposed to reflected on someone's EFL blog, it would probably get more recognition. Even more so if a university press published a dictionary devoted entirely to Korean English. The recognition I refer to is not just in terms of more people coming to know of the presence of Korean English, but recognition in the sense of having, to repeat myself, a more 'official' status. If Korean English were a taught variety in schools in Korea on a national level, as a means to avoid being locked into American English models, it would gain more recognition. Having said that, Shim (1999) argues that this is already the case, though initially at least, the variety taught was ostensibly focused on American English. And if, admittedly, Korean English were perhaps conceived of with more national pride (Porteous, 2020), it would gain more recognition. This last point is largely up to the Koreans, however, although it could be said that if the first three points raised in this paragraph were addressed, then this might lead to more national pride for Korean English, in part based on realizing that it has its time and place. This is not to suggest that Korean English is not used as indeed it is, as will be made clear. But as with expanding circle varieties in general perhaps, it can sometimes be seen as a linguistic also-ran when compared with inner-circle English (Wu and Ke, 2009; Evans and Imai, 2011; Kobayashi, 2011), which in Korea is usually the American variety.

However, Korean English need not be compared to any other variety, except within pedagogical contexts, for example, as a means to show difference – but not to make judgement. It needs to be understood as a perfectly legitimate means to express identity, culture (Bosher, 1997; Becker, 2009; Piñón and Rojas, 2011; Baratta, 2013; Parker, 2019) and, above all, to communicate, without, as may be the case, a continual quest to emulate inner circle. Koreans should use inner-circle standard when the context requires it, just as inner-circle speakers should use, or certainly understand, Korean English when the context requires it. After all, considering the number of foreigners in Korea who are learning the Korean language, then acquiring Korean English might seem a logical counterpart, especially for L1 English speakers.

Moreover, the alternate approach I take to codification should not be seen as a 'make-do' approach or second best in the current absence of more traditional methods of codification. Rather, it is an approach which merely reflects the reality of language, which does not require codification from those in power, however defined, to be viable and of use – the speakers would already agree that it is in use, perhaps daily, and as such, the speakers of a language, here Korean English, have decided. Thus, the more official outlets that Korean English is not currently attached to – homemade blogs/websites, for example, as opposed to the *OED* – does not prevent us from conferring the status of linguistic arrival for Korean English. I welcome the day when these symbols – dictionaries and grammar books, for example – are in full force across Korea, and perhaps beyond. But we can't wait that long as the language is already underway. Thus, my conceptualization of codification is one that starts with the people, and ends with them (Jørgensen, 2015; Bright, 2017; Wei, 2020) and sometimes regardless of prescriptivist notions of 'correct' language use.

To interpret codification as being synonymous with the mass production of print-based dictionaries, grammar guides and school-based textbooks is limiting and ignores the reality of language use that pre-dates such codification. Otherwise, there would be nothing to codify. Once again, the language in question is already codified and reinforced on the ground and so production of textbooks, for example, is merely reflective of such codification, and not the cause of it. Moreover, this traditional approach to linguistic codification reflects in itself notions of linguistic capital (Bourdieu, 1991). Even if a language variety is not generally viewed as reflecting a degree of capital, traditional approaches to codification suggest that a degree of linguistic approval is nonetheless bestowed on a language. This in turn can lend a degree of capital and authority to the variety, certainly if the textbooks are nationally used, published by 'trusted' sources and, even more, given government backing. One example of this concerns the word *major*, a feature of China English, and referring, as in the United States, to one's subject of study at university (though this term need not be tied solely to the United States and China, of course). I came across this word when I was applying online for a Chinese visa in 2019, as one of the questions asked me about my major in university. Here is another example of an 'official' means of codifying a language (or at least a particular lexical feature of China English): just as an application for a visa is literally government approved, so is the language used on the application.

I concede that the previous example does carry a degree of linguistic weight behind it, and can be a convincing reason to declare *major* a lexical feature of China English. But I stress again that the speakers do not need permission from governments or official sources to use their language. At best, traditional means of codification can perhaps make some speakers feel more confident about their use of a language variety and suggest that the linguistic coast is now clear for language deployment. And as important as such means of codification might be, language is once again in the hands of the community who use it. Even in cases where governments actually seek to discourage language use, in the case of Singapore's Speak Good (i.e. standard) English campaign, can this truly discourage wholesale the use of a language that, for some of its speakers at least, is regarded as more than just a communication tool, but also a badge of pride and identity? This reflects a degree of covert prestige, for a language that might not necessarily be covert in its usage.

The connection made between traditional outlets for codification and their link to subsequent prestige is partly reflective of linguistic hegemony (Eriksen, 1992; Henao, 2017; Reagan, 2018). On a more specific level related to the English language, the promotion, certainly historically, of standard inner-circle English as part of school-based textbooks for both L1 and L2 students, the idea that 'standard' equates to 'superior' is propagated by these very texts, as well as the forces behind them, such as teachers, governments and even parents (Speicher and Bielanski, 2002; Brady, 2015). Thus, once a specific language variety is promoted in school-based textbooks that are themselves sanctioned by governments (e.g. the Ministry of Education) and other official means such as renowned publishers, this will equate to said language(s) being viewed as respectable, even superior to those varieties that don't get the same treatment. The hegemony is thus seen on two levels: a dominant focus on one given variety of English, and its dissemination in equally dominant sources for output.

An EFL teacher's blog – and there are many – on the subject of Korean English does not perhaps carry the same weight as a publication on the subject by a worldwide publishing company, even though the blog might get more daily hits than the book will get readers. A university professor from Seoul National University creating a website on the subject, advocating for the use and establishment of Korean English, might be regarded with more 'respect' than a blog, yet this too would perhaps not be a match, in some people's minds, for information on this variety of English published by the British Council. Regarding the British Council, they in fact have a section on their website dedicated to Konglish: Konglish Corner:(2020) https://www.britishcouncil.kr/en/english/learn-online/konglish-video-podcast. In this case, Konglish is being approached as mistakes inherent in Koreans' use of English and is thus synonymous with Chinglish. This is another reason not to use the term; and, yet, the reputation the British Council has (which I'm not questioning) might go some way to make Koreans think Konglish is error-laden English, when in fact it need not be (and thus, another rationale for Korean English to be the term we need to use).

The issue here is one of *societal perception*, not of linguistic reality, however: standard English is not better (or worse) or more 'logical' than all other forms of English, each of which is equipped with its own internal structure, rules and usage that simply differ from a notional, or actual, 'standard'. Likewise, while a blog or personal website may not involve peer review or screening processes to get published, this does not mean that it is not informative, insightful and accurate in its content[1] (and people will disagree with the points made in peer reviewed books anyway, including my book; such is the nature of academic discussion). Indeed, teachers in Korea, both Korean and non-Korean alike, are best placed in many ways to approach this variety of English and can offer much in the way of societally codified detail. But once official organizations, establishments and publishers – essentially, trusted sources – lend their names to codification, then we arguably trust the given language variety more. Again, I am neither disparaging the pedigree of such, not arguing against traditional

---

[1] I am aware, of course, that the immediate dissemination of information provided online, which I will argue to be part of societal codification, can also be a source for misinformation, providing contradictory discussion of a wide range of subjects, to include Korean English.

codification. As I have made clear already, I merely want to approach codification from a more linguistically realistic perspective, a perspective that might not always come with much approval based on the language variety used and its relative lack of promotion through official channels, but a language variety that is nonetheless being used by a community and, in this case, has its own approval by the speakers, hence conventionalization leading to societal legitimization; this latter stage based on repeated use of the language over time which is then reflected in the production of, as I will demonstrate, online means of traditional codification (and non-traditional means of codification in general).

Thus, codification can still be regarded as 'traditional' in the sense of referring to dictionaries, for example; but from another perspective, some might say it is non-traditional precisely because the dictionaries (and other means, such as blogs and various public media) is not produced by recognizable names. Instead, established publishers need to make way for individuals producing their own content to showcase the features of a variety, here Korean English – this can be done via not only personal blogs and online dictionaries but also YouTube clips. Thus, it could be said that self-publication, whether we like it or not, is a more modern way in which the features of Korean English, largely lexical features perhaps, are being shared with the world (and this of course applies to many varieties of English, from all circles).

However, we might also consider the intersection between recognized and prestigious sources within the context of online dissemination. In this case, I again refer to the British Council as a 'name brand' and, as such, one that has the potential to be regarded as more official, whether it produces EFL study materials, textbooks or, as in this case, disseminates information on Korean English online. How might such an authority approach the subject of Korean English – and subsequently influence people's perception of it – versus online dictionaries and resources which are largely produced by 'Joe Public'? On the British Council website, we can find a 'Konglish Corner' (2020): https://www.britishcouncil.kr/en/english/learn-online/konglish-video-podcast.

Again, I am not against the recognition, and due respect, that comes with prestigious organizations such as the British Council, and others. But it is fair to say that labelling a perfectly functioning variety of English as deficient, or certainly suggesting as much, is not a linguistically realistic stance to take. What is realistic – and fair – is to characterize Korean English – and inner-circle English for that matter – as wholly appropriate for *certain* contexts, and inappropriate for others. Blanket bans, however subtly communicated, are simply not a linguistically realistic way to approach the plurality of language. On the British Council site, it reads, 'learn how to improve your English with these guys and stop making those Konglish mistakes'. This is mentioned in reference to a YouTube clip posted on the webpage, where two individuals discuss errors Koreans have when speaking English.

Of course, it depends very much on how Konglish is being understood. If it is being used to refer to pure errors, as far as we can determine, then the term *Konglish* is inappropriate. Instead, let's refer to errors as, well, errors. In this manner, we avoid conflating language errors with the national origin of the speakers. If Korean were the world's lingua franca, would American speakers of this global language want their variety of Korean to be referred to as, perhaps, *Amerean*? It appears that there might be regular updates of online content and at the time of accessing the website, podcast four was uploaded, focused on the use of modal verbs. On the podcast, two (native speaker) teachers converse in English, with subtitles provided on occasion which illustrate the use of specific English expressions, such as *you'd better go to Insadong*. This is highlighted as an error, however, on the grounds that the use of 'better' as part of advice is normally given for negative situations, such as *you'd better not stay out too late*. Grammatically speaking, the initial expression is not an error at all; the issue is one of semantic appropriateness. However, I would go further – Can we not offer the following expressions in English in entirely appropriate contexts, as suggested?

(1) *You'd better go with me* – Uttered with the implied meaning of, 'there's no room for you in the other car, so best to travel with me'.
(2) *You'd better go shopping now!* – Reflective of informal banter, meaning 'the sale is about to end – hurry before it's all over!'
(3) *You'd better go to Insadong* – Uttered as an entirely positive imperative, meaning 'they have exactly the kind of vase you want to buy in Insadong'.

Granted, the content of the online lesson is perhaps aimed more broadly, and not focused on the contextual complexities. But there are two points to be made: first, the expression that is flagged by the speakers as an 'error' is not grammatically problematic, but might be seen as a pragmalinguistic issue. Second, if indeed this kind of 'error' is flagged as a reflection of otherwise codified Korean English, then it is not an error on a pragmatic level either between Koreans. Having said that, as it might come across as somewhat inappropriate if uttered to an inner-circle speaker, then we can use one language variety to help understand the other. In other words, by approaching 'errors' such as this, rather than dismiss their use, we can simply take the time to place them alongside more appropriate expressions to help learn American English, for example.

Another expression used by the teachers involves the modal verb *could*, as in *you could talk to her*. One teacher 'corrects' the other and explains that *could* implies choice, but *should* is the correct modal to use for suggestions (*you should talk to her*). This is followed by the use of *have to* in expressions, such as *you have to go there* with the implied meaning of *you shouldn't miss it – it's a great experience*. Clearly, the implication of the video's content is that Koreans have difficulty with their use of modal verbs, such as when to use *could*, *should* and *have to*, which might point more to pragmatic competence than grammatical competence per se.

The website also contains a download – English Language Learning Tips. Here it confirms difficulties that some Koreans may have with modal verbs, seen with the statement of 'some things Korean speakers have problems with in English'. This is followed by some examples of the semantic implications of a selection of modals:

'had better' – strong advice
'should' – medium advice
'have to' – obligation
'could' – ability / choice

Overall, then, the content is very informative and engaging, both the visual and written information, but is arguably in need of a name change – delete Konglish and perhaps reframe as 'issues with English'. As I stated at the start of this book, this is not about political correctness, but *linguistic* correctness.

We should also consider the use of Korean English, and Korean itself, by fans of Korean pop culture, as part of the Korean *hallyu*. This can be seen in many ways, to include an online posting I came across in which Korean English was associated with fans of Korean drama and K-POP, for example. One telling comment stems from a post in which the writer provided a somewhat scathing comment on such fans, and used the term *oppas*. *Oppa* (오빠) is Korean, meaning *older brother*, and is used by women to refer to their older brothers per se, as well as being used as a term of affection for their boyfriends. That a Korean word is morphologically marked for the English plural, however, is interesting, and such usage is attested to by Ahn (2019), with the word having undergone Englishization and arguably becoming well known based on the mega-hit 'Gangnam Style', in which it featured. Khedun–Burgoine and Kiaer (2018) in fact refer to alternate spellings for the word *oppa*, to include *obba*, and in terms of its meanings, these now include 'sexy young Korean males, a beloved Korean boy' (Ahn, 2019: 1) when used by non-Koreans, but presumably K-POP fans in particular. Ahn further states that the Korean word for older sister *onni* (언니) is used as a term of address by younger females to older females, but can now refer to a female K-POP idol, and the word *aegyo* is also understood and used by K-POP fans, referring to the practice of young Korean women talking 'cute' as a means to perhaps get something (such as a gift from a boyfriend). Thus, *oppa*, *onni* and *aegyo* are but three Korean words which are now, in effect, used by speakers of many different languages *other* than Korean. Within K-POP circles, from the United States to Brazil, these words already exist to fans, and are used in their conversations with each other. It is therefore clear that the Korean language as used by non-Koreans, based on a K-POP/drama fandom base outside of Korea, coupled with the use of online communication, is a clear example of linguistic codification (Kim, 2016; Ahn, 2018; Lee, 2018). Though this does not pertain to Korean English per se, the mechanisms for a language to be codified are the same, here via online usage among fans.

Furthermore, Touhami and Al-Haq (2017) discuss the linguistic influence of K-POP on Algerian fans, referring to the concept of 'fandom language'. The researchers cite examples of Korean expressions used by Algerians, such as *aish*, which communicates displeasure, and *asah*, which communicates success. The authors also refer to the term *Koreaboo* used to describe obsessive fans' attitudes towards Korean music and TV drama. While many of the fans indeed use purely Korean vocabulary in their discourse with fellow fans, including *oppa*, some of the vocabulary is clearly Korean English, such as *hwaiting*, which is an expression used to give encouragement, borrowed from the English word *fighting*; other words include *skinship* (physical touching) and *selca* (selfie). Their passion even extends to pronouncing words with Korean pronunciation, such as *cop-pee* (coffee) and *pija* (pizza). As just one example of international fandom, here we can see how Korean English is not just used by Koreans, and the Algerian fans are but one of many other examples. That their use of Korean English is mostly tied to somewhat esoteric vocabulary does not discount this from being a form of language use in a larger sense.

Blommaert (2014) states that picking up aspects of a language, without mastering it, is a legitimate means of expression and communication, and this would certainly apply to the K-POP fandom community, who probably refer to *skinship* with their *oppas*: a contrived example perhaps, but not an improbable one. Potayroi (2014: 123) further states that 'in fandom, fans use specific language that people outside of their group might not understand and recognize; we call this specific language lexis'. There are further examples, such as Japanese anime fans adopting Japanese words into their conversations such as *kawaii* (cute)

(Fukunaga, 2006), and Smith (2015) refers to the fan base of *Harry Potter*, all of whom would surely know what is meant by the word *muggle* (i.e. someone who is from a non-magic family). Therefore, the use of Korean English lexis by non-Koreans, albeit as part of *hallyu* fans, would constitute a specific variety of Korean English – media English in Korea, covered in Chapter 5.

It can be said, then, that once a variety of a language takes hold and is thus understood by those who speak it, it has achieved its own conventionalization. However esoteric a given language variety might be, here a variety based on a combination of both Korean and Korean English, with semantic shift in evidence for words such as *oppa* and *onni*, and initiated as part of K-POP fandom, it is still its own language. However the fans might refer to it, whatever name they might give it, this variety of language is as real to K-POP fans as their 'day language', whether Arabic, French or Russian. While some might argue that fan-based varieties of language are somehow not the 'real thing' and therefore wouldn't be candidates for more traditional codification, the fans don't seem to notice (and linguists would not take such an attitude anyway). Moreover, this fandom base has already codified their language beyond their own particular use of it, based on the sheer numbers of internet sites which provide information on K-POP language.

Blommaert (2010) also discusses the idea of repertoires, referring to the ways in which individuals actually use language(s) as part of a globalized world, which can be applied here. For example, such linguistic 'resources' can include accents, registers and genres, both written and spoken forms, deployed at a given time and place, with specific people and for a specific purpose. Blommaert defines these resources as 'the actual and observable ways of using language' (page 102). This leads to the suggestion that there is a need to reformulate the concept of language proficiency, as 'people often communicate with bits and pieces of genres and registers' (ibid), a reference to Blommaert's designation of 'partial competence'.

By way of illustration, we could imagine a chat group of K-POP fans whose members meet online and represent first language backgrounds of, for example, French, Arabic, Portuguese and Japanese. These individuals may well use English as the overall language to communicate in, as a lingua franca, all displaying different levels of competence. In this sense, English is being deployed merely as a tool of overall communication (e.g. to greet, ask questions about one's health, and such). But when Korean is deployed, the vocabulary may well be written in the Roman alphabet and consist entirely, or certainly mostly, of fandom language (*Hi Onni*; *SUGA is my new bias*, etc.). In this sense, the limited knowledge of

Korean is entirely sufficient for the purposes of sharing an interest – and identity – with other worldwide members. Not being fluent in the language per se is not an issue; they're fluent in K-POP English, as it were.

A Google search for the otherwise generic 'K-POP fans' language' reveals 'about 45,100,000 results', thus helping to spread, and further establish, this variety.

A sample of just three sites provides ample evidence that this K-POP variety of Korean English is alive and well:

- 'Learning the KPOP language', from Richelle (2016) (https://aminoapps.com/c/k-pop/page/blog/learning-the-kpop-language/YkIb_ueZPGaMMBzXdMpm1LJbVZrw2z);
- 'K-pop 101: 21 words every fan should know', from SBS Pop Asia HQ (2018) (https://www.sbs.com.au/popasia/blog/2018/03/13/k-pop-101-21-words-every-fan-should-know);
- 'K-Pop 101: The Terms You Need To Know Before You Stan' , from Morin (2019) (https://www.refinery29.com/en-us/k-pop-music-fans-terms-meaning).

While I will focus specifically on the online codification of Korean English in Chapter 4, I feel it more appropriate to focus on an aspect of it at this point. In this case, the focus here is specifically on the use of Korean, and more relevant to this book, Korean English, within a more specific context of K-POP fandom. Thus, this dominant aspect of Korean pop culture has allowed individuals from diverse cultures and language backgrounds to learn Korean, however informal the learning might be; but in the process, K-POP culture has also spread Korean English vocabulary and, by extension, helped to create a pop culture language – K-POP language – that is perhaps something new in the process. Moreover, the comments made by fellow K-POP fans on some of these sites is part of the global online discussion community, united here by a love of K-POP, a love seen, in part, by language use. This alone is a subject for another book, but for now, I refer to this language which is indeed inclusive of Korean English vocabulary, and through both its use in society – to include its use by non-Koreans – as well as its online codification, through online dictionaries and blogs, for example, this is wholly indicative of the approach I take to societal codification.

Of the three sites referenced, we can find a range of vocabulary as part of online dictionaries. Some of the words are Korean, some are Korean English in a more general sense referring to everyday societal usage and others might be a use of Korean English tied more specifically to K-POP language. Examples are provided as follows:

Korean	Korean English	K-POP English (?)
Aegyo	*Hwaiting*	*All-kill*
Aigoo	*Selca*	*Bias*
Hallyu	*Skinship*	*Killing part*

The foregoing Korean English words were referenced earlier in this section, as were *aegyo* and *hallyu*, with *aigoo* a term used by Koreans to refer to disappointment and equating somewhat to *oh no!* In terms of K-POP English vocabulary, *all-kill* refers to a song going to number one on all eight Korean music charts; *bias* refers to one's favourite member of a group; and *killing part* refers to the part of a song which fans consider the most memorable, whether a dance move, change to a new musical key or a gesture made by one of the singers.

Clearly, then, Korean English as the starting point for a national variety of Englishes encompasses several others, with K-POP English one of them. The extent to which words such as *bias* and *all-kill* are part of everyday conversation for those who use Korean English will depend on the extent to which they do, or do not, follow K-POP perhaps. But these words, while forming part of a more niche area, instead of what we might consider 'everyday' Korean English vocabulary, are an important aspect of how Koreans – and non-Koreans alike – are using English in unique ways.

Reporting on language

As evidence that I am neither ignoring nor disparaging traditional methods of codification, this section now focuses on such examples, albeit not tied to school-based textbooks, grammar guides and print dictionaries per se. Clearly, the fact that expanding circle Englishes are the topic of discussion, presentation and analysis within academic journals and academic books (i.e. by 'books', I refer specifically to the kind of book I am now writing) is strong evidence that (a) there is something to report on in the first instance; and (b) such publications are themselves a means of codification, albeit limited to an academic audience in the main and not society as a whole.

Major publishing companies such as Bloomsbury, Palgrave, Routledge and many others have published, and continue to do so, on World Englishes, which clearly includes coverage of expanding circle varieties. My book in fact has some competition in this regard, including *Korean Englishes in Transnational Contexts*, by Christopher Jenks and Jerry Lee, published in 2017. Indeed, this book, and others, will inform my own discussion of Korean English.

That there are books focused on Korean English in large part is another reason to demonstrate how this variety clearly exists as if not, there wouldn't be much to write about. Granted, writing papers, books and articles about expanding circle varieties in specific terms of providing examples of their lexical and grammatical make-up does not necessarily equate to a firm societal establishment as such. In their discussion of China English, for example, He and Li (2009) were quick to point out that the features they referred to were, to some extent, *suggested* to be established features of China English, as opposed to absolute certainties. Nonetheless, that we can provide examples of expanding circle English in terms of grammar and lexis, suggested though they may be, is a clear example that the people are using said features with enough regularity to indicate, at least, a growing linguistic trend – and this would point to societal codification in progress, if not societal establishment and subsequent reinforcement. In addition, many universities, as I had mentioned, are now teaching World Englishes (incorporating, of course, NICE) as part of their curriculum.

Combined, these are all positive steps for several reasons:

- NICE have been identified, including expanding circle varieties of course, and as such, their linguistic components have been captured, disseminated and shared with international audiences as part of academic textbooks and relevant academic journals (e.g. *World Englishes*, *Asian Englishes*, *Asian EFL Journal* and *Language and Education*, to name a few; on the *World Englishes* journal website, a search for 'Korean English' reveals 276 articles).
- This identification can in turn help knowledge of such varieties to spread globally, potentially having a hands-on effect at the classroom level, having inspired teachers to develop new ways to teach English, by having taken on new knowledge about Englishes.
- Finally, future EFL teachers, having been given knowledge about World Englishes as part of their training programmes, are now better equipped to avoid linguistic hegemonic practices, unintentional though they may be, and work instead to create a more linguistically inclusive classroom – one that respects NICE which may of course include the variety spoken by their students.

Societal use of language

This section focuses on societal use of language that goes beyond the starting point of the speakers themselves and pertains instead to a wide range of uses that focus on written forms of Korean English found within society. This practice in itself is yet another means to societally codify a language but at this point, I would argue it is more a case of societal reinforcement. This relates quite clearly to Kruger and van Rooy's (2017: 28) illustration involving a feedback loop, which begins with a new form (and can end there, if this new feature is not picked up by societal usage) and, potentially, via codification, becomes reinforced in society (see Figure 1).

This process is also reflective of the process of societal codification that I had discussed. Consider the example in Figure 2, one that I had referenced earlier in the book (https://bjdcollectasy.com/2018/11/02/korea-dolls/), from the title page of Korea Dolls (2019).

The sign shown in Figure 2 is but one of countless examples of the Korean English expression *grand open*, which of course is the Korean English equivalent of *grand opening*. Moreover, I use the word *sign* quite broadly, as *grand open* can be seen printed on everything from banners, menus, flyers, posters and so on. As we might expect in inner-circle countries, the expression is used to launch the start of all manner of businesses: restaurants, department stores, clubs, markets and others. I had first seen this expression when I initially came to Korea in 1995; and going back on a regular basis over the past decade, I continue to see it.

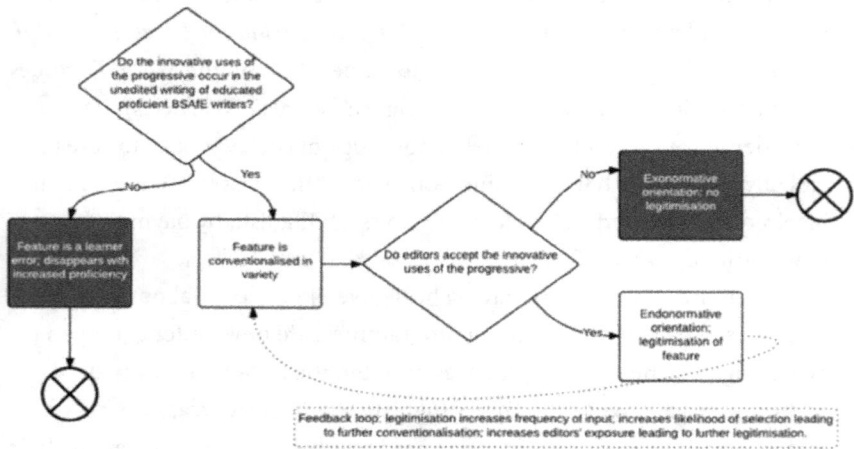

Figure 1 A previous model being applied here to the discussion of societal codification.

Figure 2 Poster as part of societal codification of Korean English. Korea Dolls (www.koreadolls.com).

That it is mostly written in the Roman alphabet is perhaps unsurprising, given that this is the writing system used of course for English. I have occasionally seen it written in the Korean alphabet, however, known as *Hangul*. This might be even more linguistically meaningful, in that by using the expression in the Korean alphabet, it might help to embed this expression that bit more into Koreans' collective psyche, and once again, reinforce the use of this expression. Therefore, *grand open* is no more 'missing' a suffix than inner-circle English is in need of deleting one (*-ing*).

Anecdotally, I don't recall seeing the inner-circle expression of *grand opening* printed in Korea, but this does not mean it doesn't exist. But what would make one use firmly Korean English, and not an error, and one firmly inner circle, is the sheer societal propagation of the Korean version and it is unlikely that once out, such usage will be put back in the bag and replaced with the 'correct' version. Of course, the inner-circle usage of this expression might be used for a range of reasons, based on the connotations it might be expected to carry. Though speculative, perhaps some Koreans wish to attract foreigners more (or at least not exclude them), and therefore use the form they're perhaps more accustomed to (though when I go to Korea, I am entirely accustomed to the Korean version); connected to the first point, perhaps some Koreans wish to simply use inner-circle English, believing it to be more international; and perhaps some Koreans are reluctant to use Korean English in such a prominent manner (e.g. on a brochure or menu), though many may of course feel the opposite. But its usage within Korea reveals that for some Koreans, there is a suggested confidence in using this variety (Ahn, 2017). This is not to ignore the literature that points out Koreans' anxieties about using English (Park, 2009), but I would suggest given the spread of Korean English used among Koreans, then this variety poses less of an issue within this intranational context.

Another example of Korean English in full public view concerns the word *officetel* (오피스텔) – this is a blended word created from *office* + *hotel*, and refers to an apartment building that combines both studio flats with places of business. The advantage of this is that individuals can both live and work in the same building, thus avoiding long commutes. Officetels often house professors, lawyers and accountants, for example, providing both work and home. It is simply wrong to label this word as anything other than what it is – a lexical innovation of Korean English that has become conventionalized, and in full use in society. This innovation is also drawing on the grammatical possibilities of English, using a blended term (as opposed to merely borrowing a word wholesale). In terms of its written usage, there is an ad in Seoul, in English, found on the following real estate website, Seoul Homes (2020): https://seoulhomes.kr/property/large-lofty-type-officetel-near-gangnam-stn-short-term-available/.

Large lofty type officetel near Gangnam Stn. short term available

The English like the foregoing phrase could easily be found within the inner circle, but the word *officetel* would not. In fact, I don't immediately know what the equivalent word would be in, say, American English. Is an officetel very much a Korean innovation? Perhaps not, but the Koreans required a word to describe a building that basically doubles as space for residents and businesses; and thus, officetel fits the linguistic bill.

However, if we look closer at the ad directly, 'lofty type' does not, to my ear at least, sound particularly 'natural'. This does not mean it is *unnatural* of course, but rather, it is a way to communicate, in the context of describing property for rent, that sounds rather unusual. In the United States, or perhaps the inner circle as a whole, *high rise* might be the more appropriate expression instead, but I'll let the readers decide for themselves on this one, in terms of any judgements made of 'lofty type' in this specific context and my suggested replacement. But deciding on whether or not *lofty type* is Korean English, we would need to analyze, in the first instance, multiple examples of officetel rental ads. This would give us a firmer linguistic picture. If, however, such analysis is inconclusive, and one ad says *lofty type,* another says *high rise* and yet another proclaims *tall building,* then this particular expression can best be understood as one, or perhaps several real estate companies' individual uses of English, but not widespread use. If so, this does not make it an error per se, certainly not in a grammatical sense. Rather, it might constitute a stylistic use of English that may be perceived, by some at least, as unnatural, but not necessarily semantically unclear. It would also form part of contextual codification, in this case pertaining to real estate English in Korea. I will come back to this discussion as part of the chapter focused on media English in Korea.

Another example of public use of Korean English concerns the word *saida* (사이다), which is based on the English word *cider*. The word refers to a brand name of soft drink, which would correspond to Sprite. That it is a borrowed word from English, but one infused with a different meaning in Korea than *cider* in the United States (a drink made from apples) and Britain (an *alcoholic* drink made from apples), is what makes it an example of Korean English. Seen from this perspective, this usage specific to Korea is akin to the word *football,* which has been appropriated by three countries – the United States, Britain and Australia – to refer to three different sports, as I had referenced earlier in the book. The societal codification of this Korean soft drink is especially unique and ubiquitous, given that it is not merely a reference to a soft drink but also a brand name, as seen in the next URL. Thus, as the drink is mass produced, so is the Korean English usage spread to the masses (Lee, 2018) (https://thetakeout.com/pop-culture-a-guide-to-korean-soft-drinks-1829732918) (see Figure 3).

A final example of societal usage of Korean English within this very public context concerns the Korean English expression *Dutch pay*. The inner-circle equivalent is *Dutch treat*, though the conventional expression is *to go Dutch*. Koreans, however, don't *go* Dutch they *do Dutch pay* instead. That this expression is codified and embedded in Korean English reveals a somewhat symbiotic relationship between society and language: the expression can be heard within society which in turn reinforces its usage and leads to, as discussed in the following paragraph, the expression *Dutch pay* being appropriated by Korean businesses.

For example, there is a Korean business named 'Dutchpay Korea', found on the following website: www.dutchpay.org. There is further evidence of its firm use in Korean English. In an article in *The Korea Times* in 2017, Ko Dong-hwan

Figure 3 Societal codification via a mass-produced soft drink. Taken from https://the takeout.com/pop-culture-a-guide-to-korean-soft-drinks-1829732918.

reports on a new app entitled 'the credit card Dutch pay service', established by the Financial Services Commission. Given that going Dutch was historically not the norm in Korea (and perhaps still isn't with older generations, for whom it is customary to either host or guest), the app contains a replica of an individual's credit card details. Thus, when one person pays for his/her guest(s), those who have had their meal paid for can then use the app to send money to the individual's account. This might seem a more indirect route, but given that the bill/check in restaurants in Korea often comes as one total and is not split, it requires the guests to know the banking details of the host. In another article from *The Korea Bizwire* (Lee, 2015), this service is discussed, integrated with KakaoTalk (http://koreabizwire.com/duth-pay-coming-to-kakaotalk/40556), with KakaoTalk (카카오톡) an instant messaging application for smartphones.

There is no shortage of examples of this kind of 'public English' to be found within Korea (Lawrence, 2012; Holmquist and Cudmore, 2013). Store fronts alone promote English-named Korean businesses with brightly coloured signs, such as *Buy The Way* (a convenience store); *Beanpole* (a fashion brand); and *Angel-in-us* (a coffee chain) – there are of course many more examples (there are also, however, some non-English examples of foreign languages which are used for businesses, such as *Tous Les Jours*, a popular Korean bakery chain). This public use of English in Korea is at once both wide and deep, extending beyond business and company names, to include its use on Korean magazine covers, within company slogans, in commercials and print ads, and within K-POP and Korea drama of course (Lee, 2006; Lee, J.S., 2007; Lee, K.Y., 2007; Baratta, 2014; Hare and Baker, 2017). Hsu (2019: 463) also addresses the use of English on magazine covers in the Taiwanese context, and aptly describes this as a means by which the 'nativization of English has been reinforced'.

In this case, however, the nativization applies more to what Blommaert perhaps has in mind – more to do with the 'bits and pieces' and ornamental use of language. Nonetheless, I would apply this to the larger picture of societal codification, in that words and phrases in English are nonetheless being spread. To what extent this spread is manifest in the English use of Taiwanese individuals who read the magazines in question is not known, but it is plausible that the English can become part of their repertoire, as opposed to merely functioning as some kind of hook.

This use of English in Korea in such a broad range of public contexts points to Korean media English. This can involve grammatical accuracy, but perhaps unusual style or semantics. This discussion will be included later and reflects a more innovative (in a non-linguistic sense), original and even 'poetic' use of English that is at once original, but not always predictable (as I had mentioned earlier), and part of contextual codification. Given the nature of media, broadly defined, to indeed position itself as original (Reinartz and Saffert, 2013), whether selling shoes, promoting a TV drama romance or singing K-POP, there is perhaps more of a need to *not* use an otherwise familiar variety of English and instead try to use English – from slogans to lyrics – in a manner that suggests originality, which can then be placed onto the product. For this reason, this particular usage of English in Korea is not necessarily tied to Korean English in the sense of a codified variety of grammar and lexis (see Chapter 4). However, as Chapter 4 will make clear, and in keeping with the work of Jenks and Lee (2017), we need to also include a variety of Englishes within the designation of 'Korean English'. And this would include its widespread usage within a variety of media in Korea.

The effects of the internet on linguistic reinforcement

The internet, with its myriad outlets for online communication, is perhaps one of the quickest ways to send information nowadays and that would include its role in spreading, and changing, language (Merchant, 2002; Gao, 2006; Hanna and De Nooy, 2009; Squires, 2010; Bokor, 2018). In the Korean context, Rhee and Kim (2017) comment that internet use is particularly high and used for a variety of functions, which are not tied solely to English use in chatting of course, but that would certainly be included within overall internet usage in Korea. The internet as a whole, chatting, emails and so on can all combine to export varieties of English from one person to another and this can include sending an email from a Korean computer room in Seoul to a friend in Delhi, or chatting with friends after school using English as the medium, when the group may otherwise have many different native languages.

Danet (2010) explains that regarding online language populations, 35.2 per cent use English, both native and non-native speakers, with English 'the de facto lingua franca of the Internet' (page 147). Thus, computer-mediated English is a force to spread English and different varieties, with 'computer-mediated English' a variety in its own right. Danet points out some of the features of what might be considered computer-mediated language overall, such as the use of emoticons, multiple punctuation (!!!) and using all capital letters. Such features are initiated with the computer users, and with each and every use, the features mentioned earlier, and others, are subsequently being reinforced. Once again, the internet is a useful tool for societal codification of language. And more recently, the Internet World Stats (2020) website indeed makes clear that as of 31 March 2020, English is the first out of the top ten languages that are used on the web. The percentage of the world's population using this language as a medium for online communication is 25.9 per cent, with the number of internet users of English given as 1,186,451,052 (and this does not include its use as a lingua franca among other L1 speakers of English!).

We should not forget the importance of film media to influence language. A filmic dialogue may indeed represent an innovation in the English language (or any other), but it is up to society to decide whether or not they wish to use it. An example I referred to previously (Baratta, 2019a) derives from the US film *Fast Times at Ridgemont High* (1982), a successful teen comedy. During an argument between two friends in the film, an individual is accused of being a *wimp* and a *pussy*, with both words referring, as they do in this scene, to a man perceived as weak or cowardly. The individual using these two words against his friend then puts them together to form the blended word *wuss*. While the film per se did not necessarily coin the term, it arguably helped the term to be used more extensively in US society. And as an American, I can confirm that the British expression *the full Monty* was unheard of until the British film of the same name came out. Its influence in the United States was such that I recall hearing a character in a US daytime soap use this term (the US equivalent would be *to go the whole hog*). Purely anecdotal, but it illustrates the point. That is, language can spread via media in this way, here film, and it is then up to society whether to continue to use new expressions or not.

In terms of the internet as a communicative tool, the internet usage for Koreans, as of 2006, is 83.8 per cent (Daniel, 2011). Daniel (2011) in fact points out how the Korean language has been affected by internet usage, part of Korean Net Lingo, or KNL. This incorporates, superficially, elements of English, largely the use of letters, but is otherwise firmly Korean. Nonetheless, this is one example of how language is in the hands of its society members, though in this case perhaps, a usage tied more to youth. In my previous research into World Englishes (Baratta, 2019a) the one Korean participant in fact echoed this suggested use of online language use in relation to Koreans' English. He referred to Konglish as being largely mediated by online usage among Korean youth, with the example provided of the word *com*, meaning *computer*. Of course, this might be more tied towards KNL. Moreover, there is evidence for Korean internet slang, which, while not tied to English per se, nonetheless offers evidence of how the internet incorporates features of English. One of many blogs on the subject – https://blogs.transparent.com/korean/korean-internet-slang/ (Ginny, 2011) – is itself testament to how the internet is also spreading linguistic norms; not merely via the use of emails and texts, for example, but also via blogs which provide online guides for such linguistic norms.

The Korean participant went on to say that the younger generation in Korea use online communication to formulate a use of English that the older generation might not understand; but a use that the current and future generations will understand. Lee (2001: 338) concurs, believing that Anglo-Korean loan words in particular as a feature of Korean English are becoming 'more native speaker-like with each generation' – again, a tie-in with societal usage which in turn cements a language, or an aspect of it. When asked about his feelings regarding the notion that Korean English is not 'proper', this individual declared that such a belief was an 'arrogant statement' and 'BS' (i.e. bullshit) further explaining that 'all languages have their own traits and characteristics' (page 220). This need not be contradictory to the view that Korean English, in his mind, was not yet official. His overall point might be that Korean English does constitute a use of language that serves its (youthful) speakers well, but is lacking officialdom in terms of not (yet) reflecting the aforementioned traditional methods of codification. He in fact also suggested that people should consider the 'Norman invasion period', a reference to the multiple linguistic influences on the English language. Park (2019) does shed light on this potential for different generations of Koreans to be more or less proficient in Korean English vocabulary, with older

Koreans perhaps less likely to use Korean English words that are Anglo-Korean borrowings; examples of this category include *stress, accent* and *Facebook* – words which are directly borrowed from English, yet exhibit Korean pronunciation as follows: 스트레스 (stress), 액센트 (accent) and 페이스북 (Facebook), which on a somewhat 'intuitive' level are respectively pronounced as *suh-tress-uh, ak-sent-uh* and *pace-book*.

Inherent in this global use of media, Warshauer, Black and Chou (2010: 490) explain that 'an estimated 55 billion emails are sent every day', with English being the dominant language (Crystal, 2001). Within this usage, it is not solely, or perhaps even mostly, business English that is used. In other words, it might well be that emails are used for informal communicative purposes, where one's local English might be deemed more appropriate than a more formal variety which might seek to emulate standard inner circle. And within this spread of English, Meriläinen (2017: 762) refers to the 'propagation' of specific linguistic features, indicating the 'entrenchment of this (new) feature in the speech community' which is driven by 'social factors'.

Seargeant and Tagg (2011) investigate online discourse use among young Thai women. This particular usage reveals features including deletion of copula verbs and articles, and while this usage might be a variety of Thai English that is tied to the specific context of computer-mediate communication, a participant nonetheless referred to the language use as reflecting 'Thainess' (page 505). Merchant (2002) further explores the use of internet chat rooms among teenage girls as a means to partly explore how language adapts to that context, including expressions such as *U, woz, wot* and *BRB* (be right back), as well as not capitalizing *I* – a means to 'save typing time and increase the pace of the dialogue' (page 301). While this study takes place in the north of England, a suggested internet language, consisting of abbreviations and emojis as but two examples, may also incorporate aspects of English and, in doing so, establish them as legitimate in the online context. The approach taken here to World Englishes allows us to thus capture variety within variety (Mesthrie and Bhatt, 2008), and thus, there is again a need to subdivide the variety of English used in Thailand, and of course Korea, as part of the broad category of 'Korean English'.

Whether online English is its own category, albeit one influenced by the relevant local English, or merely an online reflection of an expanding circle variety, is beyond the scope of the discussion here. Instead, it is felt to be sufficient to simply provide evidence that expanding circle varieties are indeed being reflected in society, to include social media usage. Ai and You (2015) focus on the continuing reinforcement of China English within the online context of a discussion forum, finding evidence of the use of new ditransitive verbs, such as *present, advise, supply* and *provide* (e.g. *I'd appreciate it if you'd present me those websites*). This is an example of how an existing expanding circle variety can be further spread by online usage, though as Chapter 5 will discuss – and as I have touched on here – we might consider internet usage as its own variety within a variety. A variety which can use the grammar and lexis of an existing English, and/or use features that might be more specific to internet usage per se more globally. So far, then, we might find beyond the initiator of Korean English, Korean internet English, Korean media English and others; and as Chapter 5 will make clear, media English can itself be further subdivided depending on the specific type of media.

We can see examples of online language within internet use on a more global scale, to include chatting, texts and of course emails, and consisting of abbreviations (LOL) and the visual language of emojis. Foster (2018) addresses how social media as a whole is changing the English language, such as the use of vocabulary (*tablet, troll, catfish, ghosting*). Such language might be part of a global internet/social media language, though this is beyond the scope of the coverage here – though there is a branch of study referred to as Internet Linguistics (Baherl, 2013). For now, the internet and its many communicative outlets offer an accessible and direct means by which its users can spread, and reinforce, online English, to include here online expanding circle Englishes. The larger picture pertains to more modern methods of communication, from emails to Facebook, chatting to texting, and I move on now to the specific ways in which Korean English has indeed been codified via the internet, providing a brief introduction to online dictionaries.

Online dictionaries and guides for Korean English

The most immediate, perhaps the most obvious means, of societal codification of Korean English nowadays, beyond the speakers themselves, is the internet. If notions of books and dictionaries are still at the forefront of people's minds with regard to codification, then these can now be found online, dictionaries in particular. With regard to the belief in dictionaries as being a powerful means of codification, Dolezal states (2006: 695) the following:

> dictionaries confer legitimacy upon a language as a comprehensive concept, or some part of a language, whether we call that register, dialect, lexicon, or vocabulary, to choose some of the more common designations. 'Legitimacy' can

be understood as a shorthand for identifying and establishing the varieties of Englishes that are used in various locations around the world. English speakers have been accustomed to relying on the dictionary as not just a reference, or look-up tool, but as an authority that tells us whether a certain locution is actually a part of the language: 'Is it in the dictionary?'

However, considering the plethora of online dictionaries for Korean English, we need to consider this as an alternate form of *the* dictionary; thus, Dolezal's question which completes his quotation is just as relevant to an online source as a print book, and just as relevant to someone's personal dictionary blog as to the *OED*. Prestige is another matter of course, as I had discussed earlier.

The internet has multiple examples of Korean English which serve to further cement this variety, as well as exposing people to it for the first time. Coverage of this modern medium as a prominent means of societal codification would make a fitting end to this section, but I have chosen to provide this coverage in Chapter 4. I have decided to do so for two reasons.

First, the focus within this chapter, while including a discussion of Korean English of course, has otherwise wished to avoid a focus *solely* on Korean English and in doing so, place Korean English within the wider discussion of expanding circle Englishes and societal language codification in general. In adopting this approach, it can help to demonstrate how, once again, society, or certainly societal groups within, decides for itself the language it will use. This applies to Korean English, as much as it applies to British youth who love to use expressions such as *that is well sick*, to the occasional anger of their parents and teachers perhaps. It also applies to each and every language variety (and varieties within), from Albanian to Gujarati to Wolof. This much is perhaps obvious, but framing a discussion of Korean English and societal codification within this broad sociolinguistic picture helps to set the scene for the remainder of the book, which is indeed focused solely on Korean English. This in itself pertains to the second reason for the separate placement and discussion of online sources of Korean English.

That is, Korean English deserves its own discussion and therefore, Chapter 4 will begin by unpacking the various aspects of this discussion to be had: (a) the status of English in Korea; (b) the differences between Konglish and Korean English – to include how I incorporate features of the former into the latter; and then, (c) a final discussion on the grammatical and lexical features of Korean English. The second and third sections of Chapter 4 will not only be informed by academic publications, but will indeed be based on the information gleaned from online publications, whether websites, blogs, YouTube videos, magazines, newspapers or Google translate. As I had mentioned earlier, online sources probably get more hits than academic ones on the subject of Korean English, and given their role in societal codification, they should not be discounted as not being 'official' or 'academic' enough (though I acknowledge the potential for disagreement and even misinformation that can occur in the more open nature of online contexts).

Chapters 4–6 now follow, which will cover Korean English and English use in Korea in detail, respectively focusing on its grammatical and lexical features; media use of Korea; and the role of Korean English in the EFL classroom.

4

The lexical and grammatical aspects of Korean English

This chapter will first present definitions from the literature of both Konglish and Korean English; and from here, I will then present numerous examples of Korean English grammar and vocabulary, relying on both the academic literature of books and journals, as well as 'societal literature' – websites, blogs and online sources overall. Just as I have argued for a more modern approach to codification, one which is based on societal use of language, I likewise approach websites on this subject as a legitimate means of revealing the extent of Korean English in terms of its establishment in Korea.

Defining Konglish and Korean English

While I have established my approach to, and definition of, Korean English, one that pertains to the systematic use of English in Korea as an established expanding circle variety, it makes sense to discuss the relevant literature regarding the two terms in the section title, as a means to provide an update as to the differing opinions and attitudes towards them. Before I explore the literature, I begin this section by problematizing the very term which I use to describe the variety of English under discussion – Korean English – by providing an extended quotation from Jenks and Lee (2017: 7–8):

> focusing on macro-level concerns of nativization of English cannot account for the vast range of proficiency levels, discourse styles, and educational attainment among individual users. In addition, such narratives can also construct a misleading view of a homogeneous collective ideology of English without attending to the necessarily heteroglossic nature of language ideology within a particular region (Jenks & Lee, 2016). Simply put, 'Korean English', in the singular form, or even expressions such as 'Korean usages of English' or 'Korean

attitudes toward English', can potentially suggest that all Koreans speak English, or even think about English, in a constant, static, and uniform way.

This is a telling point, and clearly ties in with the need for a pluralistic way of conceptualizing Englishes within Englishes (within Englishes) in the first instance. Jenks and Lee (2017) rightfully point out that the ways in which English is used in Korea do not necessarily suggest a uniformity. If we consider (as Chapter 5 will do) the media outlets for English in Korea – such as K-POP, Korean TV drama and advertising, as but three examples – then we can expect to see, and hear, a wide variety of English, as appropriated by Koreans. At times, the English that is used in such contexts need not point to a specific Korean version per se in terms of grammar and/or lexis, yet it nonetheless suggests what might be categorized as 'Korean use of English' within contextual codification. Many such examples reflect Blommaert's (2010) discussion on 'bits of language', even suggesting a 'decorative' use of English.

One example that comes to mind concerns the advertising blurb used by Korean Air some years ago to advertise its flights to Kenya, in which the Kenyans were described as 'indigenous people full of primitive energy'. This use of English, at face value, does not appear to be tied to any country per se, and perhaps this is partly due to the grammar reflecting inner-circle standard and, thus, an 'unmarked' variety. However, language is more than just grammar and lexis, as this chapter will discuss, and the overall semantics of the previous excerpt suggest that Kenyans are primitive, which could go further and imply that they are not civilized. Clearly, this is just my reading, but Korean Air nonetheless offered an apology as a reflection of the negative implications of this slogan.

I do not present this example in any way to suggest incompetence on the part of the slogan writers and by extension, Korean people's use of English. Far from it. In fact, I recall hearing of an advertisement for Parker pens, an American company, which tried to appeal to a Spanish-speaking audience by using the word *embarazada*, as part of the marketing phrase 'won't leak in your pocket and embarrass you'. However, the word *embarazada* translates as *pregnant*. I had in fact covered these kinds of errors (Baratta, 2019a), which, while not always suggesting mistranslations per se, do create a meaning that is unintended. For example, a sign in a cocktail bar in Norway declared the following: LADIES ARE REQUESTED NOT TO HAVE CHILDREN IN THE BAR. Grammatically proficient, semantically misleading. Of course, the immediate context makes it clear that children are not permitted in the bar area, and more specifically, parents – though defaulting to women only – must adhere to this. Clearly, the intended meaning is not that women are not allowed to give birth in the bar area.

So, what do we make of this one sentence? Is it a feature of Norwegian English? If applied to a pluralistic approach, perhaps it could be, but then, which particular variety would this apply to? We could suggest that it comes under 'hospitality English' (as used in Norway), or perhaps more broadly, 'tourism English' or on a very narrow level, 'hotel English'. That English is not monolithic is hardly a controversial statement, but Englishes are not monolithic either.

Beyond the use of English in Korea for advertisements, the use of code-switching from Korean to English is far from rare. Chapter 5 will cover this in more detail, but I recall many instances of TV characters switching to English, using expressions as varied as *I got it, jackpot, double crazy* and even longer stretches of dialogue. The song 'Lovin' You' by the girl band Sistar uses the English expression *what can I do* in the chorus. In fact, one wonders to what extent the hit song *Gangnam Style* has perhaps influenced English, certainly in terms of making many fans aware of the word *oppa*, as I had mentioned. As for advertisements, defined broadly, the Seoul government's use of I SEOUL U as its tourist slogan is yet another form of English, as used in Korea and by Koreans. In terms of who the uses of English are *for*, this might be regarded broadly as the Korean people, but more as a reflection of the power of English in Korea and thus, sending the message, indirectly, regarding the status of the English language in Korea (and of course the abovementioned slogan is for the world, as a means to attract tourists). Again, Chapter 5 will go into more depth on this, but this brief discussion serves to address Jenks and Lee's (2017) quotation. While some have argued that Korean English does not exist (Song, 1998), Jenks and Lee clearly suggest that it does, but it can't be narrowed down to a suggested monolithic variety.

In addressing their claim, I state again the need to investigate more than just a definable Korean English and instead look beyond to the ways the English language is used in Korea in toto. This is the purpose of the next chapter which, while not possibly being able to address all instances of English in Korea, will attempt to address additional contexts. Jumping ahead to the future, it is possible that, given the number of inner-circle English-speaking immigrants who now live in Korea, their children may well grow up bilingual, to the extent that their variety of Korean will be infused with elements of their parent's home language, which in some cases will be English. This can relate to ethnolects, varieties of languages which are emerging, and have emerged, based on the influence of immigration in a given country. For example, if we consider the German language, one of the varieties would include *Kiezdeutsch*, which is a variety of German influenced by the languages of immigration in the country, notably Turkish and Arabic. Thus, a future Korean English variety might well be centred more specifically on home use, which can of course spread beyond this immediate boundary. Though speculative, it is possible that this suggested variety could evolve, and differ from what is otherwise understood as Korean English (to be discussed shortly).

Thus, I agree with the points made by Jenks and Lee, which perhaps reflect the impracticality involved with trying to compartmentalize language, which cannot be contained as it is always on the move, dynamic and anything but static. On the other hand, there is a practical need to attempt to do so, a means to make the abstract more concrete. In this case, I refer to the importance of identifying variation within a given language in order to better understand its range of use, to include the different speakers who make it their own. In this sense, we could understand a monolith such as 'British English' on multiple levels, involving sociolects (e.g. Multicultural London English) and regional dialects (e.g. Yorkshire English), as but two examples. The ever-changing nature of language within a given community, let alone within national borders, precisely because of the plurality of language, needs some kind of systematic approach to help us attempt to understand this plurality better and keep up to date. We need a starting point, whether Korean English, American English or Indian English. It is where we go from here that can be a matter of discussion.

However, I prefer not to use terms such as 'the use of English in Korea' or 'Koreans' use of English', precisely because they are, in comparison to Korean English, rather too vague. And while terms such as *Korean English* might suggest too much 'precision', such terms help to provide needed clarity and also help recognize regions which, as I made clear in the Introduction chapter, have not always been recognized as much as inner- and outer-circle varieties of English. My discussion of Korean English will be applied to the systematic use of specific grammar and lexis that is used in everyday conversation and even in writing, to include newspapers. This, too, might be seen as broad (what is 'everyday conversation?'), but I hope the discussion to follow will clarify matters. Therefore, I will use the term *Korean English* for reasons discussed much earlier, but now continue by reflecting on the relevant literature in terms of what is meant by the key terms *Korean English* and, of course, *Konglish*.

There are differing opinions towards what defines Konglish (Hadikin, 2014), the more commonly used term of the two used in the title of this section. As I suggested earlier in the book, Konglish as a term might meet with less negative perceptions than Chinglish, and not necessarily be regarded as synonymous with translation errors to the extent that Chinglish usually is. I suggest that this is the case considering the historical influence of English in Korea, one quite different from China. While English didn't arrive in Korea until relatively recently, the first English school was nonetheless established in 1883 (Nahm, 1993). More recently, the US military has maintained a visible presence in Korea for several decades, including a military alliance between the United States and Korea, bilateral economic relations with the United States, such as the free trade agreement, and much influence from Hollywood films. This has allowed English to have a consistent, uninterrupted foothold in Korea and, as such, more time for Koreans to have perhaps developed their own unique variety. This would suggest a degree more consistency in the use of English among Koreans who have long since embraced it; and thus, Konglish might also suggest, to some, a nativized variety, despite the different terms used, and differing definitions of terms such as Konglish.

Some researchers have used the term *Korea English* (Lee, 2007; Park, 2009), perhaps a reflection of the term *China English*. While Chinese English as a term has been referred to as a reflection of errors in speech, I again prefer to use the term *Korean English*, not *Korea English*, as a reflection of an expanding circle variety that is established. Clearly, one feature that seems to unite the three terms is the borrowing of English words as a dominant factor (Kent, 1999; Lawrence, 2012; Mulholland, 2014; Fayzrakhmanova, 2016). This alone, however, does not tell us everything, notably in terms of perceptions of Korean English. In some cases, perceptions are quite negative, with Yoo (2014: 84) describing Korean English as 'broken English used by Koreans without a consistent pattern distinct from other varieties of English'. Nam (2010: 276) further describes Korean English based on 'an impoverished view of English'. Nonetheless, there is disagreement on this matter in terms of opposite views which see Korean English as being established and codified and indeed used by Koreans (Jung and Min, 1999; Shim, 1999; Park, 2009; Rüdiger, 2014; Ahn, 2017; Baratta, 2019a). Park (2009: 94), using the term *Korea English*, defines it as 'the spoken English used by the most educated Korean speakers when communicating internationally as well as intra-nationally'.

Another important factor is seen with the study by Thorkleson (2005) involving Korean university students. It was noted that when the students edited English language news articles, the edits were different in terms of linguistic choices based on whether the understood audience was Korean or international. This suggests two important factors: one, that Korean English, even if viewed as a performance variety, has use for Koreans intranationally. Two, this also shows that if individuals are making conscious choices regarding a particular variety of a language and its use in a specific context, then this would refute beliefs that the variety is somehow random and error-laden. Given the discrepancies not just in terms of differing definitions of Korean English but also in terms of attitudes, it is all the more reason why more clarity is needed. Arguably, much of the negativity stems from beliefs that Korean English needs to approximate standard inner circle and/or that it needs more official means of codification. As I have made clear already, neither belief is, linguistically speaking, valid.

Kent's (1999) pioneering work on Korean English established several features of this variety and, in doing so, points towards a level of systematicity. Kent discussed the use of loan words from English, semantically modified loan words (e.g. *eye shopping* for *window shopping*) and truncated terms (e.g. *air con* for *air conditioning*), among others. However, Lawrence (2012) goes further, arguing that Korean English has developed to the extent that it can't merely be defined on the basis of borrowing words from English. However, he does not believe that it has been codified. Perhaps one day it will be codified in a manner that some believe is befitting of established linguistic varieties; I have already made my point clear on this matter. Lawrence's approach to Korean English, however (using the term *Konglish*), is perhaps the most appropriate, and the one I would use. I base my judgement, as much as I can, not on personal feelings on the matter. Rather, I find the definition of Lawrence ideal because, in a spirit of linguistic objectivity, it avoids both negative and positive appraisals of Korean English and instead merely presents a neutral, value-free description. This is the approach that is required for linguistic analysis. Lawrence (2010b: 12) defines Korean English as 'a creative mix between English and the local language, which normally includes morphology, semantics and syntax but may also include pronunciation, pragmatics and discourse'. No judgements are passed in terms of broken English or the like, or indeed singing Korean English linguistic praises. It would be naïve, however, especially for a linguist, to ignore the potential for negative perceptions of Korean English in the classroom context; Chapter 6, however, will address this.

Ruffin (2010) offers a rather pejorative view on Konglish, published in *The Korea Herald*. This outlet alone – an online newspaper – can help spread views, positive or negative, on a host of subjects, and is potentially read by millions. This kind of dissemination, covered in this chapter, is perhaps the most relevant nowadays for information searches – the internet. The extent to which online views of Konglish influence people is unknown, but Ruffin's descriptions of Konglish are problematic, if we adopt a linguistic point of view as opposed to a societal one. Defining Konglish as the use of English words and phrases in a

Korean context (though I will argue it goes beyond this), Ruffin explains that, in reference to Konglish, 'there appears little concerted government efforts to keep the Korean language pure'. McPhail (2018) discusses Korean English, and also touches on Korean English and its lack of purity when compared with Korean, while also reflecting on its widespread use in society. The difference between the perspectives offered on a lack of 'purity' offered by Ruffin and McPhail is that Ruffin suggests some kind of linguistic impurity in language – this does not exist. McPhail, on the other hand, approaches impurity in language (and purity, for that matter), from a purely societal perspective. And on that level, notions of (im)purity in language do unfortunately exist, and in turn can affect people's attitudes to language and subsequently, the speakers themselves (Bohner and Wanke, 2002).

Negative societal attitudes towards Korean English might be a reflection of multiple societal factors in Korea. These are discussed by Park (2017) and include self-deprecation, based on viewing the West as an all-powerful point of cultural comparison and as part of this, native speakerism. The idea that native speakers of English are regarded as the 'ultimate arbiter and authority' regarding English teaching 'contributes to the propagation of self-deprecation' (page 60). However, Park goes deeper on this matter, arguing that presumed incompetence with the English language is somewhat of a proxy, a symbol of 'embarrassing evidence of the backwardness of the country' (ibid). However, it is impossible for me, a Westerner/American, to suggest how Koreans do, or should, feel on the matter of their culture and as a reflection of culture, their use of language. As I have made clear, all the linguistic objectivity in the world can sometimes not compete with societal attitudes.

Park goes on to describe another ideology tied to the English language in Korea, one which is based on viewing competence in English as tied to success in education and career, with English viewed as a symbol of 'power and privilege' (page 60). With competence in English viewed as a status symbol, then such connotations can come to be associated with competent speakers of the language, but clearly, this is afforded to the use of native speaker varieties, and then those tied to perhaps American English more so (Porteous, 2020). Having said that, there is evidence that Koreans are travelling to outer-circle countries to learn English, such as South Africa (Coetzee-van Rooy, 2009). Nonetheless, in comparison with inner, or outer-circle countries perhaps, Korean English might not be afforded such prestige (Shim, 1994; Kent, 1999; McDonald and McRae, 2010; Young and Walsh, 2010; Porteous, 2020). Young and Walsh (2010: 132) in fact claim that 'most South Koreans dream to be an NS'.

Nonetheless, attitudes towards the influence of English words on the Korean language, though only one aspect of Korean English, have been investigated. Irwin (2011: 200) found that in the Japanese context, the pervasive influence of English words in Japanese society creates a 'love-hate' relationship. Some view the influence of English as creating a more 'advanced, democratic society', while others regard English 'as a threat to Japanese culture and tradition' (ibid). In the Korean context regarding attitudes towards the influence of English, Rüdiger (2018) finds similar results, and we can suggest that the identity Koreans forge from their language (Coulmas, 1999; Park, 2010) as being a factor. This suggests that, while English per se is regarded as very important for Koreans to master, this does not suggest that its study, use and influence are necessarily desired. An illustrative quote is provided by Lee (2014: 33), who states that 'English is possibly the most revered and at the same time the most feared foreign language in contemporary Korea'.

However, we must not forget the importance of the context of communication. There are clear instances in which standard inner circle would be prescribed, and other varieties proscribed. Such instances would indeed reflect 'institutional' usage of English, such as university entrance examinations and IETLS/TOEFL, for example. However, in everyday, informal contexts, Korean English use might be regarded as wholly appropriate among its speakers, or certainly not a reflection of poor English. Likewise, its presence on a wide societal level, as discussed in the previous section, strongly suggests that this variety has a time and a place within Korean society, largely free from negative perceptions by those who choose to use it. Therefore, when discussing societal perceptions of Korean English, it makes sense to determine said perceptions within a full context of the 'where', 'when' and 'who' in terms of its deployment. Moreover, not all the literature agrees with regard to Koreans' perception of Korean English; Ahn's (2014) study largely reveals positive attitudes expressed towards this variety. While Korean perceptions of English – including their own variety – are not a specific focus within this book, it is useful to briefly touch on this important issue, as a means to help provide a backdrop to the actual use of Korean English in Korea, though, as acknowledged, the literature on this subject is somewhat inconclusive.

Considering the literature on the subject of Korean English specifically, my own definition of this term is based purely on linguistic principles, and not societal attitudes, whether positive or negative. Korean English refers to the variety of English as used in Korea which exhibits a systematic and predictable use of its own grammar and lexis. Linguistic definitions are often, admittedly, quite 'boring', free from social judgements. However, approaching language in such matter-of-fact and objective terms is wholly relevant to a focus on language, of course. Given that Konglish has been understood in such different ways, this term in particular can be problematic, whereas Korean English is more suggestive of a codified variety. Nonetheless, Konglish has been defined, as this section has made clear, on the basis of borrowed words from English which have taken hold in Korean society, as well as Koreans' use of new words based on an English linguistic base (e.g. *eye shopping*).

For this important reason, Konglish need not consistently be reflective of negative attitudes based on being regarded as 'broken English' or the like. Instead, viewing Konglish as a variety of English as used in Korea made up of predictable use of vocabulary, for example, would not be out of place within a definition of Korean English, as this latter term points wholly to linguistic predictability, establishment and, ultimately, codification. Therefore, certain definitions of Konglish would not at all be inappropriate with the definition provided by myself, and others, of Korean English. As such, the two terms might legitimately intersect, but for reasons already made clear, I prefer to use the term *Korean English*. On the other hand, in the instances where Konglish is being treated with scorn, ridicule and, essentially, as 'bad English', then clearly such perceptions have no basis in either linguistic research or in my approach towards Korean English.

Given the definition of the term as a hybrid form (McPhail, 2018) and references to a fear of English in general encroaching on Korean culture – to include the Korean language – then this can be a broad issue with regard to the negativity towards Konglish, as most people refer to it. Konglish is regarded by some perhaps as 'not one or the other', and is associated with a lower proficiency in English overall. That these understandings are a reality for some, and are subsequently applied to this term – and its speakers – can help explain some of the negativity.

I will now continue the discussion, focusing on the grammatical and lexical characteristics of Korean English.

The codification methods and features of Korean English

This section will provide evidence within the academic literature for the grammatical and lexical make-up of Korean English, to then be followed by online examples of Korean English. While some have argued that Korean English has not been codified and institutionalized and, therefore, is not a recognized variety (e.g. Song, 1998), I take the opposing view that Korean English is indeed codified (in the manner I am applying this key term), as others also argue for (Baik, 1994, 1995; Jung and Min, 1999; Shim, 1994, 1999; Ahn, 2014). Again, I base my argument on a two-part approach to societal codification: first, that Korean English is used by Koreans and non-Koreans alike and, as such, has been conventionalized by such repeated usage. Second, this conventionalized language is then codified by traditional means such as (online) dictionaries, but by many additional methods tied to media of many kinds, both entertainment media and public media.

Those who argue that Korean English has already been codified base their argument on the use of teaching materials in the Korean school system in which features of Korean English are indeed taught and disseminated as part of learning materials, and the use of Korean English in English-language newspapers in Korea (e.g. *The Korea Times*); both of these outlets will be discussed in this section and also provide further ballast for the idea of societal codification, with school-based textbooks a more traditional method of codification of course. Inherent in these opposing views as to whether or not Korean English is a codified reality is once again the rigid belief that codification must be viewed from a perspective that I have argued against as being the only perspective, and consisting of, for example, school-based learning materials and dictionaries published by authoritative sources (an individual's personal online dictionary would perhaps *not* be considered authoritative). It is the absence, or presence, of such traditional means that leads to both sides claiming victory or defeat, as it were.

As I have made clear, I am not against such traditional means to approach language with. Rather, I have argued that such means should not be viewed as the only, or even primary, way for codification to take place. Likewise, the more modern approach to codification that I have discussed should be included also as a legitimate means to approach codification. Furthermore, I have argued against waiting for traditional means of linguistic codification to take place for expanding circle varieties and instead consider the methods of linguistic establishment that I have discussed.

Going further, Song's (1998) claim that Korean English is not codified, or necessarily established, points to two additional aspects. First, Song argues that English in Korea is not an official language, nor it is used for instruction purposes at schools; and second, it is not used for intranational purposes of communication. It has in fact been made clear how Korean English is indeed used for intranational purposes of communication, both based on the relevant literature and what I have discussed as being a more societal, public use of the language, as was discussed in Chapter 3. Moreover, Seong and Lee (2008) argue against Song's claims, pointing out that English has in fact been proposed as a second language (as opposed to a 'foreign language') by former president Roh Moo-Hyun, as well as the Seoul mayor, Lee Myung-Bak, voicing a desire to establish English-only villages.

Whether or not English becomes an official second language in Korea or not, two points can be made: one, the Korean government has indeed played a large part in promoting the need for English in Korean society, under the auspices of globalization and not Americanization. These are numerous examples to be seen, which counter Song's claims: the fact English is taught to Korean children from a young age; there are English-only classes at the university level (e.g. Seoul National University and Korea University, two of the most prestigious universities in the country); and we need to consider the emphasis placed on English skills not just for Korean teachers of English but also for government positions, and English-only high schools, as I had referenced earlier. Indeed, the pursuit of English in Korea has been referred to as a fever. Considering the pedigree of leading universities, and legislation passed by the Minister of Education and Human Resources, this points to ways in which English in Korea has got backing. This can only help to promote it as a language for use in Korean society and, by extension, Korea's own unique take on this language – Korean English – a variety which has its own specific lexis and grammar. In reference to this, Seong and Lee (2008: 85) point out 'that each glocalized English needs to be served as a pedagogical model, chiefly because the bi-directionality refutes the hierarchical concept of "uni-directionality", in which the so-called non-native speakers of English all have been compelled to follow the so-called native rules, values, and norms reflected in their use of English'. Chapter 6 will address this in detail.

What now follows is a sample within a larger sample regarding instances of Korean English (Chang et al., 1989; Shim, 1999; Ahn, 2014), consisting of three notable papers by Jung and Min (1999), Shim (1999) and Seong and Lee (2008). Shim (1999) specifically discusses codified Korean English, with the point made that the sample provided is just that – a sample. Nonetheless, the examples provided are clearly not inner-circle English; and yet, in the context of widespread society usage, they are not errors either. The material is taken from *High School English I: Teacher's Guide* (Chang et al., 1989), used in both high schools and vocational schools from 1987 to 1995, and representing 'the final product of the past 50 years of the codification of Korean English' (page 250), thus suggesting that there has been considerable time for the English language to have settled in Korea.

Shim (1999) proposes syntactic and lexical features of Korean English that go back to the 1970s, suggesting that codified Korean English, even if only in development at that time, nonetheless has a history. A determining factor in the syntactic aspects in particular that will be highlighted would be the extent to which they are still used in Korean English, whether spoken or written. Despite my claims that traditional codification should not be seen as the benchmark for linguistic codification per se, no more than American English should be regarded as the benchmark for English, Shim nonetheless investigates a use of Korean English which is wholly traditional in its approach to codification – learning materials for classroom English teaching in Korean schools, themselves backed by the Ministry of Education. It doesn't get more official and traditional than this! Shim in fact refers to the English language instruction within these textbooks as reflecting a 'codified variety of Korean English [which] now serves as the endonormative standards for English education in Korea' (page 247).

Nonetheless, that we have examples of traditional codification is a positive step. Whether or not the learning materials reflected in the teachers' minds were Korean English or were a reflection of what was believed to be standard inner-circle English is not immediately clear. Having said that, Shim (1999) explains that the features in question are 'different from the American English model that they *purport* to follow' (page 250; my emphasis). Moreover, this might be considered somewhat of a linguistic chicken and egg situation; Does the societal use of Korean English lead to it being recorded for English pedagogy, or does the pedagogy lead to children using this variety of English in society? Arguably, both reinforce each other.

Seong and Lee (2008) provide corpus data for their evidence towards a codified Korean variety of English, specifically deriving from Jenkins (2006b) and her reports stemming from her English as a lingua franca projects. As Jenkins (2006b: 169) makes clear, the information revealed from corpus data is a clear source to 'find out which items are used systematically and frequently, but differently from native speaker use and without causing communication problems, by expert speakers of English from a wide range of L1s'. This is an apt description of a codified language and also of its need for communication, which can only be impeded among the speakers if there does not exist a systematic form of language to begin with. More specifically, the data that Seong and Lee rely on stems from the CCDL (Cross-Cultural Distance Learning) programme. This programme is based in Korea University and Waseda University in Japan, requiring much written discourse (in English) between students of both universities which subsequently provides the data for analysis in terms of a codified Korean variety of English.

Before concluding this section and focusing on the specific features of Korean English, I refer to the work of Pandharipande (1987) on the process of nativization, describing the ways in which English changes when it comes into contact with other languages. Pandharipande discusses how a 'transfer of logic' in the speaker's native language in turn affects their resulting English formations, whether grammatical or lexical. This suggests a degree of predictability; and as Schneider (2007: 71) points out, this can lead to 'the emergence of locally distinctive linguistic forms and structures' (page 71). Pandharipande (1987: 152) provides the example of compound words in Indian English as reflective of this compounding tendency in Indian languages, such as *India-watchers*. This can also reflect unintentional deviation in a variety of English, referring to a widespread feature used among speakers and not given much conscious thought – a feature that has thus taken hold. Pandharipande (1987) further references *intentional* deviations, in which speakers deliberately use English for creative purposes; this will have much relevance later when I discuss Koreans' use of English within inherently creative contexts, such as advertising and public signage.

Onysko (2016) further proposes a language contact typology (LCT), explaining that language contact between English and other languages is a firm starting point to better understand World Englishes. In particular, Onysko discusses the linguistic implications when contact is based on English as a learner variety, as well as English as a global language. Examples of Korean English vocabulary perhaps influenced by the global reach of English would include *pocket ball*, referring to pool or billiards, whereas the word *skinship* (physical touching) might be more reflective of a learner English, in which reanalysis is the force behind the combination of both an English word (skin) and suffix (*-ship*) to create a new word. Both words are examples of nativized words.

On a grammatical level, Platt, Weber and Ho (1984) provide a useful list of features that they discuss as being found across countries, some of which occur in inner-circle dialect, such as double negation. However, of particular interest to this discussion are the features more often seen with NICE in Asia. Such examples include article omission or a more idiosyncratic use of such;

Kortmann and Szmrecsanyi (2004) also discuss irregular article usage within such Englishes. This might be expected when a speaker's L1 does not have articles and thus we might expect there to be errors with article usage when such speakers use English. This helps to inform the features found within examples of suggested Korean English.

On the other hand, we need to also consider the pragmatic aspects of suggested innovations. There is a need to always be aware of the who, what, where and when, which will influence, if not dictate, what is or is not appropriate language use at any given moment. This much is obvious, but to see what this might mean for suggested innovations, let us take a look at a suggested feature of China English. He and Li (2009) put forward the Null Subject Parameter as a feature of this variety, such as 'Very glad to write to you again' and 'Miss you a lot' (pages 73-74). Gupta (2012) actually references this as part of standard (inner-circle) English, albeit a more informal register. There are, in fact, many times when native speakers delete personal pronouns also; expressions such as *see you tonight* and *love you* are plausible. This raises the question, if this construction can be found in both China English and inner-circle varieties, what makes it a specific feature of China English more than, say, British English?

First, He and Li argue that this feature is based on 'cross-linguistic influence' (page 74) from the native language (e.g. Mandarin). English, as a language that is otherwise not pro-drop, nonetheless has such tendencies in informal contexts. Thus, a feature found in two varieties might have different origins, one tied to L1 influence and the other tied to more informal registers of communication. Second, we should also consider the aforementioned pragmatic consideration of this feature in China English; He and Li (2009) explain that it is found in a letter or email written in English. This gives some clue as to the context, but it is not the case, but might be, that email communication necessarily defaults to informal communication between friends (though 'letters' might).

Therefore, what is at once a grammatical issue might well have pragmatic considerations at its core, and not suggest a wholesale usage. But if such grammatical features which arise in a given context(s) can nonetheless be identified with a level of predictability, this can be a contender for an innovation which has, by continued usage, taken hold and is thus conventionalized – one of the two main societal aspects by which I put forward my discussion of codification.

I now begin the presentation of some of the various features put forward as Korean English.

Lexical differences

Day by day – This is synonymous with 'daily', and not meaning 'one day at a time' as in inner-circle English

(4)   *The weather is getting warmer day by day.*

After all – This is understood as 'finally'

(5)   *She will pass the examination. After all, she studied very hard.*

The foregoing sentence, according to Shim (1999), would be confusing to a Korean, but not to an inner-circle speaker who would translate *after all* as 'when all things are considered'. But to a Korean, it wouldn't make sense on the grounds that the cause of passing the examination is being seen as the end point – the effect. The effect, of course, is passing the exam: *She studied very hard. After all, she passed the examination.*

It is also important to point out that the two preceding sentences are grammatically proficient, but as I have pointed out in an earlier paper on Korean students' writing (Baratta, 2013), grammatical proficiency does not always translate as semantic, or pragmatic, appropriateness.

Morpho-syntactic differences

The definite article

Shim (1999: 252) explains that 'in Korea, students are told that a noun phrase becomes specific and therefore must be preceded by the definite article whenever a noun phrase is modified by a prepositional phrase or a relative clause'. This in itself is reflective of a grammatical rule, certainly a tendency, and if backed up by pedagogy, then all the more reason for it to take hold perhaps. Examples of what this rule looks like when applied to usage are offered here, taken from page 252:

(6)   *He is the man who can help other people.*
(7)   *Spring is the season that can bring hope to our hearts.*

It needs to be pointed out, however, that sentences (6) and (7) directly are, in themselves, perhaps acceptable in many circles of English. To put it another way, there might not be any immediate Korean English 'flavour' to them. Clearly, if the man in question has already been identified in a previous sentence, or conversation, and is thus known to both parties, then grammatically and semantically, it is fine. The second example might be fine without previous reference to the spring season, or the seasons in general, a means for the speaker to emphasize his/her love of spring by using the definite article. The key issue for Korean English, however, is that sentences (6) and (7) would not be differentiated from the following two; in inner-circle English, they would:

(8) He is a man who can help other people.
(9) Spring is a season that can bring hope to our hearts.

It might also be considered that the definite article is a broad category and as such Koreans' use of it might have to be categorized in equally broad terms. For example, it might be impractical to categorize each and every use of the definite article by Koreans once we start to unpack its various uses, which go beyond merely identifying something that is specific and/or has been mentioned previously in the discourse.

Platt, Weber and Ho (1984) further discuss noun phrases and how articles used within can differ in NICE from inner-circle varieties, but on the basis of the speakers applying a different cognitive system. This is expanded on by Mesthrie and Bhatt (2008), describing two such systems such as 'known-unknown (to hearer)' versus 'specific – non-specific'. Three examples from Singaporean English help to illustrate:

(10) I want to buy bag (non-specific).
(11) There! Here got one stall selling soup noodles (specific, yet unknown to listener).
(12) I didn('t) buy the dress, lah (specific and known to listener).

(Platt, Weber and Ho, 1984: 52–9)

Bickerton (1981) describes article usage based on the abovementioned cognitive systems, which in turn influenced the analysis of the previous three examples by Platt, Weber and Ho (1984). For Bickerton, the zero article is used for non-specific; an indefinite article (in example (11), 'one') for presupposed-non-specific; and a definite article is used for presupposed-specific.

If we apply this to the Korean context, Ionin, Ko and Wexler (2004) analysed learner data from Korean English. Their argument is that article usage by Korean ESL students is not random and nor is it a product of L1 transfer. Instead, it is based on the more appropriate choice between specific versus definite, which, 'in the case of English, is the definiteness value' (Mesthrie and Bhatt, 2008: 48). This can also support, to some extent, a default use of the definite article, which Shim (1999) provides more specific information for in terms of its deployment.

This is a more inclusive way to approach article usage but clearly, if indeed Koreans' use of definite articles, while not reflective of the inner circle, are nonetheless predictable, then this potentially constitutes a feature of Korean English and one perhaps part of (and inspired by) codified school-based EFL textbooks. It might be more realistic, then, to discuss Korean English use of the definite article in broad terms, akin perhaps to 'Koreans use the definite article when it is not required in inner circle'. While this might be seen as broad to the point of bordering on generic, it might nonetheless be a way to approach Koreans' use of the definite article for their academic work, for example. Having said that, Shim (1999) does point out that usage of the definite article in conjunction with a prepositional phrase or a relative clause specifically is key to Koreans' use of such. This might in turn suggest that where inner-circle English would expect a definite article in the *absence* of a prepositional phrase or relative clause, we might not expect to see uniformity of Koreans' use of definite articles in this context.

Given the complexities of article usage, for both grammatical precision and even rhetorical effect, more research into this one feature is needed. But for now, there is evidence of a specific use of the definite article, from one perspective at least, that can be expected within Korean English. Seong and Lee (2008) also point out that there is non-standard usage of the definite articles in Korean English and so this is a feature which is in need of considerable attention in the EFL classroom, in terms of knowing when to categorize Koreans' use of this feature as perhaps reflective of *their* English, and not misunderstanding inner-circle English.

Seong and Lee (2008) rely on data collected from Korea University to determine corpora evidence of predictable features within Koreans' use of English, which might in turn suggest the more specific *Korean English* (as opposed to 'Koreans' use of English', which does not). Seong and Lee explain that Koreans often delete the definite article when it is otherwise required. Shim (1999) explains that Korean English uses the definite article when it might not always be required in inner-circle English, albeit in two specific contexts. Interestingly, the examples of article deletion provided by Seong and Lee do not point to those contexts of usage (i.e. definite article with a prepositional phrase or relative clause), with one exception out of a total of six examples provided:

(13)   *I believe Thanksgiving Day is the biggest holiday in* ( ) *US* (page 89).

The previous example would appear to go against the claim by Shim, in that the use of a prepositional phrase would warrant a definite article (here, *in the*

US). However, the key aspect of Shim's discussion is that Korean English uses the definite article when it otherwise might *not* be required with noun phrases – perhaps a case of hypercorrection (if seen from an inner-circle perspective perhaps). Or, the usage would treat definite and indefinite articles as effecting the same meaning when used with prepositional phrases or relative clauses, when in inner-circle English a change in article in this case would lead to a change in meaning. Thus, sentence (13) might point to a pure error, but sentence (14) is instead suggestive of Korean English:

(14) *He is the man who believes in hard work.*

Again, sentence (14) would be standard inner circle, but perhaps also acceptable Korean English. The inner-circle interpretation would be akin to a specific man known to speaker and listener, or having at least been identified by both, and who is being referred to appropriately from an article point of view. In Korean English, however, the sentence would be semantically synonymous with *he is a man who believes in hard work*.

Furthermore, the remaining examples provided by Seong and Lee regarding (pure) errors with the definite article are not suggestive of regular and predictable features of Korean English regarding the use, or lack thereof, of the definite article:

(15) ( ) *First immigrants were called pilgrims*
(16) *Pilgrims were good friends with ( ) Indians*
(17) *. . . after ( ) harvest*
(18) *. . . after they had arrived in ( ) new land*
(19) *In ( ) present, it is a huge ceremony, as big as a Christmas*

The paper written by Seong and Lee can present some additional insights into Koreans' use of the definite article. Consider the sentence that follows, as part of Seong and Lee's paper: 'The definite article "the" is frequently omitted by the Korean users of English in the following manner' (page 89). The use of the definite article here – *the Korean users of English* – makes sense, as it is indeed being used to identify a specific group. In this case, this specific group is the Korean users as opposed to the *Japanese* users (those from Waseda University). Thus, the definite article is being used here in an inner-circle manner – to identify a specific group, as opposed to 'Koreans' being used in a generic sense, in which a zero article would be used.

But if we look carefully at the surrounding text from Seong and Lee's paper prior to the quoted sentence from their paper, I strongly suggest that the use of the definite article (highlighted in bold) is a feature of Korean English, and not, as used in this specific context, a feature of inner-circle English:

> In the syntactic features of Korea English, three different types of usages in the use of **the** English articles can be recognized from the CCDL data collected on Nov. 20, 1999 at Korea University. They are the omission of articles, the addition of articles, and the misuse of articles. The definite article 'the' is frequently omitted by the Korean users of English in the following manner.
>
> Seong and Lee (2008: 89)

First, it is not grammatically incorrect, from an inner-circle or a Korean English point of view, to use the definite article as it is used earlier with *the English articles*. Nonetheless, and at the risk of claiming some kind of native speaker intuition when all else fails (which I'm not doing), I would argue instead that this otherwise 'unnecessary' use of the definite article is, in fact, wholly necessary for Korean English. It is obeying a rule which would otherwise not be required in inner-circle English, given that the reference is to article usage in English *in general* – thus, a zero article would be more appropriate. By using the definite article, however, it suggests that the focus is specifically on *English* articles and not, say, French or German. This is clearly understood in the first instance of course, and the authors are writing about English article usage in a general, overall sense. This example, then, offers support for a Koreanized use of the definite article which is being obeyed, subconsciously perhaps, by the authors in a journal that is otherwise designed for an international audience. Nonetheless, features of a local English can be observed.

Given that the audience for the publication that Seong and Lee are writing for is presumably international, then inner-circle English would be the default standard. This is another reason why this use of suggested Korean English, in terms of the use of the definite article, is classified as such – in other words, this is perhaps a use which the authors would have attempted to address based on a more inner-circle standard, but did not. If so, this would again suggest a use of a variety of English with which they are comfortable because they believe it to be correct; for Korean English, it is correct. Moreover, on page 88, the following sentence is also noted: 'However, errors in the use of the English articles ....' Again, we can see a use of the definite article as part of a prepositional phrase (*the English articles*), which would otherwise not be required in inner-circle English, given that the reference is again made to errors with article usage in English *in general*.

I now provide another example and fuller contextual picture of the usage of the definite article:

Thus, many Koreans get confused and make lots of errors related to **the** English articles. However, errors in the use of **the** English articles seem not only just from the native language (Korean)'s interference, but from the fact that it could be intralingual (i.e., errors delivered from the English language itself by looking at the fact that . . . .) (pages 88–89)

Of course, I concede that some might argue that by retaining the definite article above, it is merely a rhetorical decision, so less tied, if at all, to any inherent use of Korean English. If so, then the definite article could be used as a means to emphasize the fact that we are clearly focusing on article usage specifically in the English language, even though this is already clearly understood. Nonetheless, such emphasis might imply a degree of importance placed on this specific grammatical feature. Therefore, while I concede there is room for disagreement as to how best to categorize the uses of definite articles as described here, I can at least suggest the use is certainly more in keeping with Korean English.

However, a final example from page 90 of the publication once again demonstrates this tendency:

(20) In addition, the **followings** are **the** examples of the misuse of 'the' when 'a/an' is needed.

First, we see pluralization of a non-count word (Mesthrie and Bhatt, 2008) and the definite article used with 'examples'. The examples referred to are specific examples in one sense, but grammatically speaking the definite article is unnecessary. In fact, this use of the definite article here (*the examples*) might prompt the question in some readers' minds of *which examples do you mean?* That is, the use of definite article suggests shared knowledge between the reader and writers, but the examples in question are only provided to the reader for the first time *after* they are referred to with the definite article. But if using a zero article instead, the communication would reflect a more generic reference, which would be expected here as there is no shared knowledge of the examples in question, and no reason to imagine that the examples that follow are the *only* examples of the use of a particular linguistic feature, which, if so, would necessitate the use of the definite article. Thus, the following sentence is arguably what might be expected within inner-circle English: *In addition, the following are examples of the misuse of 'the' when 'a/an' is needed.*

Moving on to a more 'real-world' context, and based on my frequent visits to the amusement park Lotte World in Seoul, I also recall a sign which explained to parents that no responsibility would be taken by the management if any valuable items left behind in their baby stroller were to be stolen or lost. This explanation is written thus: *Please place the valuables in our custody* (https://minniehwang.

wordpress.com/2010/05/23/konglish/) (see Figure 4). This is referred to as 'Lotte World Sign' in the references.

It seems that the Korean tendency to use definite articles in this manner (here, as part of a prepositional phrase, or within a noun phrase that precedes the prepositional phrase) occurs when inner-circle speakers would not use an article in the first instance, in the context of a generic reference to the topic, in this case *please place valuables in our custody*. In other words, Korean English employs definite articles in some contexts in which inner-circle speakers would use a zero article, also seen on the sign within the phrase *for **the** valuables lost*. Again, from one perspective, the valuables in question are specific to the person who owns them, and perhaps, in keeping with previous discussion (e.g. Platt, Ho and Weber, 1984), the Korean use of the definite article is thus regarded as appropriate. But again, on a grammatical level, *valuables* are part of a generic

Figure 4 Societal codification via a public sign at an amusement park. Taken from https://minniehwang.wordpress.com/2010/05/23/konglish/.

reference, for which use of the zero article would be appropriate for inner-circle varieties; no specific valuables are being referred to, but merely 'valuables in general, whatever they might be'.

Going further, the term *custody*, in this context, would probably be translated as *care* in the inner circle. Is *custody*, as used here, a Korean English word, however? This I can't say, as confirmation would involve an analysis of all such signs which pertain to public places where parents can leave their children's buggy. The use of the definite articles in the sign, however, is more confidently a feature of Korean English. Moreover, that this usage is placed in the context of a sign for the benefit of international visitors, but which nonetheless uses a grammatical feature of Korean English, is another means of societal codification. I had mentioned earlier that public signs in Korea that use English can involve pure errors, often translation based, but I didn't, and can't, rule out the possibility of such public signs sometimes incorporating features of Korean English as opposed to incorporating errors (or using inner-circle English). Indeed, using English on public signs for the benefit of foreign visitors does not necessarily involve translation errors and can in fact help to spread an established form of English, as this example demonstrates.

In terms of indefinite article usage in the sign where it is otherwise unnecessary (i.e. *a responsibility*), is this an error or an innovation? To get to the heart of this question, it would be insufficient to declare its use here as one or the other without a thorough analysis. For example, *responsibility* is a count noun and it would indeed be grammatically correct to thus use articles with it, such as *he has **an** important responsibility in his work*. However, in the context of the previous sign, the word is being used in a generic sense, without a need to 'specify' responsibility as such. In other words, the deeper meaning of the foregoing information is Lotte World does not take responsibility *of any kind*; thus, *in general/overall*, no responsibility will be taken. If the management of Lotte World does not take responsibility of any kind, then there is no need to imply a certain 'kind' of responsibility via the use of an article, whether definite or indefinite. The bigger linguistic picture here might be a tendency for Korean English to use articles, perhaps both kinds, in contexts in which inner-circle speakers would use a zero article. This need not point to grammatical inaccuracy per se, but it might suggest Koreans' tendency to specify referents when inner-circle speakers would otherwise discuss them/refer to them in general terms and thus would not use an article in the first instance. Thus, the Korean tendency in terms of article usage can involve a degree of hypercorrection.

On page 83, Seong and Lee also display an omission of the definite article, seen in the following sentence: 'According to him, S. Korea is now undergoing a kind of language shift due to the influence of English (especially American kind).' There is a need, for inner-circle standard English, to use the definite article here (*especially the American kind*), assuming this is the standard required for this journal. Once again, however, we need to ask if the lack of the definite article is a pure error or a feature of Korean English. To determine the former, then we could expect perhaps to have evidence of randomness regarding definite article omission. Furthermore, we might benefit from a detailed analysis of the specific context in which the article is otherwise expected. In the previous sentence from page 83, the noun phrase does not contain a relative clause or an embedded prepositional phrase, and for this reason, might this be why the writers default to article deletion? It's entirely possible, but further analysis focused solely on article usage in Koreans' English writing (or speech) would be required. Seong and Lee point out that omission of articles is one of the frequent errors made in Koreans' English; but again, is it truly an error or an innovation?

Examples of this omission have been provided and clearly do not impede understanding; but in terms of the definite article usage at least, there is a strong suggestion of a use of this feature that points entirely to Korean English, and not Korean errors when using English definite articles in conjunction with relative clauses and prepositional phrases.

Non-count nouns as count nouns

Shim (1999) points towards the previous example sentence construction that would not be permitted in American English, but are used in Korean English. Mesthrie and Bhatt (2008) further describe this phenomenon as common in NICE, albeit revealing 'a great deal of variability' (page 52):

Growth – this is treated as a countable noun to refer to plants and trees.
(21) ... *hills and valleys that are covered with fresh green growths.*

The usage in (21) appears in the *Essence English-Korean Dictionary* (1987)

(22) *Although it is a hard work, I enjoy it.*
(23) *Taking a walk is a good exercise.*

While Shim (1999) declares that example (23), as with (22), would be an error in American English, I would disagree. This is based more on pragmatic considerations than grammatical ones. Without the article preceding *exercise*, example (23) would translate as something to the effect of 'talking a walk is good exercise in general/overall'. Using the indefinite article, however, might at once give the impression of counting exercise of course, which Shim is arguing against. However, the word *exercise* can exhibit both count and non-count properties. If describing exercise in general, this would be non-count (e.g. *exercise is good for you*). But we can of course refer to an actual observable example of a specific type of exercise, which would be countable (e.g. *I did three different exercises this morning*). It seems that the sentence provided by Shim is referring to exercise in the general sense and so it would not require the article immediately before it. On the other hand, how can we be sure? As is, the sentence could function perfectly well if the intended meaning is 'taking a walk is a good *type/kind* of exercise'. Clearly, we might need to see the sentence that preceded the one Shim provides in (23), to get a fuller picture of the contextual implications. These two examples, however, do offer some more information with regard to Koreans' use of articles.

The issue might not be tied solely to the use of articles with non-count words. It might also pertain to the use of articles, perhaps both kinds, when inner-circle speakers would otherwise employ a zero article – a point I had made already. This is a grammatical issue, but one that also has semantic implications. In other words, using articles when zero articles would be otherwise expected leads to a certain specification of a topic that is otherwise being referred to in a general, overall sense. I would suggest that such usage is not reflective of Koreans attempting to specify the subject under discussion necessarily, but from an inner-circle point of view, this might be the semantic interpretation.

Word order

Shim (1999) points towards the booster expression *too much* specifically, noting that its placement in Korean English would differ from what is expected in American English, if not inner-circle overall:

(24) Korean English: *No wonder you can't sleep when you have coffee too much.*
(25) Inner circle: *No wonder you can't sleep when you have too much coffee*

An illustration, however, clearly needs the rule that produces it. In Korean English, the booster expression is presented after the object of a transitive verb;

in inner-circle English, it would be expected to be placed before the object but after the transitive verb.

This rule can only be viewed as such if it is productive. This is where EFL pedagogy has a role to play. In fact, a rationale for bringing Korean English – and expanding circle varieties in general – into the EFL classroom, is indeed to allow the speakers to be the judge, and thereby avoid a singular focus on a singular variety of English and also, to allow the teacher to learn from the students. In fact, this kind of approach, ironically, allows for Korean English speakers to rely on their native speaker intuition as a guide to what does, or does not, sound 'grammatical'.

Inner-circle English

(26) *He's groggy because he had too much sleep.*

Korean English

(27) *He's groggy because he had sleep too much* (?).

Inner-circle English

(28) *She's in pain as she had too much food.*

Korean English

(29) *She's in pain as she had food too much* (?).

As a speaker of inner-circle English, the Koreanized versions in (27) and (29) do not 'sound' right at all, but the point here is that this judgement is not sufficient to assume Koreans feel the same.

Seong and Lee (2008) discuss word order further, focusing more on the use of deleting aspects of sentences which are otherwise required in inner-circle English (page 88):

(30) *Today hot* (* subject and *be* verb have been deleted) → Today was hot.
(31) *Have to teach how to study* (*subject and object deleted) → I have to teach someone how to study.
(32) *Know how to go* (*subject deleted) → I know how to go.

One chief difference between the papers of Shim (1999) and Seong and Lee (2008) is that the latter characterizes Koreans' use of English as errors, for the most part. Examples (30), (31) and (32) are errors of course, if being viewed from an inner-circle perspective. However, the three examples might represent elliptical structures even used in inner-circle varieties, as part of informal conversations perhaps; thus, these are not errors, assuming perhaps they are used as part of informal discussion. It might also be argued that sentences (30), (31) and (32) are an example of negative transfer, partly influenced by the pro-drop tendencies of Korean. If this is the case, this does not prevent the sentences from being labelled as features of Korean English; and the fact such examples are found within the corpus might suggest that this is a feature to be expected. From here, it could be an opportunity to focus on this as a means to teach inner-circle English, in terms of the need for the 'missing' elements to be added. This kind of exercise, however, is not about correcting, but *translating* from Korean English to inner-circle English, or vice versa.

Verb tense

Shim (1999: 253) and Galloway and Rose (2015) point out that in conventionalized Korean English, present tense is usually not differentiated from present progressive aspect, with past-perfect aspect and past tense also used interchangeably. Kortmann and Szmrecsanyi (2004) also find in Asian NICE that there is a lack of distinction between past and perfect; this might help to somewhat inform Korean English.

(33) Q: *What happens to the grass and trees when spring comes?*
(34) A: *The grass is turning green and trees are budding with fresh leaves.*

The present tense might be seen as more appropriate from an inner-circle perspective, as it would serve the purpose of declaring facts associated with nature, or to put it another way, a general truth/timeless statement (*the grass turns green and the trees bud with fresh leaves*).

Again, it seems that while the examples pertain to grammar on the surface, the larger picture might be connected more to the admittedly broad word of 'style'. Both the inner-circle and Korean English earlier examples do not suggest grammatical error. Using present progressive to describe facts, for example, would be unconventional in academic writing, however, as the hard sciences use present tense to describe facts, and literature uses present tense to give the text a permanent, 'everlasting' quality.

Of course, academic writing might not reflect the style of personal correspondence in an email, or even informal conversations. Nonetheless, uses of grammar deemed unconventional in inner-circle English can be perfectly acceptable in other varieties.

Both papers presented thus far contain additional examples of codified Korean English, such as the use of prepositions, passive voice and verb collocations, for example. The purpose of highlighting just a sample from within the larger sample, however, is to nonetheless demonstrate that codified Korean English, in the more traditional sense of the word, is a reality. When placed with the more societal level of codification that I have argued for, we have a more robust case to present for an expanding circle variety of English that is used intranationally and is well established. As Seong and Lee (2008: 93) point out, 'many educated users of English in S. Korea very much frequently employ those aspects of nativized English, which features part of Korea English.' Though I use the term *Korean English* of course, the telling comment of 'educated' (here, university students) and 'nativized' are highly relevant to the overall discussion. Of course, this also implies that it is only a certain group within Korean society as a whole who use this variety of English in the first instance, with Song (2016) putting forth the argument that for 'English in Korea' to be upgraded to 'Korean English', its usage must be more widespread, as we see with Indian English, for example. I counter this (as does Rüdiger), arguing that we nonetheless have evidence for grammatical features to have become part of the Korean deployment of English, and this goes some way to arguing for this to be a new variety.

Having discussed examples of Korean English in the educational context, Shim (1999) then goes on to discuss the implications of having learned a variety of English, which, while correct in its own right, can come up against inner-circle standards beyond the classroom, such as international contexts of English usage. This could include conversing with Americans, to taking tests such as TOEIC/IELTS for which inner-circle English will indeed be the benchmark. Thus, while English testing in Korea focuses on Korean English as the test standards, students are well prepared for this variety. But beyond Korea, there remains a discrepancy based on the use of English in international contexts, if not inner-circle contexts per se (e.g. passing an IELTS test, to writing an academic essay at the University of Sydney). Some might declare that the 'linguistic damage has been done', but this, again, represents flawed thinking. Clearly, students for whom English language proficiency remains a very important means to pass exams, obtain jobs and communicate for business and pleasure in a global context, have a clear need to learn the variety which will serve them well in these multiple contexts. However, as Chapter 6 will make clear, there is a need for ESL/EFL students to be made aware of more than just one variety of English. Not to the extent of linguistic overload (Baratta, 2019a), but certainly not to present a singular view of the English language. And the use of students' own variety of English is an important teaching tool, for both students *and* teacher.

Shim concludes her article, confirming that at the time of writing, the English study skills guides which accompanied textbooks in Korean schools were still displaying features described as 'uniquely Korean' (page 256). If others, whether native or non-native speakers of English, can understand Koreans' use of English, then the features that make it Korean English can be further cemented in what I believe to be the most natural language setting of all: communication with others which takes place *outside* the classroom. Moreover, it is unlikely that inner-circle speakers would necessarily correct what they perceive to be errors in Koreans' English, whether informal contexts of communication involving friends, or the workplace. Perhaps the English use in question does not need to be corrected, but inner-circle speakers may need to be more aware of English beyond their shores. Though this is perhaps an idealistic sentiment, it is also an entirely realistic and practical one. Clearly, another factor concerns who the Koreans in question are talking to. This could include a discussion with individuals from India, Japan and Mexico at a youth hostel in Germany, in which all of the speakers might default to English (though not to assume that Koreans can't speak Hindi, Japanese, Spanish or German). The context might also include conversing with other Koreans in English as part of a classroom exercise, in which there are differing levels of this language.

Moreover, Meierkord (2012) goes on to argue that when English is deployed by individuals as a lingua franca, this might involve the use of different varieties of English which in turn leads to the mixing of such varieties. Thus, if three individuals meet who derive from, say, Japan, Mexico and Morocco, English may well be the language used by all three in order to communicate. Meierkord suggests, however, that the English as used in this situation need not suggest a uniformity among the speakers in question. Each speaker, even if proficient in English, may nonetheless bring aspects of *their* English to the conversation. The result, according to Meierkord (2012: 2), is that 'the different Englishes potentially merge in these interactions', which can potentially lead to the 'development of new emergent varieties' (2012: 2). Interestingly, Meierkord does not suggest that such varieties are necessarily stable or even codified, but that they instead can involve 'a heterogenous array of new linguistic systems' (ibid). Meierkord references the 'feature pool' in terms of the different linguistic aspects that individuals who use English bring to the table; but such features might not be used by all who are otherwise aware of them. The need to take into consideration differing levels of English proficiency among the speakers is also a factor, as well as another good point that in some countries, there might be a continuum of varieties of English, involving code-mixing, basilects and acrolects.

Meierkord, then, somewhat resists what might otherwise be a linguistic temptation to classify Englishes into recognizable and 'pre-packaged' varieties. This is partly due to the sheer diversity of all such instances in which English is deployed, which may not constitute a predictable variety per se, but instead reflect what could be an otherwise spontaneous use of English (e.g. code-mixing) as part of a given context of communication. One example might involve a Korean individual who, though otherwise speaking English with somebody, nonetheless inserts a Korean expression such as *aigoo* (akin to *oh my goodness!*). Now, would this insertion within an otherwise English sentence constitute Korean English per se? Meierkord might suggest not, as code-mixing in particular can be unpredictable perhaps in terms of which words are inserted from L1 into an L2 conversation. Or, perhaps the insertions are predictable, but only from one individual to the next and not necessarily as used by a community, thus functioning as an idiolect.

Seen from this overall perspective, Meierkord does not perhaps seek to categorize first and foremost, but instead bring up for discussion the very aspects of language use which can make categorization problematic. On the other hand, categorization of some kind is a very useful way to approach Englishes, here expanding circle and Korean English in particular. Even for expanding circle Englishes, we might in fact consider a vast array of contexts in which English is deployed which then, rather than muddy the focus on what Korean English is exactly, instead allows us to approach Korean English from a more contextual perspective.

While this approach might appear to resist the identification of specific linguistic criteria per se, this is entirely because we simply can't predict specific features of English as used in broad contexts. For example, if we consider the English used by Koreans as part of internet chat rooms, the English and Korean mixing used by K-POP fans and the English used as part of Korean advertising, while there might be specific features per se (e.g. the use of the word *oppa* for K-POP fans), it might also be the case that we sometimes need to rely on broader, admittedly more vague linguistic notions, such as the use of 'creative' language for English used in Korean advertisements. Schneider does reference, for example, a degree of 'creativity' on the part of New English speakers as part of his proposed sociolinguistic conditions. Therefore, advertising slogans such as I SEOUL U and *Life's Good*, as used in Korea, would arguably display this kind of broad 'creativity' as they fit the context of advertising, whereas more academic varieties of Korean English might reflect a more predictable use of specific features (e.g. the use of the definite article, as discussed).

The complexities of trying to represent a variety of a language as somehow static and monolithic is a point clearly addressed by Mesthrie and Bhatt (2008: 3), who use the term *English Language Complex* as 'a cover term for *all* varieties of English' (original emphasis). As with Mesthrie and Bhatt's stance, I acknowledge that there is, simply put, variety within variety within variety, with regard to the various Englishes in the world.

Mesthrie and Bhatt refer to the fact that even features identified as part of a New English may not be used by all the speakers as such, given differing proficiency levels they might have with English as a foreign language. Furthermore, the frequency of use of certain linguistic features might not always be determined with certainty. Taken together, these two points suggest that the morpho-syntactic features of a variety of English might be seen as prototypical features, which, while in existence as a means to then be able to chart them, might not be features in all speakers' use of the variety.

Nonetheless, that the authors discuss a wide variety of linguistic tendencies in New Englishes provides additional support for their existence, usage and, more so, the ways in which different varieties of English might nonetheless share commonalities. For example, Mesthrie and Bhatt discuss the retention of local vocabulary pertaining to food and clothing, and the widening of English semantics (e.g. the use of *sorry* as an expression of sympathy in Africa, and not an admission of culpability). The book's focus, then, on charting examples of the linguistic directions Englishes take, with specific examples of such, does provide more concrete examples of the grammatical make-up of Englishes, which would include Korean English as one example of 'New' Englishes.

Mesthrie and Bhatt go on to provide a fuller contextual picture, referring to uses of English such as metropolitan standards English, based on influence from media, and used in big cities (e.g. London), as well as regional dialects, pidgin Englishes, immigrant Englishes and jargon Englishes. Such an approach allows for a detailed picture which does not necessarily focus solely on a particular country as its own flag-bearer of English (e.g. Indian English), but instead focuses more on the individual, seen with immigrant Englishes (e.g. Chicano English which, while tied to a location – Los Angeles/Southern California – is perhaps more relevant to the speaker's identity as an immigrant/offspring of immigrants – in this case, Mexican Americans). While the authors concede that their classification might bring 'as much controversy as clarity' (page 6), it nonetheless captures the many varieties of English that can be found within national varieties, if indeed national varieties are to be the starting point.

Considering the complexities involved with attempting to represent so much linguistic diversity, some argue that we need to go beyond outlining varieties of English in the modern world (Bruthiaux, 2003; Pennycook, 2007; Park and Wee, 2009; Blommaert, 2010). Perhaps the sheer number of World Englishes makes it somewhat impractical, visually speaking at least, to capture them all on one page and/or with one diagram. However, there are additional reasons to pursue this post-varieties approach:

- Given the level of globalization, several varieties of English come into close contact with each other; this might suggest less discrete boundaries beyond one variety and the other.
- There is much code-switching between a variety of English and several other languages (e.g. in countries such as India and Singapore); while this might not influence the country's variety of English, it also means that many societies are not monolingual, which a varieties-paradigm might suggest.
- Again, considering that there is so much variety within a variety, categorization becomes problematic.

Leimgruber (2013), for example, argues that for speakers of a variety of English there is much variability in how they themselves conceptualize the variety, again making a uniform suggestion of a variety difficult. In terms of Singlish, for example, here are a few responses from his study: 'Singlish is Singapore English; Colloquail [sic] form of English in Singapore; A dialect of English used in Singapore; It's a pidgin or creole of all the "native" languages of Singapore namely, Mandarin/Hokkien, Tamil and Malay' (page 5). These responses by Singaporeans in describing a variety of English associated with their country also raises another issue. Namely, who is best 'qualified' to conceptualize World Englishes? Would this be the researcher who studies World Englishes, or the natives who speak such varieties? This points again to a need perhaps for NICE speakers in particular to find their own ways, should they desire, to offer their own specific input for their varieties of English.

Nonetheless, there is a need to conceptualize in the first instance, I would argue, based on the benefits of doing so: a need to make the subject matter concrete, relatable and easy to approach, and a means to identify the numerous settings in which English is used and how such settings can change the variety, whether based on vocabulary or levels of formality, for example. As put forth by Onysko (2016: 197–197), another valid reason for classification is 'to achieve global comprehension on the matter'. What is required is an approach which can address the plurality, but in a manner that allows for a degree of systematic classification (see Onysko, 2016). Besides, an approach such as that advocated by Mesthrie and Bhatt (2008) that recognizes the sheer variety of Englishes within an English can also be useful. This is precisely because it takes into consideration the diversity of Englishes within a given variety (suggestive of a linguistic *matryoshka* doll, as I have discussed – see Baratta, 2019a) and this in turn can help to provide recognition for the speakers of said varieties within a variety. For example, Mesthrie (1988) discusses the many varieties of South African Indian English within the starting category of 'South African English' (this will be discussed in somewhat more detail later).

Before moving on to additional sources of academic research on this matter, I wish to now focus on differences between inner-circle English and Korean English from a pragmatic perspective. That is, we need to also consider the ways in which culture infuses the language we use and how this can sometimes lead to communication issues, or indeed *mis*communication. Shim (1999) doesn't cover this area in great detail, but pragmatic competence in some ways can be of more importance than grammatical competence, certainly in everyday conversations. One example Shim does include in this area, however, consists of the expression *what are you?* here meaning *what do you do for a living?* The former expression is grammatically correct but semantically unclear, even perhaps in the immediate context of two strangers engaging in an introduction with each other having just met.

The issue at hand concerns pragmalinguistic failure/errors, in which words/expressions which are appropriate in one's first language are transferred to a foreign language and can sound unusual or simply inappropriate for the target language or culture. Broadly, this concerns miscommunication and can be described in terms of speaking in one's second (or foreign) language while thinking in one's first language, sometimes resulting in mere misunderstandings, or possibly causing offence, and based on a lack of knowledge of sociocultural norms involving the target language in question (Amaya, 2008). Blum-Kulka and Olhstain (1986: 169) in fact remind us that 'pragmatic failure might carry serious social implications'. Thus, when we speak another language, we do, to a certain extent, speak another culture. Amaya (2008) suggests various classroom exercises involving role playing, largely focused on student A asking for a favour, with student B instructed to deny the request. While role-plays are hardly new in the language classroom, they can help students to better understand the finer points of everyday societal communication from more than just getting the grammar right.

This is an important topic to cover as part of a broader focus on intercultural communication and that which doesn't necessarily involve grammatical considerations. This is not merely about language, but extends to the way in which one's home culture influences, if not dictates, the appropriate norms for societal behaviour and interaction – but norms that might not be shared by other cultures, or if they are shared, are not expressed in the same manner linguistically. One example is Chinese people's tendency to 'reject' compliments, at least if seen perhaps from a more Western perspective. Leech (1983) refers to this as the modesty maxim and it reflects a case of obeying cultural norms which would mean, in this specific context, not to appear proud. Leech also refers to the agreement maxim, however, in which Americans might otherwise be expected to acknowledge the compliment. How this plays out linguistically might involve what is perceived as disagreement with the compliment on the one hand versus gratitude for the compliment on the other hand.

This provides some background to the pragmatic implications for communicative competence. The examples in themselves don't necessarily reveal the deeper cultural factors which influence communication, though this will be covered in detail shortly looking at the context of Koreans, and individuals from the Far East in general. As a disclaimer, one of the inherent issues with discussing intercultural communication is, in an effort to better understand the rationale behind the ways people communicate differently, the impression might be given, implicitly at least, that 'all X do/are this' (e.g. *Korean students are shy in Western classrooms*). This, of course, runs counter to the need for increased cultural understanding, which would avoid broad generalizations at least, or stereotypes at worst. However, a legitimate starting point for such a discussion may well involve some general points about, say, behaviour, but points that are made in an effort to understand the logic behind people's behaviour.

Moosavi (2020: 4), for example, addresses what might be a stereotype that students from the Far East lack critical thinking skills. 'This perception, which is persistent within academia ... tends to suggest that East Asian students struggle to: grasp alternative perspectives; think beyond common sense; and challenge the status quo.' In this case, the linguistic implications of the statement might be realized with students sometimes not responding to questions in class, but instead remaining silent. As a result, some teachers might misunderstand the silence and declare the students to be shy, unmotivated and otherwise unengaged with the class. My Chinese students have explained that their silence in this context *is* evidence of engagement, representing the students reflecting on the class content, the question just posed by the teacher and ultimately arriving at their views on the matter. Thus, silence in this situation can equate to a deep probing and pondering of the topic at hand, and not being unmotivated.

Another further example concerns my multiple experiences with students from the Far East, notably China, Japan and, of course, Korea. This is not an attempt to lump three different cultures together for ease. Rather, I have approached these three cultures based on a shared factor involving regard for their teacher, and how this is played out linguistically. Korean, for example, is a honorifics-based language, part of a vertical society, in which people essentially exist according to certain social 'ranks'. Teachers, for example, are provided with a high degree of respect and as is the case with honorific languages, this respect is conferred on the addressee via linguistic means. This can be seen with titles afforded to certain professions, such as teaching, and verb suffixes. Of course, in an attempt to explain this, my word choices of 'rank' and 'respect', for example, are perhaps not ideal – such is the challenge when describing a language and culture other than your own, which can involve word choices which might not translate well in the first instance.

In Korean, the word for teacher is 선생님 – *songsengnim*. The word *sonseng*, meaning 'teacher' is not pragmatically complete without the honorific marker of -*nim* (님).

This, however, would have no direct translation in English, though some of my Chinese students have perhaps attempted to do so, by addressing me in their email correspondence with 'My Dear Professor'. But if we take this one word – *teacher* – which clearly has a direct equivalent in Mandarin 老师, Japanese 先生 and Korean 선생님, the pragmatic issues involved with its use can be seen in how it is used – herein lies linguistic differences based on cultural ones. Many of my Asian university students have addressed me in both emails and class as 'teacher'. Based on the societal hierarchy in countries such as Korea, one's teacher, as part of a highly esteemed profession, is addressed in this manner as a show of deference and respect. To address one's teacher – even at the university level – by his/her first name would perhaps be unthinkable (Chang, 2010).

However, and making a generalization, university professors here in the United Kingdom, and in the United States, would be addressed by their first name. This perhaps reflects a more 'horizontal' relationship involving teacher and student, and perhaps a reflection of the fact that both are adults, whereas in UK high schools, for example, teachers are referred to as *miss* and *sir*. Thus, to address a US professor as *teacher* might be seen less as a reflection of respect, and actually come across as impersonal – potentially rude – when in an attempt to signal informality, the teacher indeed expects to be addressed by his/her first name.

I concede a few points, however. One, as already mentioned, is that generalizations might not always be relatively 'safe' generalizations. I am not suggesting of course that at the university level in the United States and United Kingdom, all lecturers wish to be addressed by their first name. In fact, I am reminded of a junior college teacher in the United States who I knew, and who was indeed referred to as 'Mr' followed by his surname, though he did address his students in the same manner, such as *Mr Smith* and *Ms Jones*. In this manner, this still reflects a degree of 'equality'. Second, I have come across several Asian students – including Koreans – who do not hesitate to address me by my first name, in both class and emails. Perhaps they realized that this was culturally appropriate for the country that they were studying in, if not for their home culture. Nonetheless, from illustration of this one keyword, and crucially how it is used by different cultures, we can see the potential for cultural differences to be revealed via language use. Finally, because we are dealing with cultural differences, then we cannot label such as 'errors'; however, I am not doing so of course and merely using a conventionalized term (pragmalinguistic errors).

Further linguistic considerations concern repeated expressions used in email correspondence with my Chinese students, for example, such as *please forgive me* and *sorry to disturb you*. Such expressions are usually in reference to what I perceive to be nothing more than basic enquiries and I am not suggesting that the expressions are meant to be taken literally. But they nonetheless perhaps represent conventionalized expressions based on students' home culture and language which, while not causing confusion per se, might be quite different from what Western teachers would expect. Such deference is also found in the emails of Koreans (Lee, 2020), as a direct reflection of Confucian cultural values; here, a revered status for teachers, and also the need for social harmony. In terms of the linguistic implications, qualifying requests is commonly found (e.g. *if this is OK, if this is not a problem*). This potential for differing expectations in communication is not in itself problematic; in fact, it is an opportunity to have a mutual dialogue that gets to the heart of the ways cultures communicate differently so we can obtain mutual understanding. Clearly, Western students may also write in this manner to someone in authority, such as a teacher, but we might expect such linguistic behaviour more from Korean and Chinese students. This example also reflects the research of Bjørge (2007), who found that emails to professors adopted a more formal tone when sent from students whose culture was more vertical, and stressed hierarchical differences.

Further, Chang (2010) explains how sociocultural differences between Americans and Koreans can be realized at the level of syntax, pragmatics and expectations for behaviour; this latter category can be part of non-verbal communication and so broadly connotes language. The Korean sense of collectiveness, versus American individuality can be seen with expression such as *our country* (i.e. Korea); the use of *my* (country) in this context would sound 'very egocentric or even arrogant' (page 138). Questions asked of individuals regarding their age and salary are also reflective of collectivist societies, but could be seen as rude to Americans (and others perhaps). In Korea, asking someone's age upon meeting is wholly relevant, as those who are older need to be addressed appropriately based on the honorific nature of the Korean language. Respect for those who are older is built into the language itself, consisting of suffixes and infixes added to verbs, for example, and this also includes titles, as mentioned earlier, and in some cases, changing the verb entirely (e.g. in Korean, there are two different verbs for *eat*, depending on who the addressee is). Finally, Chang explains that 'silence is golden whereas frankness and outspokenness are prized in America' (page 140), to include expressive acts such as apologizing and thanking being 'less expressive' in Korean than in English in terms of forms and frequency. This can lead to Koreans being perceived as unfriendly, and Americans as being too talkative.

There are two points to be made. First, as Chang (2010) asserts, a degree of cultural intelligence is required for effective cross-cultural communication, and this topic is ripe for classroom pedagogy and discussion: 'The main function of English as an international language is to play a role as a communication tools [*sic*] in divergent environment [*sic*]. In this environment, it is very important to understand the cultural differences among divergent countries' (page 141). This kind of cultural give and take can help individuals to understand the rationale behind the behaviour of people from a different culture, if not appreciate different cultures as a result. Second, culture is very often expressed through language, whether verbal or non-verbal. Ironically, given a suggested Korean preference, or certainly tolerance, for periods of silence between friends who are otherwise having a conversation, then here is an example of how sometimes, not speaking at all is the expected linguistic behaviour. As the local values, attitudes and worldviews of a given culture are expressed through language; then in this case, another aspect of Korean English can be understood from such a broad, but important, perspective. Thus, when Koreans speak English with non-Koreans, for example, the ways in which their home culture seeps through in their language – here, English – will allow it to take on a distinctly Korean cultural flavour, at times. However, asking personal questions is not meant to be rude, but merely reflective of a collectivist culture. Therefore, understanding Korean English means also understanding how culture is expressed through Koreans' use of English; this aspect does not suggest that 'English in Korea' is at all an appropriate moniker (Song, 2016), as Koreans' use of English, as discussed here briefly, might extend to their use of English far beyond Korea's borders.

Another illustration is provided by Harris (2003), a Canadian living in Korea, who recalls an incident in a Korean bank in which he was told that his application for a credit card had been denied. The bank employee told him that, in regard to obtaining a credit card, it would be 'almost hard' – 거의 힘들어하는. To a Korean, this would have been understood as a 'no'. But to a Westerner, perhaps more accustomed to what we might call 'direct' language, the response was anything but direct. But to a Korean, it was anything but *indirect*. How this refusal might be translated into English would perhaps go beyond a direct translation per se, but might be tied more to issues involving not wishing to give an answer which may cause the other person a loss of face. This, too, is indeed a culturally based perspective. Korea, as a high-context culture, relies on what might be regarded as indirect, sometimes more non-verbal means of communication, to understand each other, with the United States, as a low-context culture, relying on what might be considered more 'clear' and direct language to make one's statements unambiguous. Of course, there is nothing necessarily unclear about a Korean's person message to another Korean when they share the same cultural understanding and expectations.

Another area for misunderstandings concerns the use of tag questions (Zhang, 2010), whereby Koreans may give the answer to the question but in an unexpected way when speaking with inner-circle speakers of English. Of course, it is important to distinguish between non-standard uses of the tag question itself and failure to answer it as expected. For example, forms such as *He's gone now, is it?*, though non-standard, is a feature of an inner-circle English, Tyneside English (Beal, 1993: 202). What now follows, however, are instances in which Koreans' responses to tag questions by inner-circle speakers can cause misunderstandings. Avery (2015: 1) explains that in the Korean system, tag questions are fewer when compared with English. English might include 'right?, don't you?, won't I?, will he?, as but a few examples. In Korean, the equivalent would be the otherwise singular form of 아니야 (*aniya*), essentially meaning 'is it not?' This is one potential complicating factor, though Avery suggests that in the EFL context, given the common occurrence of positive-negative tag questions, these should be taught first. From this we might expect difficulties when teaching negative-positive tag questions. An example is as follows:

(35) A – I can tell you don't like this food, do you?
B – Yes.

In this case, speaker A is asserting that speaker B does not like the food he/she is eating. The expected answer of 'no' would mean of course 'no, I don't like it'. The Korean response of 'yes', however, is confirming that A's assessment is indeed correct, because by giving an affirmative response, speaker B is saying, 'yes, you are right. I don't like the food'. To an inner-circle speaker, however, 'yes' would be interpreted as 'yes, I do like this food – your assessment is wrong'. Park and Dubinsky (2019: 2) point to difficulties within negative polarity questions in terms of how they are answered in Korean. Using the example of *didn't he eat lunch?*, a Korean response of *yes* equates to 'yes (he didn't eat)'; a response of *no* equates to 'no (he ate)'. To an inner-circle speaker, the same responses would be understood in opposite ways.

At this point, I would imagine that many of the readers, regardless of your national origin, can recall instances where your own cultural expectations were seemingly not met by others, who might of course have been obeying their *own* cultural expectations and norms. Whether this has taken place while on holiday, in business or in the classroom, it is a relevant aspect of language. While this might not be tied to Korean English per se, it nonetheless relates to the larger picture of a need to understand our fellow interlocutors and addressees, in ways that go beyond the immediate context of the English they use and its grammatical and lexical components.

I now provide another real-life example, taken from my time in Korea. I leave it up to the Korean readers to determine if my understanding of the situation is valid or, indeed, if I have gotten it wrong. In this case, I was standing at a bus stop in Seoul when a car momentarily stopped at the bus stop and a woman who was exiting the car hit me in the leg with the car door as she opened it. It didn't cause any real pain and this was hardly an international incident. However, I did expect some kind of acknowledgement. The woman did so, and her reaction was to give me a brief smile and then she walked on. I didn't assume of course that her smile equated to laughter or making light of the situation. Rather, I interpreted this to essentially be a non-verbal means of showing mild embarrassment, akin to acknowledging her fault. Thus, she had apologized without saying a word. If my analysis is correct, then here is a clear example of language which might be regarded as indirect on one hand, and yet totally clear on the other – communication does not always have to rely on words. But for me to have expressed anger or annoyance, to the point of demanding an 'apology', would clearly have been inappropriate – she had already apologized. I accepted her apology by means of returning her smile with one of my own.

Continuing the discussion on codified Korean English, I now turn to a study by Jung and Min (1999), who present a corpus-based approach to features of Korean English, a means to obtain more insights into how English is used by, and for, Koreans (and the expat community, by extension). Specifically, they investigate uses of English found in English-language Korean newspapers and compare this with the English used in inner-circle newspapers. Jung and Min state that corpora can be a useful means to better understand aspects of a language which signal volition and prediction.

For the purposes of analysis, Jung and Min chose the editorials and culture sections from *The Korea Herald* from the 3rd to the 28th of May, 1996. This comes to a total of 126 articles, all of which were written in English by Koreans. The readership of the newspaper is essentially anyone who can read and understand English, or who is perhaps trying to improve their English. Therefore, the readership can range from expats, who may or may not be native speakers of English, to Korean students and businesspeople.

Jung and Min analyze the use of modal verbs *will, would* and *shall,* and compare their use in the articles with parallel corpora in American English, British English and Australian English, with frequencies of the modal verbs per 10,000 words. In terms of frequencies of use, *will* is most commonly used in Korean English (53.6), compared with the other three varieties' frequencies: British English (28.0), American English (27.0) and Australian English (34.2). In terms of the use of *would,* the frequencies are as follows, with Korean English making use of this the least (12.54), American English (28.5), British English (30.0) and Australian English (26.7). Finally, Korean English made no use of the modal verb *shall,* which appeared infrequently overall in the other three varieties.

I have chosen to highlight the use of *will* in the Korean context, given that it has the highest frequency of all four varieties of English. More specifically, in terms of the semantic implications of this modal verb, Korean English uses *will* mostly to show epistemic meaning, referring to an individual's confidence in a proposition expressed, such as *I think he will win the race*. In Korean English, the frequency is 92.93 per cent for this particular function, compared with a very close second of 92.2 per cent (American English), 71.4 per cent (British English) and 61.7 per cent (Australian English). The close correspondence with American English in this case might be based, though speculative, on the influence of American English in Korea. However, this is broad and a more close contextual analysis would be required to obtain a more nuanced perspective.

Collins (2009) also analyzes the use of modal verbs in corpora representing American, British and Australian Englishes, consisting of both speech categories (e.g. telephone calls, class lessons) and written contexts (e.g. fictions, newspapers). In terms of epistemic *will*, Collins distinguishes between predictability and prediction, as do Jung and Min (1999). Jung and Min declare that the former can be paraphrased as 'I (confidently) predict that it is the case that p' (page 28); the latter is paraphrased as 'I predict that' (page 29). This can be seen with examples such as *this language will die out in a few generations* (predictability) and 'you'll most likely strengthen your defenses' (prediction) (Collins, 2009: 128).

In Collins's data, the American corpus displayed the highest frequency of *will* in terms of its overall uses; in Jung and Min's (1999) data, the US corpus, specifically regarding use of epistemic *will*, also had higher frequencies than British or Australian data (and came in second, as mentioned, to the Korean data in Jung and Min's study). Collins does point to an 'Americanization' in terms of American English being at the forefront of shifting to new linguistic categories; in this case, Collins's research revealed fewer modal verbs in the US corpus compared with the British and Australian corpora, but a higher frequency of semi-modals in the US corpus, such as *be going to*. In this manner, we can expect different varieties of English to share common grammatical features, but one variety in particular can demonstrate a higher frequency of particular features. This can be applied to Korean English as much as American English, so that certain features might be considered 'Americanisms' and likewise, from the results here, we might expect within newspaper texts, a more frequent engagement with epistemic *will* in the Korean context.

A final point to make here concerns other uses of *will* which are higher in frequency in the inner-circle varieties than in Korean English. Once again, Korean English compares with American English in terms of low frequencies for the use of root *will* (which involves both willingness and intention); respectively, 5.29 per cent and 7.8 per cent. For British English and Australian English, the frequencies are respectively 22.7 per cent and 33.5 per cent. Intention *will* can be seen as in *he said he will do it*; willingness *will* would involve a paraphrase of 'be willing to' as in *she said she will do all she can to help*. As Collins (1991: 186) reports, a focus on an event connected to intention *will* represents 'factually objective reportage', yet a focus on a subject's state of mind, as with willingness *will*, is less relevant for newspaper reporting. Hence, the totals across all four corpora for intention *will* are higher than willingness *will*.

Perhaps the low frequency for this use of *will* in the Korean data, notably intention *will*, suggests a degree of hedging, though this would point to a stylistic device which may, or may not, point towards Korean English in toto, as seen in newspapers. And in the UK context, the type of newspaper can have significant effects perhaps on the written communication, such as whether the newspaper is a tabloid or broadsheet. Nonetheless, Jung and Min (1999) have produced research which, at least, does suggest that Koreans, when writing in English for a specific readership of an English-language newspaper, may display tendencies regarding the use of modal verbs (and other features) that show variation.

More recently, Takeshita (2012: 276) provides a discussion of Korean English in terms of the phonological inventory of this variety. Takeshita points to the fact that Korean does not have certain sounds found in inner-circle English, such as the voiceless labiodental fricative /f/. Thus, *coffee* can sound more like *cop-pee*, and another example of Korean pronunciation influencing English words is *pizza*, realized more as *pi-ja*; I had covered this earlier. There is also a tendency for Koreans to add a syllable to English words which end with a consonant, so that *card* can sound somewhat like *car-duh*. Pronunciation and accent are important aspects of language use of course, though the focus within the book is otherwise on grammar and lexis. This is not to underplay the importance of pronunciation, of course. Some NICE are perhaps immediately distinctive based on their pronunciation, such as the retroflex sounds of Indian English, /ḍ/ and /ṭ/ (Galloway and Rose, 2015). But I believe that a phonological focus on Korean English, and NICE in general, reflects a feature that might be held to less scrutiny. To put it another way, views held about a variety of English not being 'correct' in some way are often based on grammar in the first instance. It is unlikely that someone's accent would be held as being 'error'-prone in terms of their variety of English, certainly within the academic discussion concerning NICE. We might expect it to be unrealistic, for some individuals very difficult, to modify their pronunciation as adults, to the point of sounding more like a 'native'. While it makes perfect sense to capture all aspects of Korean English, I have otherwise chosen to make grammar and lexis the dominant focus.

Takeshita (2012) also focuses on lexical aspects of Korean English, however, such as loan words from English which are then modified: *one shot* (a drinking toast, such as 'bottoms up'), *eye shopping* (window shopping), *hand phone* (mobile/cell phone), *gagman* (comedian) and *one piece*, meaning 'dress'. Some words are clipped such as *air con* (for air conditioner), *apartuh* (apartment) and *notuh* (notebook), and words such as *skinship* meaning physical touching such as holding hands, which clearly demonstrates knowledge of inner-circle English in terms of the use of the suffix *-ship* when added to nouns. There are many other examples which will follow in the next section.

Hadikin (2014) reports on Koreans' use of the lexical strings *but you know, do you know* and *and you know*. The comparison is made with Koreans who reside in the UK with those who reside in Seoul, with both groups users of English. Subsequent corpora involve the Scouse corpus of Liverpool spoken English, and the spoken section of the British National Corpus. Of these three speech strings, Hadikin finds that *but you know* occurs with much more frequency in the Korean English data for both sets of Koreans, explained as a means that 'buys more time for online speech processing' (page 76). *Do you know* occurs among the Koreans as a topic introduction and to assess what shared knowledge might exist between the speaker and addressee; *and you know* demonstrates more variability among the Korean groups. Together, Hadikin declares that such specific use is 'evidence supporting the idea that Korean English is a variety in its own right' (page 178). Interestingly, there was little use among Koreans of the expression *do you know what I mean* compared with the British corpora.

Even more recently, Rüdiger (2014, 2019) continues the discussion of Korean English, drawing on data from the spoken context consisting of casual conversation between Rüdiger herself and Koreans, with English as the medium of conversation. Drawing on the data contained within the SPOKE corpus Rüdiger put together, we again see parallels with what has been discussed so far in terms of grammatical features. One example is irregular use of articles, but perhaps altogether regular for Korean English, seen with examples such as *a lot of people are complaining about different meaning of the Konglish* (2014: 13). Once again, this would tie in with what is suggested to be a rule of Korean English – using the definite article as part of a prepositional phrase within a noun phrase, whereas inner-circle English would not require the article here (i.e. *a lot of people are complaining about the different meaning of Konglish*). Rüdiger also points to semantic change, such as *talent* to mean 'actor'. There are further grammatical features discussed, such as not marking verbs for past tense, and not marking for plurality when the contextual information already suggests this, such as *I have three book*. Rüdiger refers to this as reducing redundancy, given that the numerical information provided is semantically sufficient. The lack of past-tense marking might tie in with Shim's (1999) research, which found that different tenses can be found together in one sentence. On page 253, Shim provides the following example: *He seems to be pleased when he saw me*. Thus, perhaps Rüdiger and Shim, as with the previous examples regarding the use of conditionals, are approaching the same grammatical aspects, but from different perspectives. As I had mentioned earlier in reference to Rüdiger (2019), the fact that multiple conversations with Koreans generated material put forward as grammatical features of Korean English strongly suggests that such features were used extensively, or certainly predictably, by the Korean participants, and here in the context of spoken, not written, communication.

This section has provided clear evidence about the codified nature of Korean English, which has included some of the points mentioned in Chapter 3. First, implied in the discussion provided earlier is the fact that Koreans are using a variety of English, and hence we indeed have something concrete to discuss in the first instance. Second, Korean English has been covered in the academic literature presented here, from journals to books. Given that the academic coverage spans more than two decades, this also provides strong support for a consistency in its grammatical and lexical components and given this time span, it stands to reason that Korean English can only expect to embed itself even more within society, what I have termed *societal reinforcement*. Third, given the coverage of Korean English in written contexts, from newspapers to written correspondence by Koreans, this might suggest more evidence of a codified variety of English. For example, we might expect written forms of communication, more so newspaper articles read by many people each day, to have been proofread and edited before going to print. If so, then this in turn suggests that much consideration was put into the English used and this would imply that to the writers and editors, the English was otherwise satisfactory and ready to go out – especially for a national newspaper (but one that can also be accessed online by an international audience).

Finally, we also have evidence of the traditional methods of codification – such as school-based textbooks – which have played a part in the establishment of Korean English. However, even if this were lacking, can we honestly say that Korean English would not exist as a variety in its own right? While some would see school textbooks as ultimate evidence for a language variety being codified, I do not. Platt, Weber and Ho (1984: 2–3) indeed consider a 'New English' as being in need of having developed through the education system. That some might also regard the propagation of Korean English within Korean schools as being the final authority on the matter, I defer authority back to the speakers, whose usage of specific grammatical features and lexis allows for Korean English to become conventionalized in the first instance. The final three points made by Platt, Weber and Ho regarding nativization point to (a) the development of a New English in a country where English was not the language otherwise spoken by the population, (b) it is used by those who can speak it in a range of contexts (education, the media) and (c) it has become nativized by adopting its own unique features. These final points are more valid, as they don't necessarily suggest the need for intervention by those on high, such as the government. While point (b) might include government usage, the more we rely on official means to give a language – here, Korean English – the linguistic all-clear, then we might be waiting in vain for some time, in cases where inner-circle standard is still propagated at the expense of other relevant varieties, and a language variety will still continue on its merry way each day, used by people on the ground.

While Galloway and Rose (2015: 136) declare that public opinion concerning Far East Asian Englishes in general is 'largely negative', this might have more to do with prescriptive attitudes which set inner-circle English as the default. When conversing among themselves in Korean English, however (e.g. at universities where clubs enforce an English-only rule), perhaps there is not much thought given one way or the other, or it might in fact reflect covert prestige by the speakers, who then switch to standard inner circle when it is required. For some, the switch from one variety of English to another can be effortless; and Gupta (1998) reports on this in the Singaporean context, in which individuals who have mastery of Standard Singaporean English will nonetheless move to so-called Singlish with ease, when the context requires it. As Pakir (1991: 109–110) states, 'norm-setter, norm-maker and norm-breaker may all be found in one and the same' individual. Nonetheless, the trillions of Won spent each year in Korea on English education, reflected in summer schools, private tutoring and institutes (*hagwon*), are undoubtedly for the purpose of learning inner-circle standard, but Korean English is a linguistic reality. As I had mentioned earlier, there are additional grammatical features not covered here, such as the use of prepositions (Jung and Min, 1999; Seong and Lee, 2008), participle construction (Shim, 1999), passives (Seong and Lee, 2008) and pronouns (Rüdiger, 2019). However, that there is more to cover points again to a multitude of ways that grammatical features as used in the inner circle have become Koreanized, a point with which the literature presented here agrees. Moreover, I feel that the discussion presented has been sufficient to make the points clear with regard to the grammatical features of Korean English.

I now continue the discussion of the societal codification of Korean English by drawing on the content of websites dedicated to this subject, thus providing what is perhaps one of the most common and accessible ways that a language is spread in the modern day.

Online codification of Korean English

As I write, a Google search for Konglish reveals 'about 177,000 results'; a search for Korean English reveals 'about 3,380,000,000 results'. Going further with relevant online search terms, information is provided as follows:

Konglish dictionary – 'About 15,800 results'
Korean English dictionary – 'About 396,000,000 results'
Konglish grammar – 'About 30,000 results'
Korean English grammar – 'About 210,000,000 results'

Though I have made clear my preference for the term *Korean English*, Konglish is the more commonly used term and, as such, it makes sense to investigate what comes up when using this specific term as part of online searches. No book can arguably do justice to the multiple outlets for online dictionaries and guides, which subsequently comprise many outlets: YouTube videos, blogs, Google translate and online newspaper publications, such as *The Korea Times* (and I'm sure I may have missed other examples). An analysis of each website in terms of its content is far too time consuming.

However, the definition I have provided for Korean English, which may indeed be applied by many to Konglish, is the systematic use of lexis and grammar which pertains specifically to the English as used by Koreans in as much as it differs from inner-circle standard, and before sub-varieties are considered (e.g. K-POP English, media English). Though I clearly do not have the time to look at each and every online source dedicated to the subject, I do have specific criteria in mind for the majority of online sources that provide the basis for this section. The sources need of course to be entirely relevant to the focus on Korean English. This much is clearly obvious, but some of the sites focus on different subjects. For example, on the first page when searching for 'Korean English grammar', one of the sites is actually focused on Korean grammar – Korean Grammar for Beginners: https://www.90daykorean.com/korean-grammar/. On the same page, there is another website dedicated to the differences between Korean and English grammar (The Differences between English and Korean): http://esl.fis.edu/grammar/langdiff/korean.htm.

My concerns are not with the quality of the graphics of websites, however, as, while important to an extent, they are relatively superficial concerns compared with the information and content of the site. Having said that, anyone can essentially create their own online presence; and for this reason, some might argue that 'quality control' is a relevant issue when searching the web for information on Korean English. For this reason alone perhaps, online codification, unless it comes with a name brand, might be disregarded by some. But this is an unfair judgement if applied too broadly, because some of the websites are written by people, who, in keeping with societal use of language, represent the individuals on the ground who are using, and listening, to Korean English on a daily basis.

By having their ears to the ground, as it were, they are well placed to understand not merely the linguistic features of Korean English, but also its contexts of deployment in Korean society – and beyond perhaps – and on one level, they function as real-world investigators.

In an attempt to capture the overall content and context of Korean English and its online codification, my discussion in this section is based on searching for the following listed terms, and analyzing the content of the first page that comes up for each search. The following are the key search terms and the numbers of online sources that come up on the first page:

Konglish – 7
Korean English – 9
Konglish dictionary – 9
Korean English dictionary – 10
Konglish grammar – 10
Korean English grammar – 9

Some sites appeared in more than one search, such as the Wikipedia entry for Konglish. This amounts to, at the time of writing, fifty-four sites analyzed for content. While this is not even a drop in the linguistic ocean in terms of a more thorough analysis and discussion, it is suggested that given their position on the first page following a Google search, these sites perhaps represent the most viewed sites; and taken together, a lot can be gleaned regarding online codification.

Using the search terms referenced earlier as subheadings in terms of online content for Korean English, I now present an overview of the results.

Konglish

The overall content points to Korean English as involving loan words from English – and some from Japan. Wikipedia, though much maligned, provides an overall fair account of Korean English. By 'fair' I mean that it refrains both from linguistic praise and linguistic scorn and instead refers objectively to this variety as 'a style of English used by Korean speakers'. Though perhaps a vague definition, it nonetheless avoids suggesting that Korean English – here referred to as Konglish of course – is deficient.

There are many examples provided of Korean English vocabulary, with a sample provided as follows, taken from https://en.wikipedia.org/wiki/Konglish (Konglish, 2020):

Korean English	Inner circle
Burberry	*Trench coat*
Eye shopping	*Window shopping*
Gag man	*Comedian*
Hand phone	*Mobile phone/cell phone*
Health club	*Gym*
Hunting	*Searching for a date*
Meeting	*Group blind date*
One piece	*Dress*
Overeat	*Vomiting*
Pocket ball	*Pool*
Selca	*Selfie*
Service	*Free/on the house*
Sign	*Signature/Autograph*
Soul food	*Comfort food*

The point is also made that Korean English is to be categorized as separate from errors or a temporary form of English, further suggesting that it is embedded in Korean society. But in a spirit of objectivity, the website also mentions the criticism levelled against Korean English, such as the term *Konglish* being used for 'misuse' or 'corruptions' of English by Korean EFL students. Neither term, however, has anything with which to attach itself to. Misuse of English, while this could be classed as a pure error initially, can also become an innovation, if and when such use spreads. No language can in itself be 'corrupted' – these are once again societal notions, not linguistic ones. But given that some might regard influence from other languages as evidence of losing the national character of the dominant language and in turn, affecting national identity, then we can expect to hear terms such as *corruption, decay* and so on. Clearly, such strongly held opinions are not going to be swayed perhaps by this book or others like it, but approaching language from a linguistic point of view – which is the most relevant – can help to combat negative linguistic attitudes (O'Neill, 2018). However, debates about the changing face of national identity in Korea are perhaps emotionally charged and go beyond language and instead tie in with immigration, an increase of mixed-race marriages and are even reflected in recent legislation in Korea which provides rights for foreign workers. This indeed is a subject which is beyond the scope of this book, but given that language is a proxy for identities tied to national origin, race and class, among others, then Korean English can be for some a proxy for losing one's identity as

Korean (Rüdiger, 2018), by virtue of what it means to be 'Korean' itself open to discussion (Jenks and Lee, 2017).

However, a reference is made to errors on public signs and brochures, even using the term *bad Konglish*, and, as with the discussion in Chapter 2 of Chinglish, then this too can be a potential issue. The issue in this case could sometimes, but certainly not most of the time, lead to foreigners misunderstanding the English used on public signs, but it might also lead to jokes made about Koreans' use of English. In the context described here, we are dealing with translation errors, not Korean English.

The Korean Language Blog (https://blogs.transparent.com/korean/what-is-콩글리시-konglish/) (Kyung-Hwa, 2017) again refers to Korean English in a purely matter-of-fact way, referring to it as the use of English words but whose meaning and pronunciation have been altered. This is followed by a list of Korean English vocabulary, much of it already referred to earlier, but including other examples such as *remo con* (remote control), *super* (supermarket), *back mirror* (rear-view mirror) and *auto-bike* (motorcycle).

The writer of the blog, Kyung-Hwa, explains that Korean English words 'are very useful to learn when you study Korean', and her presentation of some of the words – to include her voice recording of the pronunciation of a sample of words – is a means to stop people scratching their heads, as she puts it. In other words, the presentation is clearly for online pedagogic purposes and once again, we have online evidence of Korean English words. That the writer describes her interest in language, culture and travelling suggests that she would be unlikely to describe Korean English in negative terms. Indeed, there is nothing 'positive' or 'negative' about it, but people's attitudes are a different matter.

The website found at https://medium.com/story-of-eggbun-education/english-words-you-only-hear-in-korea-5bd3eed8f9c3 (Choi, 2017) continues a description of Korean English as, once again, a means to educate. The website is entitled 'English Words You Only Hear in Korea'. Starting with the premise that Korean English vocabulary can cause initial confusion for inner-circle speakers, with British English speakers referenced specifically, the writer Miri Choi (or Choi Miri, in Korean) provides a list of words with the inner-circle meaning. Once again, such lists reinforce, if this is even needed, words which have long since been established by Koreans' take on the English language. In fact, to the extent that many of these words are now used in Koreans' conversations which are conducted in Korean, it might be difficult for some to know where Korean ends and Korean English begins. This is no less true of American English. The reason why speakers of such might not question the origins is of course because they go further back in time. To put it another way, at what point are borrowed words no longer perceived as 'borrowed' and instead, part of the dominant language? To illustrate the point, most Americans would probably see the following sentence, contrived though it may be, as entirely English.

The moose entered the café in his pyjamas.

This sentence is English of course, but the linguistic influences in terms of vocabulary include Algonquian, French and Hindi.

On her website, Choi provides a table which gives the Korean English word, British students' attempt to define it and the actual meaning provided at the end (see Table 1).

By providing Korean English examples as part of a translation method, it can add fun to the proceedings and in fact mimic the kind of classroom exercises which can help to make language more accessible. Choi also offers a list of further vocabulary which she suggests are common expressions that people should know (see Table 2).

A useful approach might be to see how many instances of these words, and others, appear on web-based searches. However, from the online evidence so far, it can be seen how Korean English vocabulary is indeed found across sites and represents predictable use of language that, whatever its origins, is now a clear part of Korean English.

Of note in Table 1 presented by Choi is the use of the expression 'Britain students'. We could of course consider this a pure error from an inner-circle point of view, in that Britain is a country, not a nationality, and *British* students

Table 1 Choi's Table of Konglish

Konglish	The Inferred Meaning by Britain Students	The Real Meaning in Korea
스킨 (skin)	Natural covering of your body	Toner
썬크림 (suncream)	?	Sunblock
세트 메뉴 (set menu)	?	Combo
원룸 (one-room)	A room	Studio apartment
화이트 (white)	Color	Whiteout or correction fluid
세일 (sale)	Selling	Discount
비주얼 (visual)	Relating to sight, or to things that you can see	Appearance
사인 (sign)	A mark or shape that always has a particular meaning	Signature
버버리 코트 (Burberry coat)	?	Trench coat

Table 2 Choi's List of Common Konglish Expressions

Konglish	Meaning
아르바이트 (arbeit)	Part-time job
오토바이 (auto-bike)	Motorcycle
컨닝 (cunning)	Cheating on a test
린스 [(rinse)	Hair conditioner
원샷 (one-shot)	Bottoms up
핸드폰 (hand phone)	Cell/mobile phone
리모컨 (remote-con)	Remote control
개그맨 (gag man)	Comedian
비닐백 (vinyl bag)	Plastic bag
아이쇼핑 (eye shopping)	Window shopping
와이셔츠 (Y-shirts)	Dress shirts

would be the correct form. On the other hand, we might first ask if this kind of expression is used by Koreans to denote national origin (i.e. country name + noun, such as *Britain students* and *America people*). I don't claim to know the answer, but I can suggest that the expression as used by Choi reflects transfer from Korean, in which 'country name + people' is the way to express nationality (Baratta, 2013). Thus, in Korean, *American people* is expressed by saying 'America people'.

The next website, located at https://www.wired.com/2016/09/beauty-perils-konglish-korean-english-hybrid/, (Rhodes, 2016) has the title 'The Beauty and Perils of Konglish, the Korean-English Hybrid', by Margaret Rhodes. The article discusses the work of Korean graphic designer Ran Park, who, after living overseas for several years, returned to Korea to find evidence of borrowed English words used in everyday life. Examples include direct borrowings, such as *banana* and *computer*, both used in the Hangeul script and with Korean pronunciation of course, but otherwise clearly English (although if we go back to the beginning, the origins of the word *banana* derive from Wolof). This inspired Park's artwork entitled *Lost in Konglish*. As with the other sites presented thus far, a sample of Korean English words are provided, such as *manicure* for *nail polish* and *hand phone* for *cell/mobile phone*. Rhodes declares that Korean English 'follows few strict rules', though I would disagree, based on the previous content in this chapter regarding grammatical features, not to mention the vocabulary clearly having specific meanings for specific contexts of use. Perhaps Rhodes's comment is based on reducing Korean English to a series of word borrowings which would otherwise suggest a rather superficial influence, without the deeper workings of syntax.

Rhodes goes on to address Park's concerns regarding the influence of English. While acknowledging its importance in the work place, Park believes that

English is leading to Koreans 'losing' their language. One example provided is *donut*, which is cited as an example of lacking the 'descriptiveness of native words'. By comparison, the North Korean equivalent translates as 'a ring of bread'. Discussing language in purely objective linguistic terms, in which case no language can ever be 'sexy', 'common', 'ugly', 'oppressive' and so on, does little to perhaps assuage people's fears of, for example, the linguistic dominance of English at the cost of local languages and identity. To suggest that Koreans should embrace, or at least wholeheartedly accept Korean English, would be a mistake on my part. First, I am not Korean, and so I am in no position to throw linguistic fact at societal attitudes. To do so could easily suggest a certain elitism, and worse, cultural ignorance. Rather, this aspect of Korean English, or English overall, and how it can be perceived for good and bad in Korea, is an important factor in a discussion of language in society.

Additional websites include https://www.90daykorean.com/konglish/, (90 day Korean, 2020) which also provides a list of vocabulary within the overall context of educating the public about Korean English. This site discusses the use of Korean English in everyday life, encouraging people to use the relevant lexis when in Korea, suggesting that foreigners do have need of a language which the Koreans themselves are clearly using. Examples of everyday vocabulary provided on the website pertain to supermarkets and stores, and would include words such as *hot dog* for *corn dog*, *band* for *band-aid/plaster* and *wrap* for *plastic wrap*. My article on Korean English also makes an appearance on the first page when searching for 'Korean English' (Baratta, 2019b), published in *The Conversation* (Korean language speakers should take pride in Konglish – it's another wonderful example of linguistic diversity) (theconversation.com).

My own contribution to the subject is probably already understood – a discussion of the fact that Korean English is indeed legitimate and not failed English, and that we cannot judge languages from a singular perspective, in this case tied to inner-circle English. Interestingly, my article received a comment from an individual living and working in Korea, who understood 'Konglish' as English loan words with their own pronunciation and meaning. He had not come across the term *Korean English* as referring to a variety of English. Herein lies one of the contentions of course. Even for those who view Korean English as a wholly legitimate and systematic use of English and English-based words, we need to consider how it goes beyond this and indeed refers to the English language per se as used in Korea and by Koreans (and non-Koreans). Seen from this point of view, Korean English may not necessarily use vocabulary otherwise associated with it. In English-language newspapers in Korea, for example, it is possible that there may not be a need to refer to Korean English vocabulary, but the writers otherwise use grammatical features that are part and parcel of Korean English. Therefore, more needs to be understood on a societal level about this variety of English that includes more than just words, though vocabulary is of course a large part of Korean English and what makes it lexically distinctive.

The final two sites are located at https://www.koreanwikiproject.com/wiki/Konglish (Konglish), part of Wikipedia, and http://www.macmillandictionaries.com/MED-Magazine/March2003/05-korean-english.htm (Miller, 2003). The former site is dedicated to a list of vocabulary, as are the others in large part; and thus, we can see the reinforcement of Korean English as consisting in the main of words borrowed from English, whether direct borrowings or words that have since taken on semantic shift. Words will of course shift in meaning and it's unlikely that after we borrow words we're going to give them back. The final website likewise offers a list of Korean English words. The writer Jeffrey Miller introduces the subject as follows:

> In Korea, the mixture of Korean and English words to form words independent to the base of the Korean language but originating from English (in some cases from other European languages) is known as Konglish. Through a direct absorption of these loan words into the Korean language, these words have been become [sic] institutionalized into the language. While this combination of Korean and English or Koreans' interpretation of English is not necessarily wrong, these Konglish words or phrases are widely used and accepted in Korea.
>
> Konglish can be broken down into four types: (1) words whose meanings have been altered; (2) words that have been fabricated to mean something entirely different from the borrowed word or phrase; (3) words in which the pronunciation has changed; (4) and words or phrases which have been abbreviated. Konglish also incorporates 'pseudo loan-words':
>
> Taken from http://www.macmillandictionaries.com/MED-Magazine/March 2003/05-korean-english.htm.

Miller further provides categories for the borrowed vocabulary, such as English words with a different meaning (*gargle* meaning *mouthwash* and *meeting* meaning *date*). Brand names are also included, such as *Burberry* meaning *trench coat*. This is an example of overextension, which Americans and British do too: *Kleenex* for *tissue*, and *hoover* for *vacuum*. Other categories are altered phrases including *light Coke* (diet Coke), *MacGyver knife* (Swiss Army knife), *cash corner* (ATM machine) and *oil bank* (gas station/petrol station). Miller also reflects on a personal instance of being exposed to Korean English upon his arrival in the country. When shopping for men's underwear, the sales assistant used the word *panties*, which refers to both men's and women's underwear. Thus, a specific word in American English for women's underwear refers to underwear worn by both sexes in Korean English.

Miller's use of the keyword *institutionalized* suggests he is regarding English-based vocabulary as firmly established in Korea and an identifiable aspect of Korean English. However, within the literature, the term takes on a different meaning, referring instead to the use of the New English in the classroom and within local literature (Moag, 1992). Having said that, I have presented evidence for such uses of English in Korea, though it nonetheless is suggested that for Miller, the use of the term *institutionalized* is referring more specifically to legitimization.

Despite this, he goes on to say that 'Konglish can be corrected in the English classroom if the usage by students has not been fossilized'. If the focus is on standard American English in the Korean EFL classroom, which it almost certainly will be, then this pedagogic context does *not* mean Korean English is in need of correcting. Rather, as Chapter 6 will make clear, it is an opportunity instead to use one legitimate variety to teach another, for example *translating* Korean English into inner-circle, and vice versa; this is the approach that is largely taken with the content of the websites presented in this section. Furthermore, linguistic fossilization is misguided, suggesting that an error has indeed taken hold in students' English and can't be corrected. Why can't we encourage students instead to be bilingual in inner-circle standard and Korean English? Indeed, many of them probably already are, and know the contexts which warrant shifting from one variety to the other.

Miller further refers to Korean English as being 'the bane of English teachers'. This might be the case for some teachers of course, more so if Korean English is seen as something to avoid and 'bad English'. But again, the larger issue is that we are excluding a national variety of English in favour of another. While some Koreans may in fact welcome this for the EFL classroom, we should instead be using both varieties – if not more – to better understand the variety within the English language. This is not suggested as a mere tokenistic exercise. Instead, it is designed to help students realize that no language is superior to another and attitudes suggestive of such are again based on society, ascribing power to the language variety whose speakers wield the most economic power and/or political power, for example. But there is a large number of Koreans who otherwise use Korean English in their everyday lives and to ignore this linguistic reality is a missed teaching opportunity. Finally, we should not ignore the potential for inner-circle teachers to learn Korean English also, one of the purposes of some of the websites referred to in this section. If teachers move to Korea to teach, then it stands to reason that they will come into contact with a host of Korean English vocabulary and, as such, they will need to learn it, and perhaps use it.

A final point to discuss is the inclusion of several YouTube videos that appear under the heading of Konglish. There are ten in total, with titles such as *the game of guessing Konglish* (Lala Creatives, 2018), *do you know Konglish* (Seemile Korean, 2019) and *can you guess these Konglish words?* (BuzzFeedVideo, 2016) This is suggestive once again of providing inner-circle English alongside Korean English lexis, and vice versa, within the hands-on and interactive context of online learning. There are many online apps for learning a language, and in principle, this is what we can find on Korean English also, as suggested by the titles at least. It would take more time than is available to go through each and every website and YouTube video, in order to obtain an even fuller and more detailed picture of attitudes towards, and definitions of, Korean English. But from just a small sample of what's out there, it is clear that by and large, Korean English (though under the title of Konglish for the previous websites discussed) is seen as comprising borrowed words from English, which can then become abbreviated, take on new meaning or combine in new ways. This is an accurate representation of Korean English, but rather lacking without a discussion of the grammatical properties to go with it.

Perhaps because words are more 'immediate' and can be heard (and seen in written form) and are needed for everyday life in Korea (e.g. shopping needs), it is easy to focus on them, to the exclusion of grammar. Perhaps many are not aware of the grammatical properties of Korean English outside the context of academic research and instead, such properties are regarded as errors. And Konglish might still indeed be regarded overall as representative of errors. In some cases, this might be true, such as spelling errors (*baby back lips*, for *baby back ribs*), but in this case, let's call an error an error, not Korean English or Konglish.

Also of relevance is the fact that many sites and certainly YouTube allow for people to post comments. The content of such comments can be revealing in terms of attitudes and opinions regarding Korean English and this can also reveal something of how society – Koreans and non-Koreans alike – perceives this variety and if indeed it is seen in negative terms. As but one example, the YouTube entry for *can you guess these Konglish words* offers some interesting comments, such as several posts from individuals who thought *skinship* was an English word. In this case, 'English' perhaps refers to inner-circle/native speaker English, but *skinship* is English, albeit Korean English. Moreover, given the use of the suffix *-ship*, it can just as easily function as inner-circle English words do, such as *friendship* and *relationship*. Predictably, as is often the case with online comments, the discussion tends to go off topic (e.g. an individual asking for others to post comments if they like Korean drama). However, some comments do reveal a certain prejudice, including one post from an individual who makes it clear that he/she is not comfortable with K-POP fans trying to make their interests 'mainstream and normal', to which someone else posted the question which sought to ask in response if Korean culture – of which Korean English is a part – is not normal. Some comments make it clear that they are connecting, in their minds, Korean English words with Korean drama and K-POP, suggesting that they, and their fans, are the 'instigators' and propagators of Korean English vocabulary, seen in part with the word choice of 'fanfictions'. From here, another post asked for respect for Koreans, given that Korea is not just about K-POP, as he/she comments. Another comment, from a Korean, explained that if a non-Korean uses the term *selca* instead of *selfie*, he will judge them, perhaps a comment made in jest, however.

To conclude this section, I now provide a synthesis of the main points:

- The entries largely approach Korean English vocabulary with objectivity, presenting lists of words in some cases with the translation in inner-circle English, and in large part the entries function as educational tools, with this made clear on several websites. This translation approach avoids the implication that the Korean English words are incorrect.
- However, there are two issues that are noticeable, such as the influence of English in Korea leading to a loss of national identity, and presenting Korean English vocabulary as inappropriate for the EFL classroom – perhaps this is based more on avoidance of Korean English simply in order to improve one's standard inner-circle English abilities.
- Overall, however, the coverage of 'Konglish' does not suggest errors, but merely lexical borrowings from English and the ways in which Koreans have since changed the language further in terms of how such borrowings have developed.
- Finally, that so much vocabulary is indeed codified via use of online dictionaries is a clear example of the societal codification I have argued for – people are perhaps more likely to find information on this topic from an online search and having done so, will find much information on Korean English vocabulary.

Korean English, Korean English dictionary, Korean English grammar

Under these three headings, the sites that can be found are, with the exception of the Wikipedia entry on Konglish, all dedicated to learning Korean, or providing a Korean-English dictionary. Thus, the understanding, initially from these search terms at least, is translating from Korean to English, or English to Korean, or actually learning the Korean language. This might have more to do with Konglish still being the default term for many online searches, and not Korean English.

Konglish dictionary

I begin the further discussion of online material by again pointing to my approach towards societal codification. Here we can again find evidence of more traditional means of codification – largely dictionaries – as well as more modern, non-traditional online means, such as blogs. One of the obvious drawbacks, potentially, to online dictionaries is that they can be created by anyone, and not trained lexicographers (Cotter and Damaso, 2007). This can lead to inaccurate statements perhaps and certainly allows for a degree more subjectivity, which can include negative comments regarding a given topic, here Korean English. This is evident based on the definitions provided under some of the entries for 'Konglish dictionary', as will be seen.

On the other hand, the internet – awash with websites, blogs, YouTube – allows for a public forum, a unique discussion point as seen with people's comments on websites. This further allows for, as Damaso (2005) claims, a 'populist dictionary'. This has its own benefits, discussed by Cotter and Damaso (2007) as part of 'an emergent dictionary genre' (page 1) and referring to their Urban Dictionary (UD), which compiles a list of slang expressions in English. This is not to suggest I am implying that Korean English is slang; rather, I seek to investigate the rather limited data regarding this manner of suggested online codification. The following are some of the benefits of such online dictionaries:

- Lexicographic principles are joined with Web-only communication technologies to provide a context in which users collaborate, cooperate and compete for meaning-making.
- The collaborative opportunities inherent in dictionaries like UD distinguish them from traditional print dictionaries in that an authoritative editor is replaced by what can be seen as large-scale usage.

- At the same time, their creation shares many characteristics with the traditional dictionary.

Cotter and Damaso (2007: 1)

Moreover, online resources for language learning, defined broadly, can be seen with a vast array of topics. These can include academic lectures posted on YouTube (on subjects beyond just linguistics, of course); individuals posting themselves to YouTube and explaining – some with humour and some taking a more 'academic' approach – the features of various accents (I recall seeing a clip in which a native of Philadelphia explains the features of this particular accent); and indeed, much information on Korea, Korean culture (including language) and, of course, Korean English.

Green (1996: 11) argues that even traditional dictionaries 'are the products of human beings, [who] try as they may, bring their prejudices and biases into the dictionaries they make'; thus, while there is perhaps a degree more freedom regarding the content of online web material designed by individuals, in that they are not under contract by a major publisher, we should again consider that online resources, to include more than dictionaries (e.g. grammar-based materials), offer the benefits of a traditional dictionary – this can include 'authorizing usage, storing vocabulary, improving communication, strengthening the language, and affording metalinguistic reflections on language' (Cotter and Damaso, 2007: 2). The UD collects words that are part of popular culture, but perhaps gives them a home that users can appreciate. Again, the words reflect conventionalization, which is then codified by an online resource. I concede that for some, all the online dictionaries in the world are no match for one copy of, say, the *Oxford English Dictionary* (which itself does not proscribe slang entries). But the issue, once again, is that online resources are arguably easier to connect with, literally, and as I write as we slowly come out of lockdown here in the UK, access to computers (for some, not all) is easier than access to libraries when such buildings are closed. In addition, on the UD, users click the Thumbs Up button based on an entry's popularity. Thus, this can be seen as an innovative way to address Reddick's (1990) view that a dictionary is in need of consensus or it risks losing authority. Thus, we have a modern way to address established principles of dictionary creation; as the authors state, 'the attitudes and practices of users need not be abstracted into principles and trends. Instead, users themselves, in this case UD contributors, merely act and make meaning, and use the dictionary as they wish' (page 8).

From the OED online presence, it states that 'The OED requires several independent examples of the word being used, and also evidence that the word has been in use for a reasonable amount of time'. This is found in the FAQ section, the question being 'How does a word qualify for inclusion in the OED?' This points to conventionalization, with the dictionary the means to codify and in time perhaps, gain even greater acceptance in society for the word(s). But this applies equally to online dictionaries, as the Korean English words already displayed qualify, as they have been in use for a reasonable amount of time, which is reflected in large part with the fact they are included in various online dictionaries in the first instance.

Some of the sites under the heading of Konglish dictionary have already received discussion, having come up under a Google search for Konglish. Otherwise, the sites that can be found at present are as follows:

> https://glosbe.com/en/ko/Konglish (Glosbe, 2021)
> https://www.urbandictionary.com/define.php?term=Konglish
> https://www.macmillandictionary.com/dictionary/british/konglish
> https://www.yourdictionary.com/konglish
> http://leonsplanet.com/konglish.htm (Priz, 2011)
> https://tefltastic.wordpress.com/2008/12/01/konglish-a-to-z/ (Case, 2011)
> https://translation.babylon-software.com/english/konglish/ (Babylon, 2020)
> https://sydneytoseoul.wordpress.com/2013/08/02/lexical-borrowings-from-english-in-konglish/ (Z, 2020)

Most of these sites provide what appears to be a dictionary definition of the term *Konglish* and no more, illustrated as follows:

> *A disparaging term for various varieties of Korean English having distinctive lexis, syntax and phonology.*
> https://www.yourdictionary.com/konglish
> https://glosbe.com/en/ko/Konglish

Referring to Konglish as a disparaging term ties in with one of my main reasons for using Korean English instead as a symbol of linguistic arrival that goes beyond mere word borrowings and instead reflects a codified and established variety of English. Of note is the fact the definition refers to 'various varieties of Korean English' which, in keeping with the content of the next chapter, as well as the research of Jenks and Lee (2017), points to using the term *Korean English* as a starting point for conceptualizing English as used in Korea. I realize again that a change of name does not equate to a change in attitude; but if we can understand the properties of Korean English in terms of its conventions and online means of codifying such then this can be a means to address what could be seen earlier as a certain linguistic prejudice (i.e. the fact the writer is referencing Konglish as a disparaging term is perhaps not reflective of his/her views, but it shows awareness of other views in society).

Korean and English mixed together. Korean with English grammar.

I am the Keun-est sister. (Keun meaning big.)
https://www.urbandictionary.com/define.php?term=Konglish

The previous definition seems to offer two definitions, with the first a bit vague though perhaps again referring to the borrowing of English words. The two definitions, however, seem to come together with the example offered, which would appear to be a case of code-mixing. In this case, the Korean word 큰 meaning 'big' is made into a superlative by using the suffix *-est*: Korean word, English morphology. The example cited earlier of *oppas* would also be a feature of language mixing, and more so due to the influence of the Korean *hallyu*. It is unclear if the use of the blended word *keunest* is a viable feature of Korean English or simply an illustration that ties in with the broad definition given. Here is where the concept of 'authority' in terms of those doing the codifying can be relevant, applied to someone who is not merely knowledgeable regarding the subject, but is regarded as an expert. Clearly, we need more than merely a broad definition with an illustration that does not suggest the wealth of vocabulary that makes up Korean English. A question we might ask concerns the extent to which such vocabulary includes blends that incorporate Korean words with English morphology, such as the previous example. Lee (2013: 179) cites one example involving the word *baglnye*; a combination of two English words, 'baby' and 'glamour,' and the Korean feminine marking morpheme *-nye*; combined, this refers to an attractive woman who also suggests innocence. From this one example, it is hard to generalize, but perhaps such uses should not be unexpected. Indeed, Lee (2014) points to a very common outlet for hybridized expressions, a reflection of medialect and another example of a social-based means to potentially spread language to the masses, which in turn can lead to the expressions becoming conventions, which, potentially, could then be codified by the source in which they were first used: TV shows. More on this will be discussed in Chapter 5.

A blend of English and Korean

Konglish, rather than catalysing the decline of rich culture and tradition, adds something new to the Korean culture.

https://www.macmillandictionary.com/dictionary/british/konglish

Again, this definition is suggestive of combining elements of both English and Korean, which, from one perspective, is perhaps true, seen with the example of using English-based words in an otherwise Korean sentence. But as I have detailed, Korean English includes, but is certainly not limited to, its vocabulary. The value judgement, which is agreed with by some, offers something extra. That is, we see a belief that the inclusion of English words can add to Korean culture, rather than being suggestive of taking away its unique character. This adds balance to the otherwise negative views towards Konglish, but in a spirit of overall objectivity, we could perhaps argue that no language variety 'adds' or 'takes away' anything.

Nonetheless, the mixing of English and Korean is not merely a linguistic issue; it is indeed a cultural one. As Lee (2014) points out, mixing words – such as blended expressions – also involves mixing concepts, a meeting of East and West. A previous examples involved the word *baglnye*, which, through its use of English words, expresses a more Western concept of glamour, perhaps even understood as 'sexiness' (Lee, 2014). But with the use of a particular Korean suffix, this allows for the overall meaning to incorporate a connotation of 'innocence' at the same time. Arguably, there is no word within inner-circle English that can capture this. More on this subject will be discussed in Chapter 5, as part of medialect.

However, a need to preserve cultural heritage and identity is discussed by Lee (2020), who examines how the Korean cultural values of humility and social deference are expressed in the emails of Korean immigrants. While this might not relate directly to Koreans who reside in Korea and their thoughts, if any, regarding Korean English and its influence on Korean culture, it does demonstrate the importance of culture in specific relation to how it is expressed through language.

Konglish in English

Konglish (or more formally 'Korean language style English') is the macaronic use of English words or words derived from English words in a Korean context. Konglish terms, having initially been taken from the English language, are made from a combination of Korean and/or English words (such as *officetel* 오피스텔 office + hotel) which are not used in English-speaking countries. Konglish is often used by South Koreans in the Americanized period after the miracle on the Han River, but native English speakers usually don't understand Konglish, making such terms pseudo-anglicisms. Common grammar or vocabulary mistakes made by Koreans learning English as a foreign language have also been referred to as Konglish. Words and phrases borrowed from English or other languages may be shortened if Koreans feel they are too long. Kim Seong-kon, an English professor at Seoul National University, attributed these mistakes to an over-reliance on a Korean-English dictionary and a lack of understanding of culture and natural collocations; he stated Koreans should actively seek native English speakers to proofread their English.

Taken from https://translation.babylon-software.com/english/konglish/

The definition and discussion earlier is by and large an objective and detailed account of Korean English, albeit from the perspective once again of borrowed words from English. It does, however, acknowledge the use of the term *Konglish* as referring to grammatical and vocabulary errors, to also perhaps include pragmatic errors, as demonstrated earlier by the content of the British Council website. Konglish is, therefore, a term sometimes used to refer to errors, though some errors might indeed be innovations (Shim, 1999; Rüdiger, 2019); but if pure errors, then I again state that we should replace the term *Konglish* in such cases with 'errors'. There is no denying of course that for some, the term *Konglish* is used with pure affection, or without any particular emotion at all, and regarded as wholly reflective of an established language variety. Arguably, however, if the term *Korean English* can move from outside the academic context and more into the societal context, then we have gone one step further to recognize what is already established in terms of a grammatically and lexically unique take on the English language.

There are three additional websites which provide more in-depth information under the term of 'Konglish dictionary'.

http://leonsplanet.com/konglish.htm

Leon's Planet provides a very detailed analysis of Konglish, based on Leon Priz and his observations of English use in Korea since the mid-1990s. Priz defines Konglish on two levels. First, an interlanguage resulting in grammar and usage errors in Koreans' English; and second, loan words from English nativized into the Korean language. I would argue that Korean English cannot be both – it's either a nativized variety of English used in Korea in terms of grammar and lexis, or it's not. Priz acknowledges that most Koreans view Konglish in light of the second definition he provides.

Priz then goes on to give five specific examples of Konglish, which appears to be from the point of view of the second definition in that, as with most of the websites discussed, he provides a list of Korean English vocabulary.

Verbicide – The first category refers to 'killing' the meaning of a word. In reality, this is nothing more than a semantic shift. Perhaps the term is used in jest, but for some readers it might still reflect an error regarding semantic shift in Korean English when in reality, this has occurred in many languages, including English of course (e.g. consider the change in word meanings in English words such as *awful, gay* and *idiot*).

Examples provided by Priz include the following given in Table 3.

Priz also discusses 'fabricated words' which don't exist in English; a sample is provided based on Priz's website content shown in Table 4.

Using the term *correct phrase*, however, is very misleading. If Koreans desire to speak only inner-circle American English, for example, the Korean English equivalent, whether based on grammar or lexis, is still valid. I don't seek to criticize Priz, or others, for these kinds of designations. Indeed, as Priz makes clear on his website, his purpose is not to ridicule, and I don't believe implying that Korean English vocabulary is incorrect is an example of ridicule at all. However, it can give the impression, perhaps one reinforced by some in Korean society, that Korean English is somehow wrong, inferior or simply not correct English. It is correct as it is obeying its own rules for grammar and lexis, rules which differ from inner-circle English.

Priz also provides a list of abbreviations used in Korean English; again, a small sample are provided from Priz's website, see Table 5.

Table 3 Priz Website on Konglish

Accessory	jewellery	extra, secondary parts for anything, including jewellery, but not commonly used to mean jewellery
Angle	Bracket (used in construction)	The space between any two lines that intersect or come together end-to-end, relative to the 360° (degrees) of a circle. i.e., an angle can be between 0° and 360°
Bond	super glue	any binding substance or an emotional attachment
Booking	introduction request at a night club	making a reservation
Burberry	overcoat or trench coat	Trademark of light, long, waterproof coat
can 맥주	canned beer (or can of beer)	can (n.) = metallic cylinder (not adjective)
Cider	sweetened soda water (like the brand: 7up)	[US] cider = apple juice, usually homemade [UK] cider = alcoholic apple juice [CAN] hard cider = alcoholic apple juice soft cider = non-alcoholic apple juice

Table 4 Priz Examples of Fabricated Phrases

Fabricated Phrase 아시아에서 만든 구	Correct Phrase 옳은 구
A/S (After Service)	Warrantee Service (free-of-charge service)Service (not free-of-charge service)
American-style Coffee	Black Coffee
Auto-bi~(ke)	Motorcycle
Back Mirror	Rear-view Mirror
Back Number	jersey number
cash corner	ATM (Automatic Teller Machine)
Dutch pay	[US colloquialism] Dutch treat (Each person pays for themselves)
eye shopping	window shopping
game room	(video) arcade
golden ball	sudden death (in game)
hair band	head band
hand phone	[US] cell phone [UK] mobile phone
hard board	poster board
hyper market	grocery store
ice bar	[US] Popsicle (lollypop + icicle) [UK] Ice Lolly (ice + lollypop)
Interphone	intercom
kick board	scooter (non-motorized scooter)

Table 5 Priz Examples of Abbreviated Expressions

Abbreviated Expression 단축된 표현	Correct Expression 옳은 표현
A/S	After service (see also fabricated Konglish list)
Air con	Air conditioner
All ri~(only said when guiding a backer-upper in a car)	All right(said any time something is OK)
Apart	Apartment building (There are many apartments in one apartment building)
back dancer	'backup' dancer?
back music	background music
back singer	backup singer
Ball Pen	Ball Point Pen
Band	Bandage (or band aid)
Cassette	cassette player

Table 6 Priz Samples of Vocabulary

Word or Phrase	Notes
bye bye	Koreans use this parting indiscriminately, but in America, it is considered a child's parting or intimate couple parting
Condition	Koreans use this word to refer to their body's condition. So, it's partially correct
Stamina	Koreans use this word to refer to sexual stamina. So, it's partially correct
Timing	same as English
Muffler	This is UK English (in US, we say 'scarf')
Bonnet	This is UK English (in US, we say 'hood')
pants (*BBans* [Japanese pronunciation])	This is UK English (in US, we say 'underpants')
family name	This might be UK English (in US, we say 'surname' or 'last name')
check(s)	This is UK English (in US, we say 'chequered pattern')
Sofa	orig: Arab word: *suffa*, then French word: *sofa*English 'borrowed' the word from French
Diet	same as English (but only the kind of diet for losing weight)
Stove	Koreans use the original meaning of the word, i.e., heater, but modern English has changed from the original meaning – nowadays there are two kinds of stoves for cooking: a gas stove and an electric stove
Wine	same as English
ice cream	Koreans use this in a broader sense that we do in the US. It includes Popsicles and 'slushies'
Computer	same as English
Monitor	same as English
hard drive	same as English
CD	same as English
Keyboard	same as English
disk (floppy disk)	same as English
bargain sale	same as English, although in the US we would just say, 'sale'
Video	short for 'video cassette'
Motel	same as English
Hotel	same as English
Project	same as English
DJ	same as English
MC	same as English
Canvas	same as English
Paint	The Korean definition generally refers to industrial type paint, not artist paint, nor make-up paint
Internet	same as English
Website	same as English
Homepage	same as English
website I.D.	This might be British. In the US, we write 'username', not 'I.D.'
and many many more	I can't remember all the loan words. I read somewhere that there are around 10,000 English and European loan words in the Korean language (but they are only used in South Korea)

Finally, Priz offers examples of words from inner-circle English that have been largely borrowed in the original forms, both semantically and orthographically, see Table 6.

The list of words in Table 6 are referred to as an 'OK Konglish List', implying that they are OK in as much as they conform to their original meanings. Granted, Korean English does involve wholesale word borrowings, as the inner circle has borrowed wholesale from Korean vocabulary too (*kimchi, K-POP, taekwondo* and *nunchi* have made their way into English), but words cannot expect to remain static and so meanings will change over time. The key issue with expanding circle Englishes is not to regard them as a deficit against the linguistic behemoth of standard American English. Instead, we need to educate people in Korean English, especially if they are living in Korea, and this can be harnessed in the classroom as a means to teach each other, teacher and student, within a joint meaning-making atmosphere.

https://tefltastic.wordpress.com/2008/12/01/konglish-a-to-z/
On the foregoing site, entitled 'TEFLtastic', Alex Case provides a detailed list of Korean English vocabulary, but begins his discussion with what can be seen as a disclaimer. Case defines Korean English as involving borrowed words from English, including words based on English which have since undergone change in meaning. Even with such a small sample of websites provided, it seems clear that a more general reference to Korean English (or Konglish, of course, as the more commonly used term) defaults to its use of English words, whatever form they have taken (e.g. whether direct borrowings, abbreviations, new meanings and so on). The comparative lack of discussion of Korean English grammar, at least on the websites analyzed, is again perhaps due to the academic research in this area not having gone more public, as it were. On the other hand, it already has in terms of Koreans' use of English which in turn gave researchers such as Shim (1999) something to categorize in the first instance.

Case explains that Konglish is not 'wrong English' but simply a category of Korean vocabulary. As explained, this is just one part of Korean English, however. Case also explains that the vocabulary provided on his site is a source of 'error correction'. This is not a contradiction to his earlier statement about Korean English not being wrong. Rather, he is addressing the potential for Koreans to use Korean English vocabulary outside Korea, which could perhaps cause confusion for interlocutors. Nonetheless, in such situations, there are no errors to correct. This is no different to confusion that has arisen with British people while I have been in England, when I asked for the *check* at a restaurant (instead of the *bill*), and asked for *Wite-Out* in a stationery store (not *Tipp-Ex*). We need to apply this understanding to all varieties of English, no matter their age, region or speakers.

Case acknowledges the somewhat serious nature of this opening to a vocabulary list of Korean English, but he does so in an attempt to acknowledge that the purpose is not to present this variety in a negative light. Case presents an online dictionary of Korean English words, which confirms yet again the extent to which such words have become a regular and predictable part of Korean English, at least one aspect. Following this extensive list of vocabulary, comments are posted. Again, these are a valuable means to understand further the content of, and attitudes towards, Korean English. An interesting discussion can be found, in which the question is raised as to what should be corrected regarding language. Case explains that if a non-standard form is used, such as *I done it*, how should this be approached if interlocutors declare it wrong or can't understand it. He further asks if a native speaker model should even be relevant in the first instance. A response, using *I done it* as an example, explains that such language use would be declared wrong in a university setting and by educated people, more so within assessments perhaps. I would adjust this and say it is not wrong, merely based on a different set of grammatical rules, and it would be inappropriate for academic writing; likewise, at a family gathering, a switch to standard English when *I done it* is otherwise the 'standard' might be seen as putting on airs and graces.

A further discussion continues on the site, which ties in with much of what has been discussed already. One point made is that attitudes to language are a factor, in that *cell phone* might be considered 'standard' not based on logic; instead, it is based on the possibility of a majority of people suddenly deciding that *hand phone* is not 'correct'. There is some truth to this, based on lexis or grammar that differ from the standard variety. Again, the issue is one of power, not inherentness. In an alternative reality, perhaps *he done it* could have been the standard. These kinds of online discussions allow for opinions to be shared, arguments made and, sometimes, emotions to flare. Nonetheless, online discussions provide an immediate means for society to learn about language issues, among other things, and share views. A step in the right direction would be for more Koreans to take charge with such online means of information, whether websites or blogs, and provide a more authentic discussion perhaps, in that surely Korean English speakers not merely know this variety, but can also *feel* it.

https://sydneytoseoul.wordpress.com/2013/08/02/lexical-borrowings-from-english-in-konglish/

The foregoing blog is entitled 'Sydney to Seoul', written by an Australian who has an interest in language and culture, including Korean, with part of the site dedicated to Korean English.

The writer dismisses the notion that Korean English is reflective of broken English or errors, and defines it instead as a variation of English which ties in with Koreans' social and linguistic needs. The writer concurs with Lawrence (2010a: 45), who defines Konglish (though my preferred term is understood by now) as a 'potential contact vernacular [. . .] a creative mix between English and the local language, which normally include morphology, semantics and syntax but may also include pronunciation, pragmatics and discourse'. This definition is the most inclusive, as it takes into consideration more than just vocabulary.

While it is disappointing that none of the websites analyzed offer examples of grammatical features of Korean English, it is abundantly clear that, definitions aside, Konglish is otherwise presented nearly uniformly as the nativization of English-based words used by Koreans, from this small sample of websites at least. Though there is more than this involved, we are way past the starting point for Korean English. Examples provided on the site can be seen in Table 7.

Konglish grammar

Under this heading, as part of the final section, some sites appear that have already been commented on. However, there are four new entries which will be commented on in turn, with regard to their content and the implications for such.

Table 7 Sydney to Seoul: Examples of Vocabulary

Korean Term			Meaning
	팀	Team	Team
Direct loan words	버스	Bus	Bus
	셀프	Self	Self-service
Clipping	아파트	Apart	Apartment
	바바리	Burberry	Trench coat
Semantic shifts	미팅	Meeting	College student's blind date
	안전벨트	Ahn jeon belt	Seatbelt (Ahn jeon: Korean for safety)
Mixed-code combinations	감자 칩	Gam ja chip	Potato chip (Gam ja: Korean for potato)
	백미러	Back mirror	Rear-view mirror
Fabrications	베이글 녀	Bagel nyeo	Used to describe a woman with a **ba**by face and **gl**amorous body (Nyeo: Korean for girl)

http://language.exchange.free.fr/lessons_read.php?lang=konglish (Babel Polyglot, 2013)

This website is straightforward, presenting an online dictionary for people to see, under the heading of 'Konglish – Korean English 1' (and 2). The online dictionary available at the next website mentioned also shows the routes by which new vocabulary (though no longer 'new' of course) has entered Korean English. An approximation is also provided in terms of Korean pronunciation.

> apateu 아파트: apartment (from Japanese language アパート apāto)
> wonroom 원룸: studio apartment (from one room)
> babarikoteu 바바리코트: trench coat (from Burberry coat)
> hendeupon 핸드폰: cell phone (from hand phone)
> dika 디카: digital camera
> selca 셀카: self-portrait photo (from self camera)
> rimokeon 리모컨, 리모콘: remote control
> aidol 아이돌: idol
> geulleimeo 글래머: buxom woman (from glamour)
> ero 에로: erotic
> hojikiseu 호치키스: stapler (from hotchkiss)
> hwaiting or paiting 화이팅 or 파이팅: used to cheer a player in sport (from fighting)
> keoning 커닝, 컨닝 cheating (from cunning via カンニング in Japanese)
> mishing 미싱: sewing machine (from Japanese ミシン mishin)
> penshi 팬시: means stationery (from fancy)
> saida 사이다: lemon soda, lemonade (from cider)
> (from Japanese ワイシャツ wai-shatsu)

https://www.howtostudykorean.com/unit-6/lessons-134-141/lesson-134/

This website is titled 'Ultimate Konglish Guide', offering a variety of online lessons for this language variety. This offers more than just a definition of the various lexis but also offers visual guides where relevant. For example, a diagram is provided to reveal what is meant by the Korean English word *apartuh* (아파트), translated as *apartment*. While this refers to an apartment building, the architectural implications in Korea may differ from what is understood in the United States or United Kingdom, and beyond. The word is explained to often refer to tall, high-rise type buildings which are placed next to each other, providing several buildings and units in one large space. These buildings can be rented, but are usually owned. However, the word can also refer to smaller buildings, owned or rented by younger couples who can't afford the larger versions or don't need the extra space the larger apartments provide. Unlike the larger apartments, parking and extra space are usually not provided.

Also provided are contextual examples of how the word *apartment* is used by Koreans. Given that the following sentences are clearly in Korean, it is easy perhaps to consider the use of the word *apartment* (bolded) as nothing more than a borrowed word. This is perhaps one reason why Korean English – or Konglish to use the common term – can be understood in large part as reflecting borrowed English words, in what is otherwise a Korean conversation. However, examples have been provided previously of when such vocabulary is otherwise wrapped up as part of an English conversation or written communication, reflecting a unique Korean English grammar.

이 동네에는 가족들이 많이 살고 있어서 아파트가 많아요 =
There are a lot of families living in this neighbourhood, so there are a lot of **apartments.**

지금은 그냥 빌라에서 살고 있는데 나중에는 아파트에서 살았으면 좋겠어요
= Now I just live in a villa, but later I hope to live in an **apartment.**

The word *service* (서비스) refers to free samples of a certain item, such as food, provided to paying customers. Again, examples are provided on the website:

우리가 식당에서 밥을 많이 시켜서 서비스를 받았어요
= We ordered so much food at the restaurant that we got some **free food/stuff.**

만약 고객님이 차를 이 가격으로 구매하시면 저는 엔진오일을 서비스로 줄 겁니다
= If you buy this car at this price, I will give you engine oil **for free.**

제가 그 식당에 자주 가지만 거기서 일하는 사람들이 친절하지도 않고 서비스도 안 줘서 더 이상 가고 싶지 않아요
= I go to that restaurant often, but the people working there aren't nice and they never give me any **free things**, so I'm not going to go there anymore.

These examples also provide information on how the contextual use of *service* can, in turn, alter the meaning somewhat.

Another example consists of the Korean English word 파이팅 / 화이팅, which equates to *fighting* (though with Korean pronunciation, it's pronounced more like *pai-ting* or *hwai-ting*), but essentially means *good luck* or *do well!* The expression was widely used during the World Cup in Korea in 2002, accompanied by a hand gesture in which a clenched fist is used as the arm is quickly pulled down in a vertical motion. It is both an example of verbal, and non-verbal, communication, that many expats are perhaps familiar with. The term and gesture work together when trying to encourage someone, lift their spirits and the like.

The word 컨닝 – cunning – refers to cheating on an exam (more specifically, looking at someone else's paper) and was referred to earlier, often used by my students in Korea, though all were children. Examples are provided:

시험을 볼 때 컨닝을 하면 안 돼요 = When you take an exam, you shouldn't cheat.

제가 고등학교 때 컨닝을 많이 했어요 = I cheated a lot when I was in high school.

The full verb is 컨닝하다, meaning *to do cunning* (or in literal translation, *cunning to do*).

This website is very illustrative indeed, to include examples of the words as actually used in context. Its content ends with a very large list of vocabulary, with a sample now provided. I should point out that the words in Table 8 represent direct borrowings from English where the word retains the same meaning as in inner-circle English; the pronunciation, however, is Korean. Thus, *gas* sounds more like *ga-suh*; *golf* sounds more like *gol-puh* (see Table 8).

https://prezi.com/igjdocv6ryn5/konglish-vs-english-different/ (Sandy S., 2015)

The final website offers photos of English use in Korea, for the reader to detect the errors. Given that the first slide has 'Konglish' as a prominent title, it is clear that the implication is that Konglish equates to errors. For example, the first error

Table 8 How to Study Korean Samples of Vocabulary

가스	**Gas**
가스레인지	Gas range (stove)
가이드	Guide
갤러리	Gallery
거즈	Gauze
게스트	Guest
게임	Game
골	Goal
골키퍼	Goal keeper
골프	Golf
그램	Gram
글라스	Glass

consists of the sign, in Korean and English, referring to an elementary (primary) school, with the error based on spelling: *elemantery*. Another sign is for a popular coffee chain in Korea, Angel-in-us, which includes the slogan *the world best coffee*, and another designer store proclaims on its storefront *mannish elegance* (instead of *manly elegance*). Clearly, these are pure errors, but not based on my judgement. Rather, there is no evidence that I know of, so far, that posits that *elementary* can be spelled as *elemantery*; that possessive nouns can choose, or not, to use the suffix *'s*; and I don't know that *mannish*, is, as of yet, the Korean English word for *manly*. Thus far, Konglish is being equated with errors in Koreans' English, here largely focused on spelling. This suggests the need, once again, to separate errors, especially when there is clear agreement of their status (e.g. spelling errors) from what is otherwise established and thus conventionalized examples of Korean English vocabulary, which is further codified based on the presence of so many online dictionaries.

A further online slide, however, defines Konglish as follows:

Korean + English = Konglish
American English versus Korean English
= Different (Not Wrong)

1. Wrong grammar
2. Different meaning
3. Different pronunciation
4. Korean fabrication

The previous example is somewhat unclear; are the terms *Konglish* and *Korean English* being used as one and the same? If so, then referring to the grammar as 'wrong', when the writer has otherwise declared it as merely different, appears to be a contradiction. On the other hand, by comparing American English with Korean English and declaring the Korean variety as 'not wrong', but merely different, could suggest that Korean English clearly cannot be wrong – just different (and is thus being distinguished from Konglish on this site).

An example of wrong grammar provided on a further slide is 'Teacher! Sick!' The 'corrected' version is 'Teacher, I hurt my arm.' This is misleading, however. It appears that the speaker is perhaps a child, as the accompanying picture is indeed a young boy. It could be regarded as an error on the grounds of not being a complete sentence, perhaps even 'childspeak'. Perhaps, but the larger implication, at least with this example, is that Konglish is being equated to an immature form of English tied to children's speech.

Overall, then, this website offers some insights, but arguably does not go into sufficient contextual detail at times. We again see clear evidence of Konglish being viewed, in the main, as being based on borrowed words from English, but including an undercurrent, occasionally at least, of involving grammatical and spelling errors. If said errors are pure errors, such as misspellings, then misspellings and translation errors would be my preferred terms. Once we cross over into Korean English grammatical territory, then these are no longer errors. A final online entry points to the academic context, consisting of a conference paper presented by Kent (1999): 'Speaking in Tongues: Chinglish, Japlish and Konglish'.

As I conclude this chapter, I acknowledge again that there is only so much space and time available regarding the discussion of Korean English. I limited my discussion solely to the content of the first page that came up following a Google search using key terms such as Konglish and Korean English. Nonetheless, I suggest that given the online content presented within this chapter, the following main points can be made with confidence:

- Konglish is clearly the most understood term in use within (online) society, with Korean English arguably not used as much or for some, a term not otherwise known.
- Korean English vocabulary is conventionalized by its use in society, thus leaving online sources as a means to subsequently reinforce and codify its usage.
- These sites allow others to learn about such vocabulary, very practical for those who live and work in Korea, as well as being a means to teach others who have an interest in language and culture to begin with.
- There is little said about Korean English grammar, which other sites may indeed incorporate; more information on this specific area is needed, thus avoiding a definition of Konglish as solely, or mostly, based on borrowed words from English; it is time for understandings of Korean English grammar to move from the academic context and into a more everyday context, such as online sources.
- Overall, the attitudes presented towards Korean English – again, referred to almost entirely as Konglish – are largely positive, if not neutral, though with some comments presenting Konglish, despite its systematicity, as somehow 'incorrect' when compared with inner-circle English, instead of being merely different.

Chapter 5 is now presented, offering a discussion of media English in Korea, as another variety within a variety.

5

Media English in Korea

This chapter discusses a widespread use of English in Korea that goes beyond what has been defined and discussed thus far in terms of Korean English. Here, the focus is on the pervasive use of English in Korea as seen and heard in media. For the purposes of this chapter, the media focus will be centred on K-POP, TV, to include TV dramas, and advertisements. Together, these three areas use English, broadly, as a means of code-switching between Korean and English, whether heard in a song's chorus or a TV character's dialogue, creating blended words, and also using English for advertising slogans for a variety of Korean companies. Finally, I will discuss this use of societal English in a somewhat less defined area, though easy to recognize – the English used on store fronts, which can consist of slogans or sometimes extended phrases. Collectively, this forms part of 'linguistic landscapes' (Martin, 2020: 598), which also includes public signage and shops signs' use of English (Scollon and Scollon, 2003; Bolton, 2012); such is the vast array of the ways in which English can be used in a given society. This can move beyond store fronts and be found on products too, from tissue packets to notebooks. Such is the spread of English to be found in Korea. In presenting this focus, it also helps to address the implication of Jenks and Lee (2017) concerning the variety of Englishes as found within Korean English.

As Lawrence (2012: 89) states, '[i]n any region of the country, certain shops frequently have English signs, including coffee shops, sports equipment dealers, clothing stores, car dealers, fast food restaurants, hair salons, hotels, pensions, beer bars and wine stores'. There are, therefore, many categories in which public English can be seen in Korea, with a broad rationale for the use of English within Korean media being that 'a modern identity in contemporary South Korea is virtually guaranteed through . . . use of English' (Lee 2006: 59), further regarding English as 'linguistic capital'. Such uses especially pertain to contextual codification, which is certainly a fitting term for the kind of English referred to in the quote from Lawrence: widespread, unpredictable in its usage (e.g. the words used), but immediately codified as soon as it is placed on, for example, a storefront.

As presented here, the broader contextual background which helps to inform the discussion of these varied uses of the English language in Korea concerns identity and power. This can be seen in terms of how identities are signalled through English and how power is associated with the use of a language with high status. However, we must also consider the relative power afforded to the Koreans – such as celebrities on TV – who take English and use it to wield a degree of power in their own right. Such power can be seen on a purely linguistic level with the coining of new words, but also in terms of individuals bending both English and Korean to their will, in order to accommodate two cultures (Lee, 2014).

First, I wish to discuss the content of this chapter in relation to my argument on societal codification. I have argued that there is a systematicity with the use of English in Korea in terms of lexis and a suggested systematic nature of its grammar. Together, I have housed these features as part of conventionalization by the speakers, with codification being seen partly by traditional means, albeit within non-traditional media (e.g. online dictionaries). This also extends to public signage as seen with the previous examples of *Grand Open* and the sign at Lotte World; both are put forward as evidence of a societal means of codification for, respectively, Korean English lexis and grammar.

However we conceptualize codification though, there is arguably a very important aspect to this: the need for predictability. In other words, if any features of English, as used in Korea and by Koreans, cannot be determined to follow some form of predictable and conventionalized usage, then there is nothing to codify in the first instance. The purpose of mentioning this is that, within media contexts, the use of English might be very *unpredictable*. For example, a given song lyric may not suggest anything other than standard inner-circle English, and herein lies the focus on power, as perhaps American (or inner-circle) English will carry more weight with the listeners. Furthermore, within advertisements (such as slogans) and shop fronts, for example, the use of English in such cases is unpredictable precisely because attempts to attract customers to the product (e.g. through slogans) usually relies on novel or 'creative' uses of language. This would not necessarily suggest a use of language that is otherwise immediately recognized by the public.

Thus, the question implied concerns the extent to which the examples which follow pertain to any discernible examples of Korean English grammar or lexis. Some do, some perhaps do not. However, the rationale for the discussion to follow is twofold. First, in keeping with the previous statement by Jenks and Lee (2017), it is important to unpack the term *Korean English* from multiple perspectives, given the prominence with which English appears in Korean society. This is also reflective of Methrie and Bhatt's (2008) English Language Complex which seeks to uncover 'varieties within varieties' regarding English. A good example in the South African English context – using this as the linguistic starting point – is South African Indian English (SAIE), which Mesthrie (1988) further subdivides based on differences involving lexis, for example. Such differences can be based on the religious background of the speakers (e.g. those who practice Islam versus those who practice Hinduism) and ancestral language (e.g. Hindi, Telugu). Thus, we can see how there is internal variation to be seen, much like a linguistic matryoshka doll (Baratta, 2019a), as mentioned. Even with the comparatively younger Korean English, there is clear evidence of a use of English in society beyond that which has already been presented.

That the examples do not conform necessarily to the suggested systematicity that I have otherwise argued for does not mean that said examples are not, in themselves, examples of societal codification, however. At this point, the term might be regarded by some readers as being stretched a bit too far and the examples provided more in line with 'English in Korea' (Song, 2016). However, it would be limiting to not include such an obvious means of English use, which can, theoretically, solidify in Koreans' minds the influence of English, as well as provide insights into the internal variation of Korean English. Moreover, I approach the immediate use of English in the examples to follow, such as song lyrics and code-switching on TV drama, as part of the aforementioned 'contextual codification', suggesting a continued presence of English in Korea and often realized at the moment of deployment in song lyrics or TV dialogue.

Even if no two song lyrics, product slogans or shop front uses of English are alike (it would be unusual if they were, purely for copyright reasons), that they have been recorded and used, whether a lyric heard, a slogan written down as part of an advertisement or the use of cursive Roman script on a shop front to allure people to taste coffee, this is all part of a broader picture of societal use of English. This demonstrates the extent to which English has spread in Korea, to the extent that it would indeed be somewhat short-sighted to not include evidence of such, as part of a fuller contextual picture of the use of English in this broad national context.

A final point to make concerns the fact that regarding such uses of English, it is largely, if not entirely, the Koreans who are behind it. Whether it involves a boy band, screenwriter or small business owner, here are examples of Koreans using English on *their* terms. This is of relevance as very often, there have been instances of a dominant group using language to misrepresent others. For example, O' Barr (1994) discusses US advertising and its historic depiction of non-whites, such as African Americans and their language, as part of media images, such as a picture of the so-called mammy (Bogle, 1973) as the face of Aunt Jemima pancake mix (which is now being addressed as reflecting racist imagery). Hollywood also had depictions of Asians in film, but played by Caucasian actors, such as Peter Lorre as the Japanese detective Mr Moto, and the Chinese detective Charlie Chan, both depicted with suggested 'Asian' accents. Such language – both verbal and visual – contributes to a larger picture of the dominant group attempting to 'represent' minorities, to include their language use. George Lucas came under fire for his depiction of characters in *The Phantom Menace*, in which the character of Jar Jar Binks speaks with what sounded to many to be a Jamaican accent and dialect, and depicted as both a bumbling idiot and subservient. On the International Talk Like Jar Jar Binks Day website, we see evidence of the character's language: 'No, No, Mesa Stay. Mesa Culled Jar Jar Binks. Mesa Your Humble Servant' (talklikejarjarday.com). Likewise, the villain Nute Gunray speaks with what was suggested to be a vaguely 'Chinese' accent (or a 'Hollywood Chinese' accent).

These brief illustrations are perhaps extreme examples of how language can be used as more than a means to mock others' attempts to speak 'correctly', but more so a means to stereotype the group that is suggested, however subtly. If, however, a group takes charge of a language that is not their native variety, then their use of such represents a case of linguistic creativity, part of Blommaert's (2010) work on bits of language, as was referenced. Moreover, such usage can, in time, lead to further innovation (Martin, 2020). But more relevant to the discussion here, this is a case of the said group using the language on *their* terms. Bhatia (2020) offers an example of how this can then spread outward, to include the inner circle – this was seen with the term *Walkman* (and the product of course to which the term was attached) invented by Japanese advertisers. The use of English in ads within countries outside the inner circle is also part of the influence of this language; as Bhatia (2020: 623) explains in specific relation to English use in the context of advertising, 'in order to be a global citizen, some knowledge of English is a prerequisite'. But in closing, 'the purpose of learning English as an international language is not to blindly imitate native speakers of English' (Park, 2009: 94) and this can be applied to Korean media as much as everyday English language on the streets of Seoul.

What now follows is a broad overview of how Koreans have put English to work for them within various media contexts, demonstrating different ways in which English is used in society.

K-POP

K-POP is of course a major part of the Korean *hallyu*. According to the Yonhap News Agency in Korea, the number of global *hallyu* fans is close to 90 million people, consisting of fan clubs. Hallyu, by definition, refers to the global spread, or wave, of Korean culture around the world; and as I had referred to earlier, this is by no means tied to pop culture such as music and drama, and can extend to food, history, the Korean language, *nunchi* and *taekwondo*, among other aspects which constitute Korean culture. I recall a newspaper story (Daily Mail Reporter, 2011) of an English girl, Rhiannon Brooksbank-Jones, who had tongue surgery in order to better master the specific sounds of the Korean language. She and a friend would also watch Korean drama and listen to K-POP, and here is a very clear case of a devotion to Korea (Rhiannon Brooksbank-Jones has tongue lengthened to help her speak Korean | Daily Mail Online)

The use of English lyrics in Korean songs generally involves a switch from Korean to English, so essentially a case of code-switching. Reflecting on the global popularity of K-POP, Lee and Jin (2019: 2) declare that 'global youth, from the US to Chile, chant for K-pop'. Lee (2004: 429) provides a basis for this use, stating that 'English mixing in the song texts is not homogenous in its forms and functions', again suggestive of contextual codification as I have defined it. The following are some of the purposes of code-switching to English in K-POP, according to Lee (page 432):

Stylistic: This can be based on an English word rhyming with a Korean word, or English words which rhyme with other English words within the musical motif. For example, the song *Lovin' U* by Sistar has the following lyrics to its chorus:

(36) *Lovin you, you, Na ottoke what should I do?*

The expression *na ottoke* would essentially translate in this context as *what should/can I do?* But the internal rhyme with *you* and *do* is clear, and the repetition of the key phrase in both Korean and English serves to possibly drive home the point that the female singer is in distress.

Assertion of sensuality: Some Korean singers might seek to sidestep the Korean censors by using English words for more sexually suggestive lyrics or, in the case of the next example (from the song 'Everything' by Fly to the Sky), misogynistic lyrics. In this case, the Korean lyrics portray the singer's desire for his girlfriend to return to him, but the sudden switch to English with the lyrics *should've known you was a hoe* portrays a very different persona (Flattery, 2007).

Overall, however, the use of English can reflect broader connotations, involving modernity and internationalization (Lee, 2006; Park, J.S. 2006, 2009; Baratta, 2014), to also include notions of power and prestige (Shim and Baik, 2004), with such values attached to the language and to the speaker/singer/ actor as a consequence. Though this can work in both directions, with certain language use sometimes regarded negatively by interlocutors (Haddix, 2012; Baratta, 2017; 2018a; 2018b), while certain language use can also be a force for positive evaluation.

Jin and Ryoo (2012) explore the use of English lyrics in K-POP, suggesting another category of rationale for their use, which is referred to as cultural hybridity. Identity is a relevant factor and as seen earlier with the switch in the song *Everything*, the Korean lyrics suggest an identity of a man pining for his lost love; the use of the English insertion as presented suggests a more misogynistic persona indeed. That language and identity are intertwined, though not a dominant focus within this book, is a point that has been made clear already. In this sense, a switch of lyrics can effect a change of identity, certainly in terms of how the singer, or perhaps the character within the song, is perceived, as part of an ascribed identity (Baratta, 2018a).

Further reflecting the use of the internet as a means of language codification and here, information retrieval, a Google search for K-POP use of English lyrics reveals 'about 267,000,000 results'. Of note are the links to song samples on YouTube. Though unsurprising perhaps, this offers a direct link to not merely understanding the theories behind English use, or even seeing the lyrics online, but also a final culmination of how it actually all sounds.

The use of English in various ways as part of K-POP does not necessarily reflect Korean English to the extent perhaps that its grammatical features are on display, or even its lexis, though I am not discounting such uses. Rather, English in this context would fit within the variety of Korean media English, or perhaps a further variety of its own (e.g. K-POP English) within this larger category. Beyond the connotations of modernity and power, English use in media contexts would perhaps reflect a more random, certainly less predictable use, in that the systematicity of Korean English (as I have defined it) would give way perhaps for a wide range of English words and phrases, each specific to each unique song title, Korean lyrics and/or band name. It is also the case that the uses of English might reflect more an inner-circle use, as a means to project a more 'neutral', and thus global, positioning of the bands, through a more international variety of English which is theoretically used by all, or understood by most, as opposed to a local variety.

Ironically perhaps, it is arguably the *Korean* lyrics that might have more power as far as the overseas K-POP fans are concerned, as a means to cement in their minds the Korean-ness of this music brand, as one powerful example of the Korean cultural wave that is sweeping the planet. The BBC in fact reports that as a result of this fandom, many people are now learning Korean as a result (Pickles, 2018). The Modern Language Association in fact reveals that studying Korean in US universities rose by 14 per cent from 2013 to 2016. Many non-Korean fans can now write Korean, to the extent of writing Korean on banners and placards when their favourite band arrives at the airport, and can even sing the song lyrics (Lee and Jin, 2019). Ironically, this might suggest that for K-POP fans who are not Korean and non-native speakers of English, switches to English within their favourite songs might not be regarded as particularly innovative.

But in the Korean context, Lee (2004: 446) presents the idea that the mixing of English and Korean in song lyrics 'epitomizes South Korean youth's battle with their unsettling identities in dealing with the tension between the global and local dialogues to which they are simultaneously exposed'. It also ties in with the attitudes towards English in Korea, which are admittedly mixed. On the one hand, Lee (2004) discusses an anxiety towards English felt by many Koreans, in large part due to their perceived lack of abilities in this language. On the other hand, English clearly represents a large degree of linguistic capital in Korea (Lee, 2020). But beyond this broad backdrop, we might consider the more immediate concerns with the use of English in K-POP lyrics, often representing 'pleasure-seeking, self-indulgent, progressive attitudes; Korean lyrics within the same song capture reserved, wholesome, and introspective mindsets' (Lee, 2020: 596). Clearly, there are many factors involved in the use of English in K-POP: using a language of prestige and power, perhaps demonstrating a degree of said power by singing in English and projecting perhaps a modern identity, by use of a language associated with globalization (Kim and Choi, 2014).

I add to this by placing emphasis again on the ways in which Koreans have made English their own, as a means of demonstrating a degree of confidence and creativity – and suggested power. Lee (2007: 60) explains in fact that in the context of K-POP 'not just one English but several Englishes – African American

English, Standard English, Koreanized English – co-exist side by side' (page 60). Some examples of 'Koreanized English' in hip-hop include: *all round player,* 'Jack of all trades,' *B-bomb dropper* 'skillful hip-hop artist,' *B-girl* 'avid female hip-hop music fan,' *blender* 'artist who can perform in more than two genres,' *hiphoper n' rocker* 'a musician who does both hip-hop and rock n' roll' and *overground* 'mainstream music' (page 59).

Such uses again reflect a degree of societal codification – in this case, via the reproduction of English in song lyrics which are performed, listened to and perhaps even available in written form, such as that found on the artist's website, CD or on fan sites. Here we would find an example of societal codification on two levels that are non-traditional: first, song lyrics being reproduced with every performance and each time fans listen to them (and perhaps sing along); and second, that the lyrics, if they are in written form, are produced on fan sites perhaps. But again, this is a reflection that there is indeed something to reproduce in the first instance. That it is tied primarily to a particular music genre does not change the fact that it is being used in society, even if only by a particular group of Koreans (perhaps the younger generation and fans of a particular music genre). If such uses extend beyond this context, then words such as *overground* might be heard more broadly.

But overall, the use of English, and its Koreanized use in particular, again reflects a degree of confidence and creativity, in ways that might go against a suggested English anxiety. Performers are taking English and spreading it to the K-POP fans, many of whom live outside Korea. This can also help to spread a uniquely Korean style of English as heard in music genres beyond the borders of Korea. Thus, such uses of Korean English are understood, and perhaps spoken, among K-POP fans; as such, this is a legitimate part of the larger focus on Korean English overall.

Korean TV drama

Code-switching within Korean TV dramas (here, I am using the word *drama* broadly, to incorporate all genres of TV shows) is perhaps more noticeable in that it is spoken as part of what is ostensibly an everyday conversation between characters on-screen. Just based on my personal experience of having watched TV dramas in Korea while I lived there in the 1990s, I recall many switches involving dialogue such as *thank you/welcome, double crazy* and *bye-bye*. These switches can be considered marked forms, in that Korean dialogue suddenly introduces a language that is unexpected.

I had discussed the use of English switches in three dramas (Baratta, 2014), which were otherwise selected at random. The rationale for this was based on the assumption that given the fairly common occurrence of English switches in Korean TV drama, I had chosen three examples without any prior knowledge. Some TV dramas are indeed set overseas, in what we might consider broad contexts in which English would be expected. For example, several drams are set in countries in which, while English is not the dominant language, it could act as a lingua franca. Locations include France (*Shopping King Louie* and *The Package*) and Spain (*The K2* and *Memories of the Alhambra*). The fact that a Korean character in the latter drama speaks proficient Spanish might act as further evidence for Korea's desire to position itself as international, partly through overseas settings but also through the use of foreign languages other than English.

Chung (2011: 9), for example, refers to the use of English on Korean TV based on 'the increasingly cosmopolitan story settings' which again might involve an English-speaking country (or non-Korean speakers) and/or involves English-speaking foreigners. Given the youthful and attractive leading man and woman who are often depicted in these dramas, the use of English can perhaps bring a finishing touch to the connotations of 'the globalizing world' (Lee, 2006: 62).

Park (2006: 247) further discusses the 'symbolic power' of English, associated with 'high quality, internationalism, sophistication and modernity'. In the settings of many, but by no means all Korean TV dramas, there is evidence of sophistication and modernity in other ways, involving not just attractive leads, but storylines involving financially comfortable, if not powerful, business people, who live in nice new apartments, drive shiny sports cars, wear designer clothes and eat high-class food.

In the context of comedies, Park (2009) presents three reasons for the use of English in this context. First, Park suggests that characters' lack of proficiency with English in these stories serves 'various humorous purposes' (133). Second, Park refers to 'the hegemony of global English within Korean society' (134), which can apply to many genres of TV show and to other contexts, of course. Finally, Park states that the use of English can serve as a relatable plot device, in that the characters' switch to English can reflect probable situations in society, from characters who lack English skills to those who are proficient in the language. That a lack of proficiency in English is being made a source of humour might run counter to a discussion of power, but as Lee (2014) explains, such plot devices are a means to help Koreans address issues of language anxiety, but more importantly, this could be seen as liberating in that it is *Koreans* who are largely, if not entirely, behind the writing of such scripts. The fact they have choice in terms of how they portray English is an important factor.

However, we should consider the immediate context of situations in which English is used. In the TV drama *You're Beautiful* (2009), the manager of a boy band is portrayed as quite eccentric, seen with his hyperactive energy when discussing his plans and vision for the band, but also seen with his rather esoteric use of English. The following is a sample of his dialogue, all Korean save for the insertion of English in italics:

> (37) Popularity has to be raised strategically. Out of the songs that Tae Kyung has prepared, there's a really good one that's perfect for Mi Nam. After that it's going to be like bam-bam explosion, *jackpot!*

Schilling-Estes (1998: 68–9) states that a switch is 'primarily a means whereby speakers alter the images of self which they project for others'. In the previous case, and several others (though *jackpot* is arguably the manager's 'English trademark'), he is perhaps not merely providing comic relief with this use of English. It might also be seen as a means of affirming his power as the manager, as well as implicitly suggesting his big plans for the band's success, by using a language which is reflective of success within Korean society.

In another drama, *Big* (2012), we have more extensive English use beyond an insertion. In one particular scene, we have a newcomer to a high school, Kyung Joon, who is portrayed as insolent. When his teacher, Gil Da Ran, shows him around the campus, he comments that his Korean skills are a little weak, having lived in the United States for some time. The English is marked in italics:

> **Kyung Joon:** It's because my Korean is still a bit awkward, sorry.
>
> **Da Ran:** It seems that you don't know because you're from America, but this is a very famous line in Korea so listen very carefully. I'm a teacher and you're a student! *I am a teacher and you're a student, OK?*
>
> **Kyung Joon:** OK, Gil Da Ran.
>
> **Da Ran:** Gil Da Ran? *Teacher! Teacher!* Teacher! Teacher!
>
> **Kyung Joon:** OK, teacher Gil.

Having earlier established that he is proficient in English, there are several reasons why the teacher might wish to switch to English in the dialogue. First, it might act as mild sarcasm, as a means to drive home her point about the student-teacher relationship in Korea to a student who suggests he is otherwise unaware. This way, he has no excuse to feign ignorance. Specifically, the focus is on the pragmatic function of verb suffixes in Korea, as a reflection of the language's honorifics system, which Kyung Joon did not demonstrate earlier to his teacher. For example, the suffix *yo* (요) is added to verbs, to signify respect to the addressee, be it a teacher and/or someone older. Moreover, given the high rank afforded to teachers in the school system, then all the more reason why the respect must be paid to this profession, to include respect paid on a purely linguistic level.

Second, perhaps Da Ran, not to be 'outdone' by her student, switches to English to assert herself, a means to demonstrate her own proficiency in a language of power, and thus reassert her rightful place in society. In this way, she plays Kyung Joon at his own 'game', as it were, making it clear that she can speak English too and will not be outsmarted by a cocky teenage boy. Further, Da Ran's repetition of the word *teacher*, uttered in both Korean and English, also acts perhaps as linguistic reinforcement, given that Kyung Joon has broken a rule in addressing his teacher by her first name, which would certainly not occur in Korean high schools. Thus, he needs to be put in his place and reminded of the hierarchy in Korean society and notably within education.

We can, of course, argue that this is merely scripted language, but it is nonetheless chosen for a reason, as a means to move storylines, reflect the character's qualities and quirks and perhaps, simply put, grab attention. I do not wish to overstate the 'power' of English in Korea, however, as a means for its use in TV dramas. To do so might suggest a somewhat predictable interpretation. Also, as an inner-circle speaker, I cannot possibly know how Koreans react to such uses of English, and how they perceive them. While this could be gleaned from an academic study which seeks to obtain Koreans' views on this matter, I would still not be any more informed on a personal level, the kind that could only be obtained, and felt on an inner level, by Koreans themselves who are listening to TV characters use a foreign language.

There are many reasons to code-switch, whether in real life or scripted dialogue, and there are many more instances of such as part of Korean TV dramas. This has been merely a brief snapshot of switches to English as part of both K-POP and TV dramas, as a means to conceptualize Korean English beyond the immediate application of the term which refers to a systematic and codified use of lexis and grammar used by Koreans and, in some cases, non-Koreans. From the examples presented in the previous two sections, and from my own personal experience (which admittedly veers more towards TV drama and not K-POP), the examples suggest a use of English that befits inner-circle English. This can include insertions (e.g. *jackpot* would appear to be used in a manner that would not be out of place in the United States) or extended dialogue. If the English used in these media contexts is less reflective of Korean English as defined earlier, then this might be due to embarrassment of it being portrayed by characters who, often, are themselves portrayed as successful. As such, they need to use a variety of English which connotes success – standard inner-circle. It may also be a means to use a language of globalization via its suggested 'global' variety – again, standard inner-circle, thus acting as a lingua franca.

We need to also consider the use of English by Korean celebrities on Korean television, which perhaps makes a more prominent use of Koreanized English. However, at what point might these words be considered part of a larger Korean English as opposed to being tied to an esoteric use by celebrities? Indeed, that Lee (2020) reports on such usage might suggest that such words have spread beyond the confines of, for example, TV interviews. An aforementioned example is *baglnye*; Lee (2013: 179) explains how this word 'captures one modern version of a beauty in Korea' (and the use of the indefinite article here might suggest an error or an innovation, but this is beyond the immediate discussion). The word combines both 'baby' and 'glamour,' and the Korean morpheme *nye*, referring to a young woman who exudes both innocence and sexiness. Such usage represents linguistic innovation, in the sense that it is an identified feature of Korean use of English (albeit heard by one Korean, though this word might have spread beyond this TV show by now), and also represents innovation in a more general, though equally important, sense, involving a blended word which combines English lexis with Korean morphology. This is a good example of 'creativity', which as Pope (2010: 124) argues can involve the 'productive' and 'generative' capacity of affixes, which in this case leads to new words.

In this particular context of Korean English usage, Lee (2013: 186) argues that several functions are revealed: 'neutralizing and euphemizing offensive narratives, representing new concepts, repackaging old ideas and images, and projecting certain identities'. This again suggests a confidence in the language that goes beyond merely using English in songs or on TV as an attention-grabbing device and perhaps a means to sell CDs and gain fans.

I fully acknowledge the fact that many of the readers may well question the absence of references to many other songs and TV dramas, some of which they might regard as more 'obvious' choices for discussion. Indeed, what I have presented for discussion so far in this chapter is, as mentioned, merely a brief sample of what pertains to a larger societal phenomenon – the use of English in Korean media.

However, the main thrust of this book is indeed on Korean English as a codified variety, again based on the two aspects of codification I had established at the start of Chapter 3. First, this is seen with the spread of innovations by speakers which leads to conventionalization, and on a second level codification via the use of public media (e.g. menus, billboards), traditional means of codification (school-based English textbooks) and examples of traditional codification within a non-traditional medium (e.g. online dictionaries). The uses discussed here address the plurality of this variety, in a way that goes beyond Korean English but instead reflects Koreans' use of English, here in a media context, and in doing so, also reflects a confidence to take English and make it into something new. The fact that it is being used for an intranational audience in some cases, such as on Korean TV shows, is an important factor regarding an expanding circle English in particular. Thus, Korean English – even if tied to narrow uses such as the examples provided – is not just for conversations with non-Koreans using English as a lingua franca.

Lee (2013) further references *medialect*, which is often manifest in the use of blended and clipped expressions within Korean media, notably TV which is the focus in her paper. The individuals who are the driving force behind such innovations are again largely Korean entertainers and celebrities, using the expressions for varied purposes. These can include a need to use euphemistic expressions and to represent new concepts; all of this is packaged as linguistic hybridization. The Korean television context where such hybrid expressions are used can involve comedy shows, reality shows and talk shows, which could point to both scripted language and even words which are essentially coined on the spot. A few examples now follow:

Cimsungidol – this is a blend made up of *cimsung* (animal) + idol. The term *idol* is used largely, and herein represents how a Korean English word has already shown a degree of change. The term *idol* was originally applied to young women singing in pop bands; now it applies equally to men as well, though in both sexes there is an age range of being in their twenties. The addition of *cimsung* connotes a masculine sexual energy, which is different from previous idols. Lee (2013: 172) talks of these *cimsungdols* as often showing their toned physique on TV.

Chocolate-pokkun ('chocolate' + *pokkun* – abdominal muscles). This word refers to the six-pack of, for example, a *cimsungdol*, so called due to the suggested resemblance to the lines on a chocolate bar.

Motaysolo – a blend of *motay* (in the womb) and *solo*, referring to a man or woman without dating experience.

The use of blended expressions from a linguistic perspective also ties in with cultural blending. As Lee (2013: 173) explains, 'concepts, values, images and identities are also hybridized . . . traditional and modern, old and new, Korean and Western'. Again, one such example is the term *baglnye* in which a suggested Western 'sexiness' is applied to Korean 'innocence'; thus, a combination of ideals is captured in a combination of languages.

The extent to which this particular category of medialect in Korea – consisting of linguistic hybridization – has spread from the TV to larger society is not commented on by Lee (2013). She does, however, make clear that for the bilingual viewing audience, it provides entertainment, in large part because the connotations of the words are understood, as well as Lee explaining that for entertainers in Korea who are bilingual, it can enhance their career opportunities.

Thus, what could be considered nonce words does not change the potential for them to become more widely used if adopted by the viewing public, who in turn spread the words further within Korean society. The fact that English is being used in this manner reflects more than just proficiency in two languages; it also shows how hybridity can be expressed through concepts which require two languages in the first instance, in addition to the cultural connotations behind them.

Advertisements

This section will focus on advertisements in Korea, be it commercials or print ads, which employ English in some way. Very often, this can be part of product slogans, or more broadly, as part of brief summaries written in English, and often on the product itself, which seek to create a certain impression of the product beyond the use, or not, of an English slogan. I have seen these summaries on notebooks, wrappers for cookies/biscuits and chocolate bars, to give but a few examples. Collectively, then, the use of English in an advertisement context applies here to slogans and the use of English, often just a sentence, which serves to create an impression of the product. One example already mentioned was the blurb used to advertise the launch of Korean Air's flights to Kenya, which goes beyond the slogan, *Excellence in Flight*. Many other companies in Korea employ English for their slogans in particular, such as *Life's Good* (LG), *Do What You Can't* (Samsung) and *Always With You* (Asiana Airlines).

Whether or not a slogan employs inner-circle grammar or dialect, or uses long stretches of text or incomplete sentences is not the issue per se; nor is the variety of English used. Rather, the whole point of slogans is to be 'catchy', to the extent that people can readily associate the slogan with the brand and, theoretically, be attracted to the product, whether a car, airline or make-up product. Domzal,

Hunt and Kernan (1995: 100) consider that the use of foreign languages in advertisements is an 'attention getting device' as it is unexpected and not the norm. This can be a means to allow the product to stay in the viewers' minds. On the other hand, the frequent use of a given language, here English, when it is otherwise foreign, might not be as effective as hoped, as 'habituation' might occur (Nederstigt and Hilberink-Schulpen, 2018: 3), thus losing its marked status. Nonetheless, Ahn, Ferle and Lee (2017: 481), in discussing the use of English in Korean advertisements, explain that 'Koreans have a positive attitude toward the English language' and English 'is often associated with positive perceptions such as practical importance, global status, prestigious image, and high social status'. If, however, English in Korean advertising has suffered any loss of its otherwise marked status in this context, might it nonetheless reflect a growing expectation, and acceptance, of its use? Though speculative, rather than a case of English fatigue regarding Korean advertising, perhaps English is now afforded a kind of honorary status in this context.

The slogan for Audi is *Vorsprung durch Technik*, German for *progress through technology*. Considering, however, that this slogan was used in English-speaking countries, potentially meaning most of the viewers would not understand, might seem an unusual choice. But might the use of German, even for those who can't speak it, nonetheless come with specific connotations? If we consider the connotations, perhaps even stereotypes, of German cars, we might think efficiency, professionalism and reliability, among other things. Thus, to use German for an advertising slogan outside of Germany may well serve to reinforce this concept, precisely because language, as a proxy for nationhood in this case, can serve to produce favourable perceptions of, here, a car that is German. As stated by Nederstigt and Hilberink-Schulpen (2018: 3), 'German triggers all kinds of associations (intended are usually only the positive ones) that are transferred to the product advertised.' This ties in with the work of Kelly-Holmes (2000), who discusses the use of foreign languages in advertisements based on their symbolic function, regardless of whether the words are understood or not. Given the association of English with modernity and internalization, and not necessarily with the inner-circle countries in which it is spoken, then there is the potential for the products it is associated with to be seen in a similar light.

Therefore, deciding what is or is not 'catchy' and 'clever' with regard to the use of slogans in any language is not always straightforward, as much of the interpretation will be highly personal to the viewer. Seen from this point of view, Koreans' use of English within an advertising context should be understood more on the basis of creativity, and not errors. To illustrate, let us consider the slogan of I SEOUL U, used to promote tourism in Seoul, if not Korea as a whole. It was generally considered a failure, being held up in part as an example of Konglish, in this case referring to 'adopting English words in a way that English speakers often cannot understand' (BBC, 2015). There are three issues to discuss here, especially since the ad is not targeted solely at (native) English speakers.

First, that 'English speakers' can't understand it does not make it wrong. I didn't know as a boy that *robot* refers to a traffic light in South African English, nor until a few days ago that *dunny* means a toilet/bathroom in Australian English. And an advertisement on buses in Manchester, England recently asked the questions: *footy? telly? tenner?* This would mean little, if anything, to Americans; indeed, in American English, it would need to be translated to *soccer? TV? Ten pounds* (or *ten dollars*)? Even then, would soccer still be a means to attract people, given that it is not as fanatically played in the United States as it is in the United Kingdom. My second point concerns a somewhat societal knee jerk response to declare the slogan to be Konglish, here used as a catch-all for suggested problems with Koreans' use of the English language. It seems that the potential for English speakers not to understand is being seen as evidence of errors, and that Konglish is automatically brought into the conversation to suggest incompetence on the grounds that the slogan was not generally thought to be successful.

Marshall (2017) discusses the suggested 'failure' of this slogan as based on ridicule from the native speakers of English living in Korea. Salmon (2015) had earlier posted his views on the matter, in specific relation to the negativity towards the slogan by native English speakers:

> Judging from the Interweb chitchat, you could be forgiven for thinking that every English-speaking resident of this fair city holds an advanced degree in marketing communications, or has 20 years' experience in a global advertising or PR agency under his or her belt. One of the key messages emerging from this colossal group whine is, 'I am a native speaker of English, by God! How dare Seoul come up with a new slogan without consulting me!' Another is, 'I don't like it. So it must be balderdash!' The arrogance, the vitriol and the self-appointed expertise evident in this explosion of online bile is extraordinary.

The specific argument here is once again based on the use of English in Korea and by Koreans. Even though the slogan is clearly targeted at non-Koreans in the main, given its purposes, this does not change the fact that it represents Koreans' use of English for a specific purpose. And at this stage in their relationship with English, their use of this language should be seen as *their* use and not necessarily in need of a final seal of (native speaker) approval – a point clearly made by Salmon.

Going further, using a proper noun – Seoul – as a verb is an 'error' (unless it becomes part of linguistic conversion and widely used in society). If this were an academic essay, for example, it would be wrong, in which case we could rightfully ask *what does Seoul mean?* But we're in the world of advertising and so we can employ all kinds of rhetorical devices to make our product – here, Korea itself to an extent – more memorable. This is part of my final point: a use of English within the advertising context often relies on linguistic creativity of all kinds.

Lee (2006: 60) rightly points to 'the creative use of word play and hybrid linguistic forms' in advertisements and this can apply equally to using a country's native language as much as using a foreign one. In this case, we have an example of linguistic conversion, where a noun is being used as a verb. Why the linguistic double standards? Here in the UK, I recall a commercial for Spam around 2005–6, which used the expression, as part of a song, *Spam Up*. Spam is a noun, not a verb, and not a phrasal verb at that. So what does *Spam Up* actually mean? We need to use a bit of creative thinking here as members of the viewing public, and potentially as consumers of Spam. Given the overall upbeat commercial jingle and scenes of people very excitedly tucking into Spam, then we can suggest a semantic approximate of 'live life', 'enjoy Spam' and so on. I also recall a US commercial for Ortega chilis in the early 1980s, whose commercial jingle told the viewers to 'chili up your life'. How does one *chili up* his/her life? And we can also consider the question *do you Yahoo*, used in the United States as part of a TV commercial. I am also reminded of the McDonald's slogan of *I'm lovin' it*. Inner-circle English, unlike Indian English, does not allow for progressive forms for stative verbs, but some might disagree. In conversations with my linguistics students, expressions such as *I'm really loving this coffee* tend to 'sound' acceptable. Do we blame McDonalds's for corrupting the English language? There is no reason to either blame it or praise it, assuming it has had a linguistic influence at all, and while languages change, they do not become corrupted.

My own interpretation of the slogan for Seoul, given the unique nature of slogans, is that, as Seoul is being advertised as a place to visit, then Seoul here is synonymous with beauty and excitement, and perhaps even being used in place of the verb *love*. Thus, you may fall in love with Seoul and, going further, could this bring forth the homophone of *soul* to people's minds? However, if the public view this slogan as a failure, then so be it. But to designate a failed slogan as *failed English* reflects a certain ignorance of the creative and innovative need for language embedded within advertising, which reflects a context of language use that can be anything but 'standard' (indeed, I don't believe that *Spam Up* has entered British English, and perhaps will only ever exist as part of the commercial world). In the end, if slogans appear ambiguous, then the amount of subsequent discussion and guessing can only be a good thing and perhaps that was the intention – to let the public decide what *I Seoul U* means and in all their guessing and pondering, end up thinking about a trip to Seoul.

Lee (2006) further argues that English in advertisements and commercials in Korea is not solely based on its suggested global appeal and connotations of modernity. Instead, she argues that there are indeed uses of Korean English on occasion, as a means to appeal to the domestic viewers who are of course predominantly Korean. One example concerns the use of the expression *moving bra*, which equates to inner-circle usage of *push-up bra*. In this instance, commercials can act as yet another example of societal codification of Korean English, by reinforcing Korean English lexis. What this tells us from the perspective taken in this chapter is again a twofold consideration. First, that Koreans are using English in ways that go beyond the inner-circle standard, even reflecting inner-circle dialects in music and using Koreanized English expressions, which are more broadly part of the larger picture of how languages innovate and also, tied to the fact Koreans are doing the innovating and using English for intranational purposes in a variety of media contexts. Second, such uses are part of a societal approach to codification, which begins with society itself who are the users and propagators of a given language. Whether through music or TV interviews, Koreans' use of English is being heard and spread, at least to the extent that we have evidence of such to report on.

Bhatia and Ritchie (2006: 529) further postulate a hierarchy for the use of English in advertisements, arguing that for English to be used within the body of an ad, as part of product description (discussed earlier under my term of product 'summaries'), then it must first pass through the lower steps, starting with the product name, and followed by the company name, label, header/footer, and slogan, this culminating with the use of English in the body of the ad. The Korean use of English within advertising arguably reveals something of all of these steps, seen with product names and then extending to the top rung regarding the use of English in the body of the ad. We can see this with the product Custard Pie, a popular snack in Korea. Referring to the use of English on the box of this product, we can take each aspect one at a time:

Product name: *Custard Pie*

Company name: *Lotte*

Lotte is a Korean company, but the name is neither English nor Korean. Its origins are actually German, based on the character of Charlotte from a character in Johann Wolfgang von Goethe's novel *The Sorrows of Young Werther*.

Header/footer: *Happy Promise*

Label: *Moist cake filled with soft custard cream*

Slogan: *Happy promise* (based on the position of this expression above the product name, I labelled it, broadly defined, as a header, and yet it also appears to function as a slogan given its short, punchy use of just two words)

English use in the body: *For all people's happiness. We are baking fresh custard cakes everyday*

From just this one example, we can see the extent to which English use in Korea has become quite dominant. Apart from what I believe to be a pure error with the word *everyday* (which should be written as *every day*), the English use reflects an otherwise global variety, that which would not suggest any one locality and, as such, can be understood by English speakers from around the world for the most part. If, however, *everyday* becomes more frequent in Korean use as a reference to *every day* (i.e. *everyday* is an adjective meaning 'customary', such as *everyday use*) then it has reached the level of Korean English. Advertising may indeed be a key way for this one term, and others, to be spread and thus codified on a large societal level, whether on-screen slogans as part of commercials and/or print ads. There is, in fact, evidence of errors within inner-circle countries as part of advertising contexts, though very broadly defined. Just a short walk up and down a main road in Manchester near my home reveals this. There are many shops, from vegetarian markets to newsagents to fruit and vegetable stands, and very often their daily offers are written on a board placed outside. I have, within this inner-circle context, seen examples of what are otherwise errors such as *potatoe's* and *cellery*.

I am particularly interested in the use of English text in Korean advertisements that belongs to the category of 'text in the body of the product'. This is a cumbersome way to explain things, but I can think of none better (though I had earlier used the vague word *summaries*). Essentially, this refers to the use of English text – often just a sentence – which is placed on the product. This can refer to text placed on the 'container' itself, whether this is a packet of tissues, a box of pies, a pencil case, a school notebook and so on and so on. Beyond this, however, we can include such texts as that which is printed on store fronts, in shop windows, and on menus, placards, brochures and such. Indeed, it is difficult to narrow down the categories of 'linguistic receptacles' in Korea for English text, but I would specify the text itself as, once again, usually being fairly short, such as a sentence in length, and in terms of style quite 'poetic'. This would consist, in the example of Custard Pie, of the text which declares *For all people's happiness. We are baking fresh custard cakes everyday*.

Going further, on the store front of a coffee shop in Korea, whose name is *The Table*, I recall seeing the embedded text as follows: *Delicious love making just for you!* Grammatically proficient, semantically questionable perhaps (if not irrelevant to the context). But again, under the broad contextual banner of 'advertising', whether print-based ads, TV commercials or here, business promotion, might this more creative use of language be appropriate? The schema that might be activated by this expression might be one of sensuality, comfort, high-class surroundings and, indeed, great coffee. Further, in a Korean shop which sells cheese, a sign next to the product declared *I fall in love with this cheese*. From just these two examples, we can see a trend towards a form of English which seeks to explore perhaps semantic and stylistic boundaries, if not go beyond the latter. Regarding the specific context of English use in Korea as seen as product plugs, via these poetic expressions (I can think of no better way to describe them). Dougill (2008: 19), citing similar examples of English in Japan, suggests that such usage is decorative and 'chic', such as *funny bunny, cute life* (as used on writing paper), *no human, go ape* (a carrier bag) and *ambitious Japan* (written on the sides of bullet trains).

While this kind of English might not be the norm in, say, the United States, it is not for me or anyone else to dictate to Koreans what form of English they use simply on the basis of its style not being what an inner-circle audience is used to. In the United States, the preceding two uses might be reflected more as *delicious coffee just for you* and *you'll fall in love with this cheese*. However, who am I to say? Just as I cannot speak for the stylistic preferences of all Americans regarding language, I cannot do so for Koreans who are exploring their own English knowledge in a context which allows for such linguistic and stylistic exploration. Baumgardner (2006: 257) further states that the use of English in a shop name 'adds a certain *je ne sais quoi* to the shop's aura', perhaps as much as the use of French in this quote adds a linguistic aura. Blommaert's (2010) work, referenced earlier, is again relevant, in terms of 'bits of language' as part of an overall repertoire. Here, within the context of advertising, the use of English need not consist of more than a few words as part of a slogan. Blommaert (2010) discusses such use, in this case the use of French as the name of a Tokyo chocolate shop, *Nina's Derrière*. Some of the clientele will understand the meaning of this word, which is not immediately relevant to the product. But assuming some potential customers at least identify it as French, without knowing the meaning, then the connotations of this language, which can suggest perhaps class and sophistication, are the actual selling points.

As I said earlier, the use of English within public signs in Korea (with 'signs' translated broadly here), whether road signs, store fronts, brochures and so on, is arguably more for international use, a means to not merely look 'trendy' but to simply communicate with the world using a global language. As such, I argue that Korean English (as defined in Chapter 4) is probably not to be found as much in such contexts, despite its potential to act as yet another means of societal codification. While Lee (2006) has provided evidence that this is not always the case, I would suggest that Korean English is that which is (partly) used for intranational communication, and yet can be found beyond Korea and in use by non-Koreans.

The three topics covered in this chapter could easily fill their own books, as I cannot possibly do justice to the copious examples in Korea to be found within advertising, itself a huge area, let alone TV drama and K-POP. However, this brief discussion is not meant to be merely an adjunct to the overall focus on codified Korean English. Instead, the purpose is to make clear the myriad ways in which Korean English can be seen beyond the immediate application of a codified variety of English. It also includes a variety of societal contexts, from store fronts to candy wrappers and cans of beer, and includes a variety of Englishes for that matter, from creative, punchy slogans to a more poetic use of English. These latter categories also tie in with contextual codification, as it is unlikely that the same slogan/text will be shared by different products (this might be illegal anyway) and yet, despite the unpredictability, codification is cemented once the text is applied to the product, be it a chocolate wrapper or store front.

I conclude this chapter by providing a visual regarding Korean English, from the perspective of advertisements discussed in this section, though I leave it to the readers to subdivide further, based on any contextual levels that I might have missed:

KOREAN ENGLISH
↓
The Use of English in Korean Advertising
↓ ↓ ↓
TV Commercial   English Print Ad English   Shop Front English
↓ ↓ ↓
**Slogans   Slogans/In-Text English   Company Names/
                                                            Creative Expressions**

The final chapter now discusses the implications for the use of Korean English in the EFL classroom.

6

Korean English in the EFL classroom

The final chapter discusses the ways in which Korean English can be used within the EFL classroom. This can apply not only to English teachers in Korea but also to those teaching outside of Korea, and even if there are no Korean students in a given class. The point here is that EFL students from all cultural and linguistic backgrounds need to understand a variety of Englishes that will serve them well within international contexts of communication, help them pass IELTS/TOEFL tests, university entrance examinations and secure employment, as part of a job interview and beyond. That variety is standard inner circle, regardless of where it derives from, though British and American English are perhaps the most familiar to EFL students (Matsuda, 2020). However, just as it is quite usual to teach students a variety of inner-circle Englishes, if only to make students aware of differences in spelling, vocabulary and accent, we also need to educate students in more than just inner-circle standard English. This can include inner-circle dialects, and indeed move beyond the inner circle altogether, thus allowing for inclusion of NICE in the EFL classroom. In this way, while the focus is on the use of Korean English in the EFL classroom, teachers can easily bring in other varieties to suit their particular teaching location (e.g. Indian English), and/or to provide information on several varieties for the benefit of students. The idea is not to overload the students, but not to present a singular picture of the English language either. Even students' encounters with so-called native speakers may not necessarily reflect the textbook style of English that they have used in the classroom. As Matsuda (2020: 688) points out, 'it is impossible to introduce every single variety of English that students may encounter in the future'; but we can't allow English instruction to be monolithic either.

I acknowledge that much of the introductory material here is hardly new information for much of the readership, but it is not being presented as such. Rather, I believe it is necessary to first provide some broad background information on the role of NICE within EFL classrooms in order to then help better inform, and locate, the role of Korean English specifically within this context. Matsuda (2020) acknowledges the plurality of the English language and the implications this has for EFL teaching. She makes clear that the students' overall communicative needs and goals should be taken into consideration. This would not rule out a local variety of English, such as Korean English, but of course a larger consideration is where the teaching is taking place. If a group of Korean students are studying English as part of a university preparation course in Manchester, England, then Korean English may be of little use; British English, of course, will be. Indeed, choosing an appropriate variety may well be decided for the teacher in the first instance, as individual classes might be rather prescriptive in terms of the content that is expected to be taught. Clearly, IELTS preparation courses would need to focus on, say, standard British English – certainly for the written part of the test – and New Englishes might again be of little practical value.

Matsuda (2020), however, suggests the need to choose a 'well-established' variety of English, which, Matsuda explains, should be codified (presumably in the traditional sense of the word) and one used for various means of communication in society. Again, if teachers believe that Konglish, the term perhaps more likely to be used, is, in some way, deficient, then it is unlikely to be selected. Before teachers consider issues of linguistic establishment (and I have offered evidence for the establishment of this variety), more immediate concerns might simply reflect a general perception that Korean English is, at worst, broken English or somehow not fully formed English, or at least a variety which does indeed have communicative function, but is simply not the prestige variety that students may wish to learn, or teachers wish to teach. Moreover, at Korean *hagwons*, where students pay to receive English instruction, the expectation, for students of all ages, is perhaps to learn standard inner-circle varieties.

However, and in agreement with Matsuda (2020), the implication of using Korean English, or any NICE for that matter, is that it can be used in the classroom without being the sole focus. In other words, while teaching the features of Korean English per se can benefit students, Korean English can also be used as a means to help teach other varieties, such as inner-circle standard. In this latter situation, it is being used as a pedagogic tool, a means to help teach a variety that might otherwise be expected within the classroom. Whether Korean English is the sole focus of a lesson, or an entire class, or indeed used as a means to contrast it with other varieties, for example, in order to make students aware of the plurality of English, there are many ways it can be used. This can include its function in a high school English class in Korea, in which the teacher, whether

Korean or from elsewhere, dedicates some class time to help expose students to their own variety of English and realize that it does indeed have a time, place and purpose; not to pass IELTS tests perhaps, but certainly a means to engage with friends after school, when English use is not being 'tested'. Likewise, educating inner-circle speakers on the diversity of English, as part of university TESOL programmes, is another good use for an inclusion of New Englishes in general.

Dinh (2017: 134) further references a 'dire need' for the inclusion of cultural practices which go beyond Western/American models of reference; and Renandya (2012: 65) points out that teachers need to 'develop a favorable attitude toward the teaching of EIL (English as an International Language)'. Mukminatien (2012: 224) further asks, 'which standard should be adopted in response to learners' linguistic needs for international communication?' As a response to this question, Galloway and Rose (2015: 208) discuss a Global Englishes Language Teaching (GELT) framework, which puts the focus 'on diversity and the function of English as an international lingua franca, rather than traditional approaches to ELT which aim to teach people to speak with native English speakers'.

The rationale for the inclusion of NICE in the EFL classroom is threefold. First, as already made clear, the real world of English does not always conform to classroom English, and as such, students need to be prepared for multiple communicative contexts in which English is used, even within a single country. Differences in vocabulary and accent can be enough to cause confusion between an English person from London and a New Yorker, both of whom might be talking in Paris. Moreover, teaching students about inner-circle dialects can be useful for communicative purposes, as even if students do not wish to use dialect, they can nonetheless be taught how to understand someone who uses it with *them*.

Second, by educating students in the linguistic realities of language change and development, it can help to dispel any negativity and ignorance surrounding their country's variety of English, whether it is Korean English or Ghanaian English. This is not to suggest an approach which seeks to force linguistic respect on students and ignore the realities of their immediate English needs, which may well be more reflective of education and work and not on learning the syntactic properties of other varieties. Nonetheless, this kind of approach can help to dispel myths about what is or is not 'proper' and 'correct' English and help students realize that the reality of everyday communication will simply not be standard American English. Matsuda (2003: 438) also reflects on the value of World Englishes pedagogy as a means to promote international understanding, as an incomplete presentation of the English language may . . . lead to confusion or resistance when students are confronted with different types of English users or uses. Students may be shocked by varieties of English that deviate from Inner Circle English, view them as deficient (rather than different), or grow disrespectful to such varieties and users, which seems counter-productive to facilitating international understanding.

Again, I realize that linguistic realities are not necessarily a match for sociocultural realities and thus, educating students about the inner workings of NICE, which are as equally 'logical' as inner-circle English, will not change the fact that inner-circle English is the dominant variety. However, by approaching language attitudes and addressing the reality of linguistic dominance and prejudice in the EFL classroom, then attitudes might subsequently start to change. After all, it makes sense to address this within the language classroom in the first instance, as this is perhaps a logical starting point.

Finally, the inclusion of NICE can be a learning experience for EFL teachers who themselves speak an inner-circle English. This learning need not be tied solely to their own previous education as part of TESOL programmes, for example. Instead, it can also be a learning experience from their students, as part of a joint meaning-making classroom exercise. This is not naïve idealism, as a key to language learning success in the classroom is to make the instruction accessible and ultimately, fun. By incorporating aspects of NICE in the classroom, it can be a means to engage students, more so if they can recognize the varieties as reflective of their own country's English. This can lead to more than just lessons in English per se as reflected from the textbook, but can also lead to classroom discussion, even debate, and a means for students to share their views and have them heard. While this might be more conducive to an advanced level English class, there is no reason why this pedagogic approach cannot be included in elementary level EFL classes, incorporating, for example, more inclusive lessons in vocabulary, such as teaching students words in groups: *cell phone* (American English), *mobile phone* (British English) and *hand phone* (Korean English).

Matsuda (2020: 689) explains that 'incorporating materials from learners' own culture encourages them to critically reflect on what they may take for granted and to work on skills to explain it in a way that is comprehensible to outsiders'. Given the collective benefits regarding the use of NICE in the EFL classroom – and by extension in TESOL and teacher preparation courses – we can help to address the argument that 'a new pedagogic model is urgently needed' (Alptekin, 2002: 63). Crystal (2008: 17) further argues that 'the absolutist concept of "proper English" or "correct English", which is so widespread, needs to be replaced by relativistic models'; Matsuda (2020: 693) addresses this comment in terms of moving away from a focus on classroom success as being tied to approximation of a native speaker of English and a focus instead on addressing the learners' needs: 'Can learners *do* what they need to do in English?' (original emphasis).

Nuske (2017: 385) offers even more specific guidance regarding a change to pedagogy within the EFL classroom, advocating as follows:

> Teacher trainers could therefore encourage apprentices . . . in determining a practical yet forward-thinking method in which NS (native speaker) varieties are not radically displaced from their position of prominence but rather augmented with routine explorations of localized Englishes through film clips, tales of personal experience, and other formats likely to be considered authentic and enjoyable. Such tactics could minimize initial resistance by meeting students' expectations of studying codes that are viewed as prestigious while subtly challenging assumptions and laying the foundation for the development of more tolerant and self-empowering outlooks in the long-term.

Having provided relevant background into the topic of English teaching from a more culturally informed and linguistically informed perspective, I now move on to a discussion of the implications of such specifically within the Korean context.

The implications for teaching English in Korea

In terms of the Korean teaching context, Lee (2019) advocates more joint discussion between university professors and English teachers at the primary/secondary level, stemming from the use of Korean English lexical items and their use as part of curriculum development. Students' familiarity with Korean English, certainly in terms of lexis, could be a starting point for a simple, but effective, exercise in which Korean English is translated into the relevant inner-circle variety, and vice versa. This approach could be used, then, as opposed to 'correcting' the Korean English variety. This reflects classroom practice in the United States, in which the sociolect of Ebonics is used as a means to teach standard English (Rickford 1998; Perez 1999), whose approach could consist of exercises such as the following:

Ebonics	Standard English
He go to school	*He goes to school*
He happy	*He is happy*
He be happy	*He is usually/habitually happy*

A visual display of differing Englishes as seen above can hopefully help to take away some of the stigma that students might have, but it is of course the case that seeing the differences up close and personal, as it were, can also help to highlight them in a negative way, with the mindset of different = incorrect. Furthermore, at the grammatical level, it is entirely possible that Korean students might not be aware of the grammatical features of Korean English. While there is clearly evidence for its codification through more traditional means (Shim, 1999), it is possible that students might not equate Korean English grammar with anything other than errors, merely on the basis of its deviation from inner-circle standard. In such cases, it is up to the teacher to step in and offer some guidance as to the grammatical features of Korean English, as a means to have a deep discussion about the origins of such (e.g. the use of the definite article). Being educated about language, and not merely practising its use, is a key aspect of the EFL classroom.

Going further, Ahn (2014: 205), based on a survey of 204 English teachers in Korea, both Korean and foreign, investigated their attitudes towards Korean English; the results do not suggest positive feelings, as some reported their attitudes as being 'conflicted and mixed', to include 'a strong resistance to a full acceptance'. It is possible that within the context of education, participants feel this way based on the push for American English. Again, the classroom can be a means to re-educate, reflecting on societal use of Korean English, as I have pointed out, that many might not consider. Or if people do consider it, then once again they might feel it is not the variety of English to teach. My approach is suggesting that we indeed teach whatever the variety is that is expected and/or desired by a given group of students, but that we can do this partly based on taking a 'side by side' approach with other varieties, particularly a variety that students know of, perhaps use and one that exists in their own country(ies).

Ra (2019: 305) argues that 'given the steadily diversifying demographics in Korea and the spread of global English, ELT in Korea ought to reflect English used in the "real world".' Joo, Chik and Djonov (2020) report on the curriculum requirement to develop the use of English that serves as a connector among different cultures and countries, which would clearly suggest the role of English as a lingua franca. However, the authors point to the English textbooks used for children, which still reflect a bias towards native-speaker models. The research of Song (2013) presents a similar picture, with analysis of English textbooks in use in Korea reflecting a dominant focus on white, male American culture. Song refers to the Korean national English curriculum implemented in 2009, in which 'English is viewed as a language of global and cosmopolitan citizenship. The curriculum promotes cultural diversity and attempts to embrace cross-cultural and cross-linguistic differences' (page 382). Thus, Song suggests that in terms of textbooks, this reflection of, and push for, global citizenship has perhaps not caught up yet. This finding is echoed in the study of Shin, Eslami and Chen (2011), which found that despite the role of English as an international language – which again reflects a variety of cultures and at times, Englishes – internationally distributed EFL textbooks still dominate with a focus on inner-circle culture. Ahn (2019) also reflects on the favouritism for American English within English teaching in Korea.

Collectively, this strongly suggests that there is an awareness of the need to educate beyond a singular variety of English, but any such desire comes up against the dominant reality of inner-circle English, and beyond this, a more American/Western cultural picture, despite the fact that many who use English represent a global spread of cultures and countries. Given the role of textbooks as a means of traditional codification, there is no doubt that their use can cement ideologies, whether based on grammar use or more broadly, suggesting *who* the native speakers are; they clearly are not all white males, however. As I have said, I don't suggest that the societal reality of codification and language use will necessarily be able to compete with more traditional methods in the minds of some, and it seems that the reality of language use on the ground – where it is actually used in realistic, everyday settings – is not always reflected with textbook learning. And this suggests a disservice to the students who need to learn English to communicate, as opposed to having a somewhat conceptualized notion of an 'ideal' English which may not always be used when they communicate with others.

Kang (2017: 54) does point to a change of sorts, in that the teacher education programmes in Korea refer to American English, and perhaps its culture implicitly, as 'merely one of the varieties of English that can be spoken in the use of English as an International Language'. This is a positive step in the right direction, as if the classroom is going to change, then we need to change teacher training first (Bayyurt and Sifakis, 2017). To give a brief example of dominant culture expressed through textbooks, if not classroom practice, Canagarajah (1999: 87) offers the illustration of 'the situations represented [in foreign textbooks] – such as commuting by plane, cooking with a microwave, or shopping in department stores – assume an urbanized, Western culture that is still largely alien to rural students, and likely to clash with their traditional values'. This comment is made in relation to teaching contexts in the Sri Lankan city of Jaffna. Doan (2014: 87) further points out that the focus on inner-circle culture in EFL classrooms might not be relevant for Vietnamese students' 'real life'. Thus, a focus on standard American English and American culture, from sports to holidays, should be part of the classroom, but as part of a cultural exchange, in which teachers, and students alike, can bring in the local culture, as a means to compare and contrast with American culture, for example. In this approach, neither culture is being regarded as 'superior'; likewise, a linguistic focus which covers standard inner-circle English alongside other varieties is making the same point. And a final point here is that 'American culture' is not singular either; as such, this term should not default to the suggested dominant culture of Anglo-Americans.

There is evidence of the ways this suggested linguistic exchange can be facilitated, certainly in terms of a pedagogic approach. Lee and Green (2020: 4) investigate the sociocultural differences as expressed in language, both Korean and English, with a sample of Korean university students who are English majors. The students discussed certain differences, such as the use of *my* and *our* as a reflection of group versus individual perspectives. This can be seen with the Korean expression, among others, of *our country*, as opposed to *my country*. More embedded differences concern the Korean use of honorifics, whereas English is seen as more 'informal'; the emphasis on the family, as revealed through multiple kinship terms in Korean which English lacks; and in terms of grammar, English and its 'precise' use of articles and plurals was referred to by the students. Collectively, these examples, and others that students brought up, can indicate potential difficulties Koreans might have, and Americans too, when communicating. For example, the respect afforded to teachers might mean that some Korean students do not feel comfortable addressing their Western teacher by his/her first name (Baratta, 2021a).

At which stage of education such linguistic inclusion is initiated is difficult to suggest. In Korea, from kindergarten to grade 12, the focus is on 'teaching to the test' (Lee, 2019: 293), involving in large part a focus on English which will serve to get students into prestigious universities, both at home and abroad. This will probably be for many their first major challenge in actually deploying their English skills in a more official context, and the skills required are, theoretically, focused on standard American English in large part, though we must be mindful of Shim's (1999) research which suggests that Korean English is the variety used in Korean schools. Nonetheless, to make Korean English a more explicit aspect of the classroom, focusing on translation exercises, for example, involving vocabulary, might not find initial acceptance. It could be seen as unnecessary and even time-wasting, but the reality is that standard inner circle is still the focus, merely taught using the assistance of a more familiar variety perhaps.

At the university level, however, and perhaps more so for English majors, there is ideally more support for such an inclusive approach, one that can help understand language neither with fanfare nor scorn, but pure objectivity. As such, students can have a better understanding of the role that Korean English already plays in Korean society, and can play in the classroom, to aid both the teacher's, and the students', overall linguistic understanding.

The use of NICE in English teaching

Reflecting on the various conceptualizations of the English language(s) as used throughout the world (e.g. Brutt-Griffler, 2002; Matsuda, 2003; Canagarajah, 2006; Jenkins, 2006a), Lee and Green (2020) summarize its features and functions thus:

- Englishes exist and reflect a variety of grammars and norms for use in real-life communication;
- Englishes are multicultural, reflecting the reality of the speakers who often represent a variety of cultures and languages;
- Importantly, the approach to multiple varieties of English needs to be descriptive as a reflection of their use throughout the world, and not prescriptive in terms of how they 'should' be used or taught;
- Varieties of English serve to reflect the communicative needs of the speech communities who use it, and this suggests the initial aspect of societal codification, by means of language use on the ground by those in society.

Ultimately, the variety of English that is used in the classroom will often be prescribed by the school, reflected in the textbooks used, and this need not suggest any inherent issues. Clearly, if students need to get ready for university life in an inner-circle country, then academic English – which would equate to standard English – is key. I have taught on several pre-sessional courses here in the UK, consisting of a two-month programme of study in the summer, and ending just before the new school year, when students had been exposed to an intensive programme of English. However, the focus was not solely on standard British English as a reflection of academic English. Indeed, students were also taught 'general English', and the teachers were in fact given a great deal of freedom to supplement the textbook with their own ideas and examples. One aspect of this class indeed allowed us to focus on dialectal usage of British English, consisting of expressions, words and grammar that students could expect to hear on the streets of Manchester, but perhaps not find in most textbooks. The following is a sample:

Alright?	*How are you?*
Not too bad	*Fine* (in response to the previous greeting)
Telly	*Television*
Mate	*Friend*
I could murder a Chinese!	*I'm really in the mood for Chinese food!*
Love	A term of affection used by older people to younger people
I were // he/she/it were	Local dialect for *I was // he/she/it was*
Them books	Local dialect (i.e. plural pronoun in object case+ plural noun)
Cheers	*Thank you* (used in informal contexts)
I can't suss this out	*I can't understand this/how to do this*
I'm chuffed	*I'm proud (of my achievement)*

This is merely a partial list, but some of it does not conform to notions of 'standard' English, precisely because it is not in some of the examples. The issue is not with standard inner-circle English per se as a pedagogical model. The importance of having a standard language, whatever its grammatical make-up might be, has been discussed. A standard allows for individuals to use a form of language that, simply put, gets them in the door of universities and jobs, based on the use of entrance exams and cover letters. I believe that the issue is more to do with regarding standard inner-circle English as *the* standard, suggestive of all else being, at best, less relevant or worst-case, bad English (or whatever the language variety might be). The true standard, difficult though it may be to achieve, is one of linguistic balance. A need to teach a variety of English that will best serve the students' current – and future – English needs, but not at the expense of ignoring additional varieties which (a) can also serve as a fruitful means of communication, perhaps outside educational contexts and (b) also reflect students' local variety.

There are many ways EFL can be taught that can be accessible to students and, as such, help them to hopefully engage more in the class. I am not assuming of course that EFL teachers are not already way ahead of me and have been including a focus on more than just American English in their teaching, and that which involves Korean English, or NICE in general. But I offer these suggestions, as I had done previously (Baratta, 2019a), as merely a means to share pedagogic practice.

Lee (2019) offers suggestions for English teaching in Korea as part of IDLE (Informal Digital Learning of English) which takes advantage of students' abilities with, for example, social media and the virtual community. Lee further states that this kind of communication also has a built-in focus on English as an international language, given that Koreans' online communication allows them to come into contact with other NICE speakers (e.g. Indian English), which can reap positive rewards. Lee (2019: 294) explains thus:

> if Korean students befriend and socialize with other English users in various IDLE settings (e.g. social media and virtual community), they tend to think positively about different varieties of English (e.g. Japanese English and Indian English). Additionally, if Korean students practice IDLE activities to better understand diverse cultures, they are likely to improve their perceived ability to employ cross-cultural communication strategies.

In terms of how this translates into pedagogy, Lee suggests starting with media that students are already comfortable with, such as YouTube, Skype, digital games and so on. From here, students can create their own media, such as a website or blog, on a topic that they are familiar with, the teacher then acting as a guide to suggest further strategies for improvement.

This kind of approach can be facilitated more broadly in terms of the use of online resources to teach English. For example, a basic, but effective means, can consist of watching YouTube clips which now provide all manner of English-related content. This need not be educational resources per se, but can include examples of different accents and dialects within the inner-circle (for the former, Amy Walker is highly recommended); clips from the TV show *Saturday Night Live* in the United States can be useful also, which Lee (2019) refers to, and here again we can hear various accents, though exaggerated, such as Chicago (as part of *Da Bears* sketch) and New York City (as part of the *Bronx Beat* sketch). Of course, more specific educational resources exist, such as online clips on YouTube which educate viewers regarding the different Australian accents. A Google search is truly all that is needed to get started.

Given the focus on online codification in this book, this could also be a useful means to expose students to what is out there on Korean English, which some might not be aware of. Here is an opportunity for students to educate the teacher – how much do they agree, or not, with the content of some of these online sites? Not solely in terms of the accuracy of the vocabulary, for example, but more so regarding how Korean English is conceptualized on some of these sites, under the name of Konglish. For example, using just a few sites as a prompt, how do Korean students feel about having their English seen as legitimate, or being seen as errors, the latter suggested by the British Council. Just as Lee advocates for students creating their own resources, this could involve the creation of an online dictionary and/or grammar book for Korean English.

Essentially, many of the classroom exercises revolve around showing difference as merely that – difference, but not deficit. We know that societal attitudes cannot change overnight, but to encourage students to adopt an objective classroom stance regarding language – in this case, that no language or variety of a given language is inherently 'better', 'more logical' and so on than others is key. And for language study, what other approach would be more relevant? Exercises which help students to hone in on differences, as part of translation exercises from inner- to outer-circle Englishes (or vice versa), can be a creative way to approach EFL. Another suggested approach can thereby focus on translation from one variety of English into another, this time in the specific context of newspapers. Baumgardner (1987) provides information on just such an approach involving English-language newspapers in Pakistan to help teach inner-circle standard to Pakistani EFL students. A sample of text from the *Pakistan Times* is provided as a prompt, taken from 3 October 1986:

> The Secretary, Finance, Punjab, has issued a circular letter under which peons, chowkidars, baildars, watermen, malis, behishtis, sweepers and other work-charged employees have been granted a special benefit. But it is very strange that the Secretary, Finance, has extended this gracious concession to three departments only. Why a step-motherly treatment is being meted out to the poor peons, naib qasids, chowkidars and malis of the Education Department?

Having Pakistani students then translate the text into, say, British English, as if writing for a British audience, would allow for a more active engagement with the lesson. Likewise, if brought into the Korean English context, students could be asked to read texts written by Koreans, whether English-language newspapers, online sites or anything else. While I make suggestions for teaching, they are not rigid and can be adapted in many ways of course. Clearly, the institution will play a role (a *hagwon* versus a university) and the students' level of English (elementary English to advanced speaking).

Analyzing English texts as written by Koreans need not suggest errors or, in fact, reflect Korean English at all. We can in fact ask students to analyze such texts in order to determine if they sound 'natural' or not. This might be more suited to advanced students, but it again points to giving students the chance to offer their views and have a degree more proactivity. Likewise, analysis of

Konglish examples in terms of road signs and so on can be a means to equate pure errors as translation based, as opposed to being reflective of a codified variety of English in use in Korea. Can Korean students recognize the error? What are their thoughts? This can lead to classroom discussion and debate on the very subject of whether or not NICE have a role to play in the EFL classroom, and what the students' views on Korean English are. Such questions can be used as the impetus for classroom discussion, in which teachers and students alike have a part to play, but this can also be incorporated as part of study games per se.

Matsuda (2020) also suggests what could involve a variety of classroom exercises, under the broad suggestion of drawing from learners' culture, referred to by Cortazzi and Jin (1999: 204) as 'source cultural materials'. Clearly, this is less an actual class exercise or teaching method per se, but more a suggestion as to how classroom teaching can be informed. Matsuda makes clear that 'our goal now is often to establish and sustain an equal, mutually respectful relationship with others, and for this, the ability to perceive, analyze, and express one's own values, opinions, and practices is crucial' (page 689). By allowing for the inclusion of students' own culture, then this allows for a shared learning experience, a means to address potential ethnocentrism (Phillipson, 1992) and simply put, for the teacher to learn something, but in a manner that is perhaps less incidental, but more explicit. A word as broad as *culture* involves many aspects, some of which go beyond language. It can also involve what is or is not deemed to be appropriate behaviour in society, also explaining to the teacher the history of the country in which he/she is teaching, and learning about national holidays. How such examples, and many more, can be manifest is where both teachers and students can come together. Is this part of an assessment or merely a spontaneous discussion that often arises naturally? Is the discussion – or indeed, the cultural 'show and tell' – a regular part of classroom instruction, perhaps offered once a week? In terms of the 'cultural materials' Matsuda references, these can range from fashion magazines as a means to explain Korean beauty standards to the teacher, to food items.

One final example I would like to share derives from my days teaching English in Korea and concerns the word 합승 (*hapsung*). This is a word I had come across while I was learning Korean from a textbook, with the English translation provided for this word being *jitney*. I had never come across this English word, but it refers essentially to some kind of public transport, whether taxi or bus, which several passengers share for a lower fare than perhaps a regular bus or taxi service. The relevant aspect is that I had asked my Korean students to explain this word to me, providing them with the Korean word first. They explained the word refers more specifically in Korea to situations in which several passengers with different destinations share a taxi. The key factor here, however, is that it was clear that my students were happy to engage with me on this, a means for them to share aspects of their language and culture. Ironically, students might not consider such instances as being particularly reflective of cultural exchange or the like, or view them particularly deeply. Instead, such instances are arguably seen more simply, a chance to engage on a 'home topic', but this can nonetheless be enjoyable for the students. A final point to make is that the word *jitney* perhaps derives from *jeepney*, a reference to the vehicle itself used as a common mode of transportation in the Philippines. In this case, an outer-circle English has made some influence in an inner-circle variety.

Conclusion

I conclude by restating the main points that this book has sought to make clear already. All varieties of English, and any other language, are legitimate. Legitimacy is not determined by the use of a specific set of grammatical rules and words, which is subsequently given approval by a certain group, whether this group is native speakers as a whole, educators, the government, or anyone else. Legitimacy is based, from a purely linguistic point of view, on whether or not the language variety does its job, and acts as a means of communication for its speakers. On that level, Korean English works just fine. Likewise, we cannot wait for institutions to grant official status to a language which its speakers have already granted such status to. Societal codification at the grass roots level is based on a community, if not a country, using a language in varied contexts and situations. It is only from here that we can expect to then see dictionaries and grammar books being published in the first instance. And for those who might be more wedded to such means of codification, we might need to consider them in a different environment – the internet, and then specifically personal sites created by individuals. While there is clearly value in a language variety being approved by trusted sources, such as language learning organizations, respected publishers or the government itself, languages are kept alive and well – and legitimized – by their speakers. It is largely standard inner-circle varieties that get the royal linguistic treatment, however, inner-circle dialects and NICE less so perhaps.

However, we can't ignore the power that is afforded to standard inner-circle English in particular, a power which is of course by no means inherent, but is granted to this variety. This bestowed power is then reflected in areas which are desired by many people: a good education and subsequent success leading to a good career, reflected in the use of standard English for academic essays, university entrance exams and personal statements. And in the work context, standard inner-circle English is used to write cover letters, conduct job interviews and possibly used on the job itself. Education and career are intertwined; and to assume a standard that will give people sway in both areas is not problematic. A standard in many ways makes things easier, for teachers marking essays and for teachers who are charged with teaching our children grammar. A standard also means that by acquiring it, we are, in theory, offered a means to achieve linguistic equality with others who might never have used anything but standard inner-circle English from birth. And armed with this variety, we are enabled to seek out greater opportunities. As I have stated, there is no reason, however, why a standard inner-circle English cannot coexist with a NICE within the classroom, as this reflects the reality outside the classroom, in which a multitude of Englishes are being used at any given moment.

I would hope that in the near future, there will be more books, journal articles and by all means websites and blogs on the subject of Korean English, offering evidence of its codified status, notably its grammar, and as such, it will be accepted on a wider level, in Korean society and worldwide. The future of EFL teaching as a whole and teacher training will need to reflect the real linguistic world of English, and this is a strong reason why NICE and their role within EFL classrooms will hopefully expand. Until then, Korean English speakers will continue their use of this variety in society, whether as part of classroom English materials, newspaper articles, personal blogs and everyday conversation. Likewise, inner-circle speakers will hopefully become more open to the reality that inner-circle English has a *certain* time and place, as does Korean English. And if teachers can help students to become more bilingual, as it were, with different varieties of English, then this reflects the communicative needs that they may have in the future, from university entrance examinations, to conversing with Indian university students about the weather to offering directions to a Norwegian tourist who is lost in downtown Seoul.

I concede yet again what I perceive to be a key omission from my book, yet one which is unavoidable. Given the spread of English in Korea, I have barely scratched the surface regarding English as used in K-POP, TV drama and advertisements, let alone respective further examples within each of these categories, such as English band names which use the Roman alphabet, the myriad of reasons for code-switching in TV drama and, representing a particular interest of mine, the use of the more 'poetic' English expressions as used in the body of texts. A future study may well involve a sole focus on this area. In terms of the number of varieties contained within the national variety of Korean English, there are many. The primary focus within this book has been on codified Korean English, as I have defined and explored it in Chapter 4; however, we have evidence of further Korean Englishes, such as K-POP English. The broader category of media English can of course be separated into further varieties, such as TV drama and advertising, and then we can go further still, such as 'slogan

English in Korea' and 'English summaries of products'. These latter terms are perhaps a bit cumbersome but whatever terms we use (whether 'slogan English' or 'product English', or any other), the terms are perhaps less important than the simple fact that such diversity within the term *Korean English* can, and has, been recognized.

I further concede that no matter the level of detail that I hope to have provided in this book, many will not be swayed, still regarding my illustrations as confirming 'English in Korea', and certainly not a codified New English variety. A future study, involving large samples of Koreans from all ages and walks of life, and incorporating analysis of their speech and writing in English, would undoubtedly offer more ballast to the discussion on the status of English in Korea. But I hope that what I have managed to demonstrate in this book, however, is some evidence that (a) the use of English in Korea goes beyond lexis; (b) its use is indeed intranational to some extent; (c) English in Korea extends across multiple sites of deployment, from signs to TV shows; and (d) that it is codified in a manner more reflective of the social nature of language.

The larger picture is indeed centred on Korean English from the more specific definition and use promoted here, referring to a codified variety of English and in use by Koreans, both internationally and intranationally. And given the strength of the Korean wave, it may well be the case that non-Koreans' use of Korean English, perhaps encouraged by their interest in Korean pop culture, will also continue to grow, as well as an interest in learning Korean. For now, I hope I have added some new insights regarding the focus on this particular variety of English, and its varieties within, and in doing so, continued the ongoing discussion in what is expected to be a growing area of research interest, and societal use.

References

Ahn, H. (2014), '"Teachers" Attitudes towards Korean English in South Korea', *World Englishes*, 33 (2): 195–222.

Ahn, H. (2017), 'English as a Discursive and Social Communication Resource for Contemporary South Koreans', in C. Jenks and J. Lee (eds.), *Korean Englishes in Transnational Contexts*, 157–79, London: Palgrave Macmillan.

Ahn, H. (2018), 'Modelling the Englishization of Vocabulary in Contemporary Korean', *World Englishes*, 37 (4): 570–89.

Ahn, H. (2019), *Attitudes to World Englishes: Implications for Teaching English in South Korea*, London: Routledge.

Ahn, H. (2021), 'Spelling Variations of Translingual Korean English Words', *English Today*, 37 (1): 42–9.

Ahn, J., La Fearle, C. and Lee, D. (2017), 'Language and Advertising Effectiveness: Code- Switching in the Korean Marketplace', *International Journal of Advertising*, 36 (3): 477–95.

Ai, H. and You, X. (2015), 'The Grammatical Features of English in a Chinese Internet Discussion Forum', *World Englishes*, 34 (2): 211–30.

Alptekin, C. (2002), 'Towards Intercultural Communicative Competence in ELT', *ELT Journal*, 56 (1): 57–64.

Alsagoff, L. and Ho, C. (1998), 'The Grammar of Singapore English', in J. Foley, T. Kandiah, L. Gupta, H. Alsagoff, I. Lick, L. Wee, I. Talib and W. Bokhorst-Heng (eds.), *English in New Cultural Contexts: Reflections from Singapore*, 215–46, Singapore: Singapore Institute of Management and Oxford University Press.

Amaya, L. (2008), 'Teaching Culture: Is It Possible to Avoid Pragmatic Failure?', *Revista Alicantina de Estudios Ingleses*, 21: 11–24.

Archangeli, D., Barss, A., Bever, T., Carnie, A., Chan, E., Fong, S., Fountain, A., Hammond, M., Harley, H., Karimi, S., McKee, C., Nicol, J., Ohala, D., Piatelli-Palmarini, M., Ussishkin, A., Warner, N., Wedel, A., Willie, M. and Zepeda, O. (2010), 'Teachers' English Fluency Initiative in Arizona', Available online: https://www.u.arizona.edu/~hammond/ling_statement_final.pdf (accessed 5 April 2020).

Ates, B., Eslami, Z. and Wright, K. (2015), 'Incorporating World Englishes into Undergraduate ESL Education Courses', *World Englishes*, 34 (3): 485–501.

Avery, T. (2015), 'Tag Questions in English', *(PDF) Tag Questions in English*, Available online: (PDF) Tag Questions in English | Thomas S Avery - Academia.edu (accessed 3 March 2021).

Babel Polyglot Babel Polyglot (2013), Available online: http://language.exchange.free.fr/lessons_read.php?lang=konglish, (accessed 3 June 2020).

BabylonBabylon (2020), Available online: https://translation.babylon-software.com/english/konglish/ (accessed 7 June 2020).

Baherl, T. (2013), 'Your Ability to Can Even: A Defense of Internet Linguistics', *The Toast*, Available online: http://the-toast.net/2013/11/20/yes-you-can-even/ (accessed 15 May 2020).

Baik, M. (1994), 'Syntactic Features of Englishization in Korean', *World Englishes*, 13 (2): 155–66.

Baik, M. (1995), *Language, Ideology, and Power: English Textbooks of Two Koreas*, Seoul: Thaekaksa.

Bamgbose, A. (1998), 'Torn Between the Norms?: Innovations in World Englishes', *World Englishes*, 17 (1): 1–14.

Baratta, A. (2013), 'Semantic and Lexical Issues in Writings by Korean Children', *ESL Journal*, 1–21.

Baratta, A. (2014), 'The Use of English in Korean TV Drama to Signal a Modern Identity', *English Today*, 30 (3): 54–60.

Baratta, A. (2016), 'Keeping It Real or Selling Out: The Effects of Accent Modification on Personal Identity', *Pragmatics and Society*, 7 (2): 291–319.

Baratta, A. (2017), 'Accent and Linguistic Prejudice in British Teacher Training', *Journal of Language, Identity & Education*, 16: 416–23.

Baratta, A. (2018a), *Accent and Teacher Identity in Britain: Linguistic Favouritism and Imposed Identities*, London: Bloomsbury.

Baratta, A. (2018b), 'I Speak How I Speak: A Discussion of Accent and Identity within Teachers of ELT', in B. Yazan and N. Rudolph (eds.), *Criticality, Teacher Identity and (In)equity in English Language Teaching: Issues and Implications*, 163–78, Dordrecht, The Netherlands: Springer.

Baratta, A. (2019a), *World Englishes in English Language Teaching*, London: Palgrave Macmillan.

Baratta, A. (2019b), 'Korean Language Speakers Should Take Pride in Konglish – It's Another Wonderful Example of Linguistic Diversity', *The Conversation*, 14 June 2019, Available online: https://theconversation.com/korean-language-speakers-should-take-pride-in-konglish-its-another-wonderful-example-of-linguistic-diversity-118790 (accessed 1 May 2020).

Baratta, A. (2021a), 'What's in a Name? A Discussion of the Linguistic Implications for the Student-Teacher Relationship in the EFL Classroom', in B. Yazan and A. Selvi (eds.), *Global Englishes Language Teacher Education*, 144–149, London: Routledge.

Baratta, A. (2021b), 'A Lack of Phonological Inherentness: Perceptions of Accents in British Education', in G. Planchenault (ed.), *Pragmatics of Accents*, London: John Benjamins Publishing Company. Forthcoming.

Baugh, J. (2017), 'Linguistic Profiling and Discrimination', in O. García, N. Flores, and M. Spotti (eds.), *The Oxford Handbook of Language and Society*, 155–68, Oxford: Oxford University Press.

Baumgardner, R. (1987), 'Utilising Pakistani English Newspaper to Teach Grammar', *World Englishes*, 6 (3): 241–53.

Baumgardner, R. (2006), 'The Appeal of English in Mexican Commerce', *World Englishes*, 25 (2): 251–66.

Bayyurt, Y. and Sifakis, N. (2017), 'Foundations of an EIL-Aware Teacher Education', in A. Matsuda (ed.), *Preparing Teachers to Teach English as an International Language*, 3–18, Bristol: Multilingual Matters; Channel Gate Publishers.

BBC News (2015), 'South Korea: New Seoul Slogan Sparks 'Konglish' Debate', Available online : https://www.bbc.co.uk/news/blogs-news-from-elsewhere-34667315 (accessed 31 May 2020).

Beal, J. (1993), 'The Grammar of Tyneside and Northumbrian English', in J. Milroy and L. Milroy (eds.), *The Grammar of Tyneside and Northumbrian English*, 187–213, London: Longman.

Becker, K. (2009), '/r/and the Construction of Place Identity on New York City's Lower East Side', *Journal of Sociolinguistics*, 13 (5): 634–58.

Bhatia, T. and Ritchie, W. (2006), 'Bilingualism in the Global Media and Advertising', in T. Bhatia and W. Ritchie (eds.), *The Handbook of Bilingualism*, 513–46, Oxford: Blackwell.

Bhatia, T. (2020), 'World Englishes and Global Advertising', in C. Nelson, Z. Proshina and D. Davis (eds.), *The Handbook of World Englishes*, 616–34, Chichester: John Wiley.

Bickerton, D. (1981), *Roots of Language*, Ann Arbor: Karoma.

Bindel, J. (2013), 'From Cockney to Jafaican', *The Spectator*, 23 March, Available online: From Cockney to Jafaican | The Spectator (accessed 2 February 2021).

Bjørge, A.K. (2007), 'Power Distance in English Lingua Franca Email Communication', *International Journal of Applied Linguistics*, 17 (1): 60–80.

Blommaert, J. (2010), *The Sociolinguistics of Globalization*, Cambridge: Cambridge University Press.

Blommaert, J. (2014), 'Sociolinguistics', in C. Leung and B.V. Street (eds.), *The Routledge Companion to English Studies*, 131–44, London; New York: Routledge.

Blum-Kulka, S. and Olshtain, E. (1986), 'Too Many Words: Length of Utterance and Pragmatic Failure', *SSLA* 8: 165–80.

Bogle, D. (1973), *Toms, Coons, Mulattoes, Mammies and Bucks: An Interpretative History of Blacks in Films*, New York: Viking Press.

Bohner, G. and Wanke, M. (2002), *Attitudes and Attitude Change*, Hove, UK: Psychology Press.

Bokor, M. (2018), 'English Dominance on the Internet: Sociocultural Aspects of English Language Teaching', Available online: https://onlinelibrary.wiley.com/doi/abs/10.1002/9781118784235.eelt0281 (accessed 6 June 2020).

Bolton, K. (2012), 'Varieties of World Englishes', in C. Chapelle (ed.), *The Encyclopedia of Applied Linguistics*, 1–6, Chicester, UK: Wiley-Blackwell.

Bosher, S. (1997), 'Language and Cultural Identity: A Study of Hmong Students at the Postsecondary Level', *TESOL Quarterly*, 31 (3): 593–603.

Bourdieu, P. (1991), *Language and Symbolic Power*, Cambridge: Polity Press.

Brady, J. (2015), 'Dialect, Power and Politics: Standard English and Adolescent Identities', *Literacy*, 49 (3): 149–57.

Braine, G. (1999a), 'Introduction', in G. Braine (ed.), *Non-Native Educators in English Language Teaching*, xiii–xx, Mahwah, NJ: Lawrence Erlbaum Associates.

Bright, W. (2017), 'Social Factors in Language Change', in F. Coulmas (ed.), *The Handbook of Sociolinguistics*, 81–91, London: Blackwell.

Brown, K. (1995), 'World Englishes: to Teach or Not to Teach?', *World Englishes*, 14 (2): 233–45.

Bruthiaux, P. (2003), 'Squaring the Circles: Issues in Modeling English Worldwide', *International Journal of Applied Linguistics*, 3 (2): 159–78.

Brutt-Griffler, J. (2002), *World English: A Study of Its Development*, Clevedon: Multilingual Matters.

Butler, Y. (2007b), 'Factors Associated with the Notion that Native Speakers are the Ideal Language Teachers: An Examination of Elementary school teachers in Japan', *JALT Journal*, 29 (1): 7–39.

BuzzFeedVideo (2016), 'Can You Guess These Konglish Words?', Available online: https://www.youtube.com/watch?v=QAvBhXzytnU (accessed 25 May 2020).

Canagarajah, A.S. (1999), 'Interrogating the "Native Speaker Fallacy": Non-Linguistics Roots, Non-Pedagogical Results', in G. Braine (ed.), *Non-Native Educators in English Language Teaching*, 77–92, Mahwah, NJ: Lawrence Erlbaum Associates.

Canagarajah, A.S., ed. (2005), *Reclaiming the Local in Language Policy and Practice*, Mahwah, NJ: Lawrence Erlbaum.

Canagarajah, A.S. (2006), 'Negotiating the Local in English as a Lingua Franca', *Annual Review of Applied Linguistics*, 26: 197–218.

Cantone, J.A., Martinez, L.N., Willis-Esqueda, C. and Miller, T. (2019), 'Sounding Guilty: How Accent Bias Affects Juror Judgments of Culpability', *Journal of Ethnicity in Criminal Justice*, 17 (3): 228–53.

Case, A. (2011), 'An A to Z of Korean English (Konglish) Expressions', *TEFLtastic*, Available online: https://tefltastic.wordpress.com/2008/12/01/konglish-a-to-z/ (accessed 28 May 2020).

Chand, V. (2016), 'The Rise and Rise of Hinglish in India', *The Conversation*, 11 February 2016, Available online: https://theconversation.com/the-rise-and-rise-of-hinglish-in-india-53476 (accessed 5 June 2020).

Chang, W., Park, Y., Kim, C. and Chang, D, (1989), *High School English I: Teacher's Guide*, Seoul, Korea: Donga Publishing.

Chang, B.M. (2010), 'Cultural Identity in Korean English', *Pan-Pacific Association of Applied Linguistics*, 14 (1): 131–45.

Chung, K. (2011), 'Korean English Fever in the U.S.: Temporary Migrant Parents' Evolving Beliefs about Normal Parenting Practices and Children's Natural Language Learning', PhD thesis, University of Illinois, Urbana-Champaign.

Chelliah, S. (2001), 'Constructs of Indian English in Language "Guidebooks"', *World Englishes*, 20 (2): 161–78.

Choi, M. (2017), 'English Words You Only Hear in Korea', Available online: https://medium.com/story-of-eggbun-education/english-words-you-only-hear-in-korea-5bd3eed8f9c3 (accessed 30 May 2020).

Collins, P. (1991), 'Will and Shall in Australian English', in S. Johansson and A.S. Stenström (eds.), *English Computer Corpora: Selected Papers and Research Guide*, 181–200, Berlin: Mouton de Gruyter.

Collins, P. (2009), *Modals and Quasi-Modals in English*, New York: Brill.

Collins, P. and Blair, D., eds. (1989), *Australian English: The Language of a New Society*, Brisbane: University of Queensland Press.

Cook, V. (1999), 'Going beyond the Native Speaker in Language Teaching', *TESOL Quarterly*, 33 (2): 185–209.

Cook, V. (2005), 'Basing Teaching on the L2 User', in E. Llurda (ed.), *Non-Native Language Teachers: Perceptions, Challenges and Contributions to the Profession*, 47–61, New York: Springer.

Cootzee-van Rooy, S. (2009), 'Intelligibility and Perceptions of English Proficiency', *English Today*, 28 (1): 15–34.

Cortazzi, M., and Jin, L.X. (1999), 'Cultural Mirrors: Materials and Methods in the EFL Classroom', in E. Hinkel (ed.), *Culture in Second Language Teaching and Learning*, 196–219, Cambridge: Cambridge University Press.

Cotter, C. and Damaso, J. (2007), 'Online Dictionaries as Emergent Archives of Contemporary Usage and Collaborative Codification', *Queen Mary's OPAL #9 Occasional Papers Advancing Linguistics*.

Coulmas, F. (1999), 'The Far East', in J. Fisherman (ed.), *Handbook of Language and Ethnic Identity*, 399–413, Oxford: Oxford University Press.

Coupland, N. and Bishop, H. (2007), 'Ideologised Values for British Accents', *Journal of Sociolinguistics*, 11: 74–93.

Crystal, D. (2001), *Language and the Internet*, Cambridge: Cambridge University Press.

Crystal, D. (2008), 'Two Thousand Million?', *English Today*, 24 (1): 3–6.

Damaso, J. (2005), 'The New Populist Dictionary: A Computer-Mediated, Ethnographic Case Study of an Online, Collaboratively Authored English Slang Dictionary', MA dissertation, Queen Mary, University of London.

Danet, B. (2010), 'English and Creativity', in J. Maybin and J. Swann (eds.), *The Routledge Companion to English Language Studies*, 146–56, New York: Routledge.

Daniel, J. (2011), 'Language Contact between Korean and English in Online Communication', *Journal of Global Initiatives: Policy, Pedagogy, Perspective*, 5 (9): 115–29.

Davis, A. (2003), *The Native Speaker: Myth and Reality*, Clevedon: Multilingual Matters.

Davis, A. (2013), *Native Speakers and Native Users: Loss and Gain*, Cambridge: Cambridge University Press.

Dinh, T.N. (2017), 'Preparing Preservice Teachers with EIL/WE-Oriented Materials Development', in A. Matsuda (ed.), *Preparing Teachers to Teach English as an International Language*, 131–46, Bristol: Multilingual Matters.

Daily Mail Reporter (2011), 'Student Obsessed with Korean Culture Has Tongue Surgically Lengthened on NHS to Help Her Speak the Language', *Daily Mail*, 16 August, Available online: Rhiannon Brooksbank-Jones has tongue lengthened to help her speak Korean | Daily Mail Online (accessed 14 May 2021).

Doan, N. (2014), 'Teaching the Target Culture in English Teacher Education Programs: Issues of EIL in Vietnam', in M. Roby and R. Giri (eds.), *The Pedagogy of English as an International Language*, 79–93, New York: Springer.

Dolezal, F. (2006), 'World Englishes and Lexicography', in B. Kachru, Y. Kachru and C. Nelson (eds.), *The Handbook of World Englishes*, 694–708, Chichester: Blackwell.

Domzal, T.J., Hunt, J.M. and Kernan, J.B. (1995), Achtung! The Information Processing of Foreign Words in Advertising', *International Journal of Advertising*, 14 (2): 94–114.

Dougill, J. (2008), 'Japan and English as an Alien Language', *English Today*, 24 (1): 18–22.

Dutchpay Korea (2020), Available online : www.dutchpay.org/ (accessed 14 June 2021).

Eaves, M. (2011), 'English, Chinglish or China English?', *English Today*, 27 (4): 64–70.

Eriksen, T. (1992), 'Linguistic Hegemony and Minority Resistance', *Journal of Peace Research*, 29 (3): 313–32.

Evans, B.E. and Imai, T. (2011), 'If We Say English, That Means America: Japanese Students' Perceptions of Varieties of English', *Language Awareness*, 20 (4): 315–26.

Fang, F. (2017), 'Ideology and Identity Debate of English in China: Past, Present and Future', *Asian Englishes*, 20 (1): 15–26.

Fang, G. (2020), *Re-Positioning Accent Attitudes in the Global English Paradigm*, London: Routledge.

Farrar, L. (2010), '"Korean Wave" of Pop Culture Sweeps across Asia', *CNN*, 31 December, Available online: http://edition.cnn.com/2010/WORLD/asiapcf/12/31/korea.entertainment/index.html (accessed 20 April 2020).

Fayzrakhmanova, Y. (2016), 'Koreanized English Words from Perspectives of Korean – English Language Contact', *Asian Englishes*, 18 (3): 216–31.

Flattery, B. (2007), 'Language, Culture, and Pedagogy: An Overview of English in South Korea', Available online: http://homes.chass.utoronto.ca/~cpercy/courses/eng6365-flattery.htm (accessed 2 June 2020).

Foster, H. (2018), 'How is Social Media Changing the English Language?', Available online: https://www.languageservicesdirect.co.uk/social-media-changing-english-language/ (accessed June 8 2020).

Friedrich, P. (2002), 'Teaching World Englishes in Two South American Countries', *World Englishes*, 21 (3): 441–4.

Friedrich, P. and Berns, M. (2003), Introduction: English in South America, the Other Forgotten Continent', *World Englishes*, 22 (2): 83–90.

Frumkin, L. (2007), 'Influences of Accent and Ethnic Background on Perceptions of Eyewitness Testimony', *Psychology Crime and Law Crime & Law*, 13 (3): 317–31.

Fukunaga, N. (2006), '"Those Anime Students": Foreign Language Literacy Development through Japanese Popular Culture', *Journal of Adolescent & Adult Literacy*, 50 (3): 206–22.

Galloway, N. and Rose, H. (2015), *Introducing Global Englishes*, London: Routledge.
Gao, L. (2006), 'Language Contact and Convergence in Computer-Mediated Communication', *World Englishes*, 25 (2): 299–308.
Garner, R. (2013), 'Teacher 'Told to Sound Less Northern' after Southern Ofsted Inspection', *The Independent*, Available online: https://www.independent.co.uk/news/uk/home-news/ teacher-told-sound-less-northern-after-southern-ofsted-inspection-8947332.html (accessed 5 March 2021).
Ginny (2011), 'Korean Language Blog: Korean Internet Slang', Available online: https://blogs.transparent.com/korean/korean-internet-slang/ (accessed 1 June 2020).
Glosbe. (2021). Konglish. Available online: https://glosbe.com/en/ko/Konglish
Görlach, M. (2002), *Still More Englishes*, Amsterdam: John Benjamins.
Gough, D. (1996), 'Black English in South Africa', in V. De Klerk (ed.), *Focus on South Africa*, 53–77, Amsterdam: John Benjamins.
Green, J. (1996), *Chasing the Sun: Dictionary-Makers and the Dictionaries They Made*, London: Jonathan Cape.
Gupta, A. (1998), 'Singapore Colloquial English? Or Deviant Standard English?', in J. Tent and F. Mugler (eds.), *SICOL, Proceedings of the Second International Conference on Oceanic Linguistics: Vol. 1 .Language Contact: Canberra: Pacific Linguistics*, 4357.
Gupta, A. (2012), 'Grammar Teaching and Standards', in L. Alsagoff, S. McKay, G. Hu, and W. Renandya (eds.), *Principles and Practices for Teaching English as an International Language*, 244–60, New York: Routledge.
Gut, U. (2011), 'Studying Structural Innovation in New English Varieties', in J. Mukherjee and M. Hundt (eds.), *Exploring Second-Language Varieties of English and Learner Englishes*, 101–24, Amsterdam: John Benjamins.
Haarmann, H. (1986), 'Verbal Strategies in Japanese Fashion Magazines – A Study in Impersonal Bilingualism and Ethnosymbolism', *International Journal of the Sociology of Language*, 58: 107–21.
Haddix, M. (2012), 'Talkin' in the Company of My Sistas: The Counterlanguages and Deliberate Silences of Black Female Students in Teacher Education', *Linguistics & Education*, 23 (2): 169–81.
Hadikin, G. (2014), *Korean English: A Corpus-Driven Study of a New English*, Amsterdam: John Benjamins.
Hamid, M. and Baldauf, R. (2013), 'Second Language Errors and Features of World Englishes', *World Englishes*, 32 (4): 476–94.
Hanna, B. and de Nooy, J. (2009), *Learning Language and Culture Via Public Internet Discussion Forums*, London: Palgrave Macmillan.
Harding, N. (2013), 'Why Are So Many Middle-Class Children Speaking in Jamaican Patois? A Father of an 11-Year-Old Girl Laments a Baffling Trend', *Mail Online*, 13 October, Available online: Why are so many middle class children speaking in Jamaican patois? A father of an 11-year-old girl laments a baffling trend | Daily Mail Online (accessed 16 April 2021).

Hare, S. and Baker, A. (2017), 'Keepin' It Real: Authenticity, Commercialization, and the Media in Korean Hip Hop', *SAGE Open*, 1–12.

Harris, R. (2003), *Roadmap to Korean*, New Jersey: Hollym.

Hashem, A. (2015), *Common Errors in English*, New Delhi: Ramesh Publishing House.

He, D. and Li, D. (2009), 'Language Attitudes and Linguistic Features in the 'China English' Debate', *World Englishes*, 28 (1): 70–89.

He, D. and Zhang, Q. (2010), 'Native Speaker Norms and China English: From the Perspective of Learners and Teachers in China', *TESOL Quarterly*, 44 (4): 769–89.

Henao, J. (2017), 'Linguistic Hegemony in Academia and the Devaluation of Minority Identity in Higher Education', *Inquiries*, 9 (1): 1.

Hewings, A., and Tagg, C. (2012), 'General Introduction', in A. Hewings and C. Tagg (eds.), *The Politics of English: Conflict, Competition, Co-existence*, 1–3, New York, NY: Routledge.

Higgins, C. (2003), '"Ownership" of English in the Outer Circle: An Alternative to the NS-NNS Dichotomy', *TESOL Quarterly*, 37 (4): 615–44.

Hino, N. (2017), 'Teaching Graduate Students in Japan to be EIL Teachers', in A. Matsuda (ed.), *Preparing Teachers to Teach English as an International Language*, 87–99, Bristol: Multilingual Matters.

Holliday, A. (2005), *The Struggle to Teach English an International Language*, Oxford: Oxford University Press.

Holmquist, J. and Cudmore, A. (2013), 'English in Korean Advertising: An Exploratory Study', *International Journal of Marketing Studies*, 5 (3): 94–103.

Hong, E. (2019), *The Power of Nunchi: The Korean Secret to Happiness and Success*, London: Hutchinsons.

Honna, N. (2008), *English as a Multicultural Language in Asian Contexts: Issues and Ideas*, Tokyo: Kurosio Publishers.

Hsu, J.L. (2019), 'The Nativization of English in Taiwanese Magazine Advertisements', *World Englishes*, 38 (3): 463–85.

Hu, X. (2004), 'Why China English Should Stand Alongside British, American, and the Other "World Englishes"', *English Today*, 20 (2): 26–33.

Hu, X. (2005), 'China English, at Home and in the World', *English Today*, 21 (3): 27–38.

Huddart, D. (2014), *Involuntary Associations – Postcolonial Studies and World Englishes*, Liverpool: Liverpool University Press.

Internet World Stats, (2020). 'Top Ten Internet Languages in The World - Internet Statistics', Available online: internetworldstats.com (accessed 13 May 2021).

International Talk Like Jar Jar Binks Day, Available online: talklikejarjarday.com (accessed 1 May 2021).

Ionin, T., Ko, H., and Wexler, K. (2004), 'Article Semantics in L2 Acquisition: The Role of Specificity', *Language Acquisition*, 12: 3–69.

Irwin, M. (2011), *Loanwords in Japanese*, Amsterdam: John Benjamins.

Jee, Y. (2016), 'Critical Perspectives of World Englishes on EFL Teachers' Identity and Employment in Korea: An Autoethnography', *Multicultural Education Review*, 8 (4): 240–52.

Jenkins, J. (2000), *The Phonology of English as an International Language*, Oxford: Oxford University Press.

Jenkins, J. (2006a), 'Current Perspectives on Teaching World Englishes and English as a Lingua Franca', *TESOL Quarterly*, 40 (1): 157–81.

Jenkins, J. (2006b), 'Points of View and Blind Spots: ELF and SLA', *International Journal of Applied Linguistics*, 16 (2): 137–291.

Jenkins, J. (2007), *English as a Lingua Franca: Attitude and Identity*, Oxford: Oxford University Press.

Jenkins, J. (2009), *World Englishes: A Resource Book for Students*, London: Routledge.

Jenks, C., and Lee, J. (2016), 'Heteroglossic Ideologies in World Englishes: An Examination of the Hong Kong Context', *International Journal of Applied Linguistics*, 26 (3): 384–402.

Jenks, C. and Lee, J. (2017), *Korean Englishes in Transnational Contexts*, London: Palgrave Macmillan.

Jiang, Y. (2002), 'China English: Issues, Studies and Features', *Asian Englishes*, 5: 4–23.

Jin, D.Y. and Ryoo, W. (2012), 'Critical Interpretation of Hybrid K-Pop: The Global-Local Paradigm of English Mixing in Lyrics', *Popular Music and Society*, 37 (2): 113–31.

Jones, K. (2001), '"I've Called 'em Tom-ah-toes All My Life and I'm Not Going to Change!": Maintaining Linguistic Control over English Identity in the U.S', *Social Forces*, 79 (3): 1061–94.

Joo, S.J., Chik, A. and Djonov, E. (2020), 'The Construal of English as a Global Language in Korean EFL Textbooks for Primary School Children', *Asian Englishes*, 22 (1): 68–84.

Jørgensen, J. (2015), 'Ideologies and Norms in Language and Education Policies in Europe and their Relationship with Everyday Language Behaviours', *Language, Culture and Curriculum*, 25 (1): 57–71.

Jung, K. and Min, S. (1999), 'Some Lexico-Grammatical Features of Korean English Newspapers', *World Englishes*, 18 (1): 23–37.

Kachru B.B. (1981), 'The Pragmatics of Non-Native Varieties of English', in L.E. Smith (ed.), *English for Cross-Cultural Communication*, 15–39, London: Palgrave Macmillan.

Kachru, B.B. (1982), *The Other Tongue. English Across Cultures*, Urbana, IL: University of Illinois Press.

Kachru, B.B. (1983), *The Indianization of English: The English language in India*, Oxford: Oxford University Press.

Kachru, B.B. (1985), 'Standards, Codification and Sociolinguistic Realism: The English Language in the Outer Circle', in R. Quirk and H. Widdowson (eds.), *English in the World: Teaching and Learning the Language and Literatures*, 11–30, Cambridge: Cambridge University Press.

Kachru, B.B. (1991), 'Liberation Linguistics and the Quirk Concern', *English Today*, 7 (1): 3–13.

Kachru, B.B., ed. (1992a), *The Other Tongue: English across Cultures*, Chicago, IL: University of Illinois Press.

Kachru, B.B. (1992c), 'Teaching World Englishes', in B.B. Kachru, (ed.), *The Other Tongue: English across Cultures*, 355–65, Chicago, IL: University of Illinois Press.

Kachru, B.B. (1998), 'English as an Asian Language', *Links & Letters*, 5: 89–108.

Kachru, B.B. (2006), 'World Englishes and Culture Wars', in B.B. Kachru, Y. Kachru and C. Nelson (eds.), *The Handbook of World Englishes*, 446–72, Oxford: Blackwell.

Kachru, Y. and Nelson, C.L. (2006), *World Englishes in Asian Contexts*, Hong Kong: Hong Kong University Press.

Kachru, Y. and Smith, L. (2008), *Cultures, Contexts, and World Englishes*, London: Routledge.

Kang, S.Y. (2017), 'US-Based Teacher Education Program for 'Local' EIL Teachers', in A. Matsuda (ed.), *Preparing Teachers to Teach English as an International Language*, 51–68, Bristol: Multilingual Matters.

Kelly-Holmes, H. (2000), 'Bier, Parfum, Kaas: Language Fetish in European Advertising', *European Journal of Cultural Studies*, 3 (1): 67–82.

Kent, D. (1999), 'Speaking in Tongues: Chinglish, Japlish and Konglish', Conference: 2nd Pan-Asian International Conference - Teaching English: Asian Contexts and Cultures, Seoul, Korea, October 1999.

Kerswill, P. (2014), 'The Objectification of 'Jafaican': The Discoursal Embedding of Multicultural London English in the British Media', in J. Androutsopoulos (ed.), *The Media and Sociolinguistic Change*, 428–55, Berlin: De Gruyter.

Khedun-Burgoine, B. and Kiaer, J. (2018), 'What is an Oppa? Is it a Korean Word or an English Word?', Paper presented at the 23rd Annual Conference of the International Association for World Englishes, Quezon City, Philippines.

Kim, E. (2016), 'Anglicized Korean Neologisms of the New Millennium: An Overview', *English Today*, 32 (3): 52–60.

Kim, J., and Choi, J. (2014), 'English for University Administrative Work: English Officialization Policy and Foreign Language Learning Motivation', *English Language Teaching*, 7 (9): 1–13.

Kirkpatrick, A. (2006), 'Which Model of English: Native-Speaker, Nativized or Lingua Franca?', in R. Rubdy and M. Saraceni (eds.), *English in the World: Global Rules, Global Roles*, 71–83, London: Continuum.

Kirkpatrick, A. and Xu, Z. (2002), 'Chinese Pragmatic Norms and "China English"', *World Englishes*, 21 (2): 269–79.

Ko, D.H. (2017), 'Going 'Dutch' Viral in Korea as More Apps Fit the Bill', *The Korea Times*, 22 September 2017.

Kobayashi, Y. (2011), 'Expanding-Circle Students Learning 'Standard English' in the Outer-Circle Asia', *Journal of Multilingual and Multicultural Development*, 32 (3): 235–48.

Kortmann, B. and Szmrecsanyi, B. (2004), 'Global Synopsis: Morphological and Syntactic Variation in English', in B. Kortmann et al. (eds.), *A Handbook of Varieties of English*, 1142–202, New York: Mouton de Gruyter.

Kruger, H. and van Rooy, B. (2017), 'Editorial Practice and the Progressive in Black South African English', *World Englishes*, 36 (1): 20–41.

Kyung-Hwa (2017), 'Korean Language Blog. What is 콩글리시 (Konglish)?', Available online : https://blogs.transparent.com/korean/what-is-콩글리시-konglish/ (accessed 4 June 2020).

Lala Creatives (2018), 'The Game of Guessing Konglish', Available online: https://www.youtube.com/watch?v=lxnn8Xf3ykM (6 June 2020).

Lawrence, C.B. (2010a), 'The Verbal Art of Borrowing: Analysis of English Borrowing in Korean Pop Songs', *Asian Englishes*, 13 (2): 42–63.

Lawrence, C.B. (2010b), 'Konglish, Chinglish and Janglish: Definitions and Implications for Korea and East Asia', Paper presented at The 7th annual Seoul KOTESOL Chapter Conference, Seoul, South Korea.

Lawrence, C.B. (2012), 'The Korean English Linguistic Landscape', *World Englishes*, 31 (1): 70–92.

Lee, J.A. (2001), 'Korean Speakers', in M. Swan and B. Smith, (eds.), *Learner English: A Teacher's Guide to Interference and other Problems*, 325–42, Cambridge, NY: Cambridge University Press.

Lee, J.S. (2004), 'Linguistic Hybridization in K-Pop: Discourse of Self-Assertion and Resistance', *World Englishes*, 23 (3): 429–50.

Lee, J. (2006), 'Linguistic Constructions of Modernity: English Mixing in Korean Television Commercials', *Language in Society*, 35 (1): 59–91.

Lee, J.S. (2007), 'I'm the illest fucka', *English Today*, 23 (2): 54–60.

Lee, K.Y. (2007), 'Korea English', in K.J. Park and M. Nakano (eds.), *Asia Englishes and Miscommunication*, 241–315, Seoul: Korea University Press.

Lee, J.S. (2013), 'Hybridizing Medialect and Entertaining TV: Changing Korean Reality', in R. Rubdy and L. Alsagoff (eds.), *The Global-Local Interface and Hybridity: Exploring Language and Identity*, 170–88, Bristol: Multilingual Matters.

Lee, J.S. (2014), 'English on Korean Television', *World Englishes*, 33 (1): 33–49.

Lee, K. (2015), 'Dutch Pay Coming to Kakao', *Talk. The Korea Bizwire*, Available online: http://koreabizwire.com/duth-pay-coming-to-kakaotalk/40556 (accessed 8 June 2020).

Lee, D. (2018), 'Pop Culture: A Guide to Korean Soft Drinks', Available online: https://thetakeout.com/pop-culture-a-guide-to-korean-soft-drinks-1829732918 (accessed 4 June 2020).

Lee, J.S. (2018), 'The Korean Wave, K-Pop Fandom, and Multilingual Microblogging', in C. Cutler and U. Røyneland (eds.), *Multilingual Youth Language in Computer Mediated Communication*, 205–23, Cambridge: Cambridge University Press.

Lee, H.J. and Jin, D.Y. (2019), *K-Pop Idols: Popular Culture and the Emergence of the Korean Music Industry*, London: Lexington Books.

Lee, J.S. (2019), 'An Emerging Path to English in Korea: Informal Digital Learning of English', in M. Dressman and R. Sadler (eds.), *The Handbook of Informal Language Learning*, 289–302, Chichester: Wiley-Blackwell.

Lee, H. (2020), 'Preserving Cultural Identity in English Language Use by Korean Immigrants', *Inquiries*, 12 (10): 1.

Lee, J.S. (2020) 'English in Korea', in K. Bolton, W. Botha and A. Kirkpatrick (eds.), *The Handbook of Asian Englishes*, 585–604, Hoboken, NJ: Wiley-Blackwell.

Lee, S. (2020), 'Attitudes Toward English Borrowings in South Korea: A Comparative Study of University Professors and Primary/Secondary Teachers of English', *Asian Englishes*, 3: 238–56.

Lee, K.Y. and Green, R. (2020), 'Student Perceptions of Sociocultural Aspects of Korean and the Korean Variety of English (KVE): A Study of Korean University Students', *English Today*, 1–7.

Leech, G. (1983), *Principles of Pragmatics*, London: Longman Group Ltd.

Leimgruber, J. (2013), 'The Trouble with World Englishes', *World Englishes*, 29 (3): 3–7.

Li, J., Moraveji, N., Ding, J., O'Kelley, P. and Woolf, S. (2007), 'Designing Games to Address 'Mute English' among Children in China', in C. Stephanidis (ed.), *Universal Access in Human Computer Interaction*, 697–706, New York: Springer.

Li, D. (2010), 'When Does an Unconventional Form Become an Innovation?', In A. Kirkpatrick (eds.), *The Routledge Handbook of World Englishes*, 617–33, London: Routledge.

Lippi-Green, R. (1997), *English with an Accent: Language, Ideology, and Discrimination in the United States*, New York: Routledge.

Lotte World Sign, Available online: https://minniehwang.wordpress.com/2010/05/23/konglish/ (accessed 5 March 2021).

Lowenberg, P. (1993), 'Issues of Validity in Tests of English as a World Language: Whose Standards?', *World Englishes*, 12 (1): 95–106.

Lyu, H. (2011), *Error Analysis and Norms for Chinese-English Translation of Signs*, Beijing: National Defense Industry Press.

Ma, Q. and Xu, Z. (2017), 'The Nativization of English in China', in Z. Xu, D. He, and D. Deterding (eds.), *Researching Chinese English: The State of the Art*, 189–201, Cham: Springer.

Mahboob, A. (2014), 'English in the Kingdom of Saudi Arabia', *World Englishes*, 33 (1): 128–42.

Marshall, C. (2017), 'Lacking Seoul? Why South Korea's Thriving Capital is Having an Identity Crisis', *The Guardian*, 18 July, Available online: Lacking Seoul? Why South Korea's thriving capital is having an identity crisis | Cities | The Guardian (accessed 15 May 2021).

Martin, E. (2020), 'World Englishes in the Media', in C. Nelson, Z. Proshina and D. Davis (eds.), *The Handbook of World Englishes*, 597–615, Chichester: John Wiley.

Matsuda, A. (2003), '"International Understanding" through Teaching World Englishes', *World Englishes*, 21 (3), 436–40.

Matsuda, A., ed. (2017), *Preparing Teachers to Teach English as an International Language*, Bristol: Multilingual Matters.

Matsuda, A. (2020), 'World Englishes and Pedagogy', in C. Nelson, Z. Proshina and D. Davis (eds.), *The Handbook of World Englishes*, 686–702, Chichester: John Wiley.

Mauranen, A. (2012), *Exploring ELF: Academic English Shaped by Non-Native Speakers*, Cambridge: Cambridge University Press.

McDonald, C. and McRae, S. (2010), 'A Pre-Trial Collection and Investigation of What Perceptions and Attitudes of Konglish Exist among Foreign and Korean English Language Teachers in Terms of English Education in Korea', *Asian EFL*, 12 (1): 134–64.

McKenzie, R. (2008), 'The Role of Variety Recognition in Japanese University Students' Attitudes Towards English Speech Varieties', *Journal of Multilingual & Multicultural Development*, 29 (2): 139–53.

McKenzie, R. (2013), 'Changing Perceptions? A Variationist Sociolinguistic Perspective on Native Speaker Ideologies and Standard English in Japan', in S.A. Houghton and D.J. Rivers (eds.), *Native-speakerism in Japan: Intergroup Dynamics in Foreign Language Education*, 89–115, Bristol: Multilingual Matters.

McPhail, S. (2018), 'South Korea's Linguistic Tangle: English vs. Korean vs. Konglish: A Study of the Relative Status of Konglish and its Parent Languages in South Korea', *English Today*, 34 (1): 45–51.

Medgyes, P. (2001), 'When the Teacher is a Non-Native Speaker', *Teaching Pronunciation*, 429–442.

Meierkord, K. (2012), *Interactions across Englishes*, Cambridge: Cambridge University Press.

Merchant, G. (2002), 'Teenagers in Cyberspace: An Investigation of Language Use and Language Change in Internet Chatrooms', *Journal of Research in Reading*, 24 (3): 293–306.

Meriläinen, L. (2017), 'The Progressive Form in Learner Englishes: Examining Variation across Corpora', *World Englishes*, 36 (4): 760–83.

Mesthrie, R. (1988), 'Toward a Lexicon of South African Indian English', *World Englishes* 7 (1), 5–14.

Mesthrie, R. and Bhatt, R. (2008), *World Englishes: The Study of New Linguistic Varieties, In the Series Key Topics in Sociolinguistics*, Cambridge: Cambridge University Press.

Miller, J. (2003), 'A Word by any Other Meaning: Konglish', *MED Magazine*, Available online: http://www.macmillandictionaries.com/MED-Magazine/March2003/05-korean-english.htm (accessed 1 June 2020).

Milroy, J. and Milroy, L. (1999), *Authority in Language*, New York: Routledge.

Moag, R. (1992), 'The Life Cycle of Non-Native Englishes: A Case Study', in B.B. Kachru (ed.), *The Other Tongue: English Across Cultures*, 233–52, Urbana, IL: University of Illinois Press.

Moore, J., Higham, L., Mountford-Zimdars, A., Ashley, L., Birkett, H., Duberley, J. and Kenny, E. (2016), *Socio-Economic Diversity in Life Sciences and Investment Banking*, London: Social Mobility Commission.

Moosavi, L. (2020), '"Can East Asian Students Think?": Orientalism, Critical Thinking, and the Decolonial Project', *Education Studies*, 10: 1–20.

Morin, N. (2019), 'K-Pop 101: The Terms You Need To Know Before You Stan', Available online: https://www.refinery29.com/en-us/k-pop-music-fans-terms-meaning (accessed 5 June 2020).

Morrow, P.R. (2004), 'English in Japan: The World Englishes Perspective', *JALT Journal*, 26 (1): 79–100.

Mufwene, S. (1994), 'New Englishes and Criteria for Naming Them', *World Englishes*, 13 (1): 21–31.

Mufwene, S. (2001), *The Ecology of Language Evolution*, Cambridge: Cambridge University Press.

Mulholland, N. (2014), 'The Art of Konglish', *Babel*, 36–38, Available online: https://babelzine.co.uk/ArticlePDFs/No8%20Article%20-%20The%20art%20of%20Konglish.pdf (accessed 4 June 2020).

Mukminatien, N. (2012), 'Pedagogical Movements in Teaching English in the Emerging Issues of World Englishes. ELT in Asia in the Digital Era: Global Citizenship and Identity', Proceedings of the 15th Asia TEFL and 64th TEFLIN International Conference on English Language Teaching, Yogyakarta, Indonesia, 13–15 July , 2017.

Nahm, A. (1993), *Introduction to Korean History and Culture*, Carlsbad, CA: Hollym.

Nam, H. (2010), 'Konglish, Korean L2 Learners' Unique Interlanguage: Its Definition, Categories and Lexical Entries', *Korean Journal of Applied Linguistics*, 26 (4): 275–308.

Nederstigt, U. and Hilberink-Schulpen, B. (2018), 'Advertising in a Foreign Language or the Consumers' Native Language?', *Journal of International Consumer Marketing*, 30 (1): 2–13.

Nelson, C. (2008), 'Intelligibility since 1969', *World Englishes*, 27 (3/4): 297–308.

Nicoll, J. (1990), 'The King's English', *Newsgroup: rec.arts.sf-lovers*.

Nuske, K. (2017), '"I Mean I'm Kind of Discriminating My Own People": A Chinese TESOL Graduate Student's Shifting Perceptions of China English', *TESOL Quarterly*, 52 (2): 360–90.

O: (2020), 'The Differences between English and Korean', *Frankfurt International School*, Available online: http://esl.fis.edu/grammar/langdiff/korean.htm (accessed 8 May 2020).

O: (2020), 'How to Study Korean: Ultimate Konglish Guide', Available online: https://www.howtostudykorean.com/unit-6/lessons-134-141/lesson-134/ (accessed 28 May 2020).

O: 90 Day Korean (2020), 'Korean Grammar for Beginners', Available online: https://www.90daykorean.com/korean-grammar/ (accessed 5 June 2020).

O: 90 day Korean (2020), 'Konglish: The Ultimate List in 2020', Available online: https://www.90daykorean.com/konglish/ (accessed 30 May 2020).

O: Konglish Corner (2020), Available online: https://www.britishcouncil.kr/en/english/learn-online/konglish-video-podcast (accessed 6 April 2020).

O: Konglish (2015), 'Macmillan Dictionary', Available online: https://www.macmillandictionary.com/dictionary/british/konglish (accessed 3 June 2020).
O: Konglish (2005), 'Urban Dictionary', Available online: https://www.urbandictionary.com/define.php?term=Konglish (accessed 19 May 2020).
O: Konglish (2020), 'Wikipedia', Available online: https://en.wikipedia.org/wiki/Konglish (accessed 28 April 2020).
O: Konglish. Your Dictionary (2020), Available online: https://www.yourdictionary.com/konglish (accessed 16 May 2020).
O: Konglish (2020), Available online: https://www.koreanwikiproject.com/wiki/Konglish (accessed 7 June 2020).
O: Korea Dolls (2018), Available online: https://bjdcollectasy.com/2018/11/02/korea-dolls/ (accessed 3 June 2020).
O'Barr, William (1994), *Culture and the Ad: Exploring Otherness in the World of Advertising*, Oxford: Westview Press.
O'Neill, P. (2018), 'What is Linguistic Prejudice?', Linguistic Prejudice Conference, University of Sheffield, United Kingdom, 9–10 July 2018.
Onysko, A. (2016), 'Modeling World Englishes from the Perspective of Language Contact', *World Englishes*, 35 (2): 196–220.
Paikeday, T.M. (1985), *The Native Speaker is Dead!*, New York: Paikeday Publishing.
Pakir, A (1991), 'The Range and Depth of English-Knowing Bilinguals', *World Englishes*, 10(2): 167–79.
Pandharipande, R. (1987), 'On Nativization of English', *World Englishes* 6 (2), 149–58.
Park, H. (2006), 'English as Fashion: English Mixing in Women's Fashion Magazines', PhD thesis, University of Illinois, Urbana-Champaign.
Park, J.K. (2009), '"English Fever" in South Korea: Its History and Symptoms', *English Today*, 25 (1): 50–7.
Park, J.S.Y. and Wee, L. (2009), 'The Three Circles Redux: A Market-Theoretic Perspective on World Englishes', *Applied Linguistics*, 30 (3): 389–406.
Park, J.S.Y. (2009), *The Local Construction of a Global Language, Ideologies of English in South Korea*, Boston: De Gruyter Mouton.
Park, K.J. (2009), 'Characteristics of Korea English as a glocalized variety', in K. Murata and J. Jenkins (eds.), *Global Englishes in Asian Contexts: Current and Future Debates*, 94–107, New York: Palgrave Macmillan.
Park, J.S.Y. (2010), 'Naturalization of Competence and the Neoliberal Subject: Success Stories of English Language Learning in the Korean Conservative Press', *Journal of Linguistic Anthropology*, 20 (1): 22–38.
Park, J.S.Y. (2017), 'Class, Competence, and Language Ideology: Beyond Korean Englishes', in C. Jenks and J. Lee (eds.), *Korean English in Transnational Contexts*, 53–72, London: Palgrave Macmillan.
Park, L. (2019), 'Language Varieties and Variation in English Usage Among Native Korean Speakers in Seoul', PhD thesis, University of Iowa.

Park, K. and Dubinsky, S. (2019), 'The Syntax and Semantics of Negative Questions and Answers in Korean and English', *Proceedings of the Linguistic Society of America* 4 (1): 19.

Parker, J. (2019), 'Second Language Learning and Cultural Identity: Reconceptualizing the French Curriculum in Louisiana Colleges and Universities', *Journal of Curriculum Studies Research*, 1 (1): 33–42.

Pennycook, A. (2001), *Critical Applied Linguistics: A Critical Introduction*, Mahwah, NJ: Lawrence Erlbaum Associates.

Pennycook, A. (2007), *Global Englishes and Transcultural Flows*, London: Routledge.

Perez, S. (1999), 'Using Ebonics or Black English as a Bridge to Teaching Standard English', *Race, Class and Culture*, 2, Available online: http://www.ascd.org/publicatio ns/classroom-leadership/apr1999/Using-Ebonics-or-Black-English-as-a-Bridge-to -Teaching-Standard-English.aspx (accessed 5 June 2020).

Phillipson, R. (1992), *Linguistic Imperialism*, London: Oxford University Press.

Pickles, M. (2018), 'K-pop Drives Boom in Korean Language Lessons', *BBC News*, Available online: https://www.bbc.co.uk/news/business-44770777 (accessed 25 May 2020).

Pinkham, J. (2000), *The Translator's Guide to Chinglish*, Beijing: Foreign Language Teaching and Research Press.

Piñón, J. and Rojas, V. (2011), 'Language and Cultural Identity in the New Configuration of the US Latino TV Industry', *Global Media and Communication*, 7 (2): 129–47.

Platt, J., Weber, H. and Ho, M.L. (1984), *The New Englishes*, London: Routledge and Kegan Paul.

Pope, R. (2010), 'English and Creativity', in J. Maybin and J. Swann (eds.), *The Routledge Companion to English Language Studies*, 122–33, New York: Routledge.

Porteous, N. (2020), 'South Korea, English and Globalisation: Investigating Young Korean Adults' English Regard', PhD thesis, Aston University, Birmingham, UK.

Potayroi. (2014), 'Fandom as a Discourse Community', Available online: https://thanson g123.wordpress.com/2014/04/24/fandom-as-a-discourse-community/, accessed 6 June 2020.

Priz, L. (2011), 'Konglish', Available online: http://leonsplanet.com/konglish.htm (accessed 14 May 2020).

Prodromou, L. (2006), 'Defining the "Successful Bilingual Speaker" of English', in R. Rubdy and M. Saraceni (eds.), *English in the World: Global Rules, Global Roles*, 51–70, London: Continuum.

Quirk, R. (1990), 'Language Varieties and Standard Language', *English Today*, 6 (1): 3–10.

Ra, J. (2019), 'Exploring the Spread of English Language Learning in South Korea and Reflections of the Diversifying Sociolinguistic Context for Future English Language Teaching Practices', *Asian Englishes*, 21 (3): 305–19.

Rajagopalan, K. (2005), 'Non-Native Speaker Teachers of English and Their Anxieties: Ingredients for an Experiment in Action Research', in E. Llurda (ed.), *Non-Native Language Teachers: Perceptions, Challenges and Contributions to the Profession*, 283–303, London: Spinger.

Reagan, T. (2018), 'Linguistic Hegemony and "Official Languages"', in A. Canestrani and B. Marlowe (eds.), *The Wiley International Handbook of Educational Foundations*, 89–106, Hoboken, NJ: John Wiley.

Reddick, A. (1990), *The Making of Johnson's Dictionary: 1746-1773*. Cambridge: Cambridge University Press.

Renandya, W. (2012), 'Teacher Roles in EIL', *The European Journal of Applied Linguistics and TEFL*, 1 (2): 65–80.

Rhee, K.Y. and Kim, W.B. (2017), 'The Adoption and Use of the Internet in South Korea', *Journal of Computer Mediated Communication*, 9 (4): No page range, Available online: https://onlinelibrary.wiley.com/doi/full/10.1111/j.1083-6101.2004.tb00299.x

Reinartz, W. and Saffert, P. (2013), 'Creativity in Advertising: When It Works and When It Doesn't', Available online: https://hbr.org/2013/06/creativity-in-advertising-when-it-works-and-when-it-doesnt (accessed 5 June 2020).

Rhodes, M. (2016), 'The Beauty and Perils of Konglish, the Korean-English Hybrid', Available online: https://www.wired.com/2016/09/beauty-perils-konglish-korean-english-hybrid/ (accessed 18 May 2020).

Richelle (2016), 'Learning the KPOP Language', Available online: https://aminoapps.com/c/k-pop/page/blog/learning-the-kpop-language/YkIb_ueZPGaMMBzXdMpm1LJbVZrw2z (accessed 16 June 2020).

Rickford, J. (1998), 'Using the Vernacular to Teach the Standard', Available online: https://web.stanford.edu/~rickford/papers/VernacularToTeachStandard.html, (accessed 8 June 2020).

Rose, H. (2017), 'A Global Approach to English Language Teaching: Integrating an International Perspective into a Teaching Methods Course', in A. Matsuda (ed.), *Preparing Teachers to Teach English as an International Language*, 169–80, Bristol: Multilingual Matters.

Rosen, A. (2016), 'The Fate of Linguistic Innovations: Jersey English and French Learner English Compared', *International Journal of Learner Corpus Research*, 2 (2): 302–22.

Rüdiger, S. (2014), 'The Nativization of English in the Korean Context: Uncharted Territory for World Englishes: Investigating Emerging Patterns of Koreanized English', *English Today*, 30 (4): 11–14.

Rüdiger, S. (2018), 'Mixed Feelings: Attitudes towards English Loanwords and Their Use in South Korea', *Open Linguistics*, 4 (1): 184–98.

Rüdiger, S. (2019), *Morpho-Syntactic Patterns in Spoken Korean English*, Amsterdam: John Benjamins.

Ruffin, R. (2010), 'Korean Language Suffers as Konglish Takes Hold', *The Korea Herald*, 2 November 2010, Available online: Korean language suffers as Konglish takes hold (koreaherald.com) (accessed 14 May 2021).

Salmon, A. (2015), 'I.Seoul.U: The Case For', *The Korea Times*, 9 November, Available online: I.Seoul.U: The case for (koreatimes.co.kr) (accessed 14 May 2021).

Sandy S. (2015), 'Konglish vs. English = Different', Available online: https://prezi.com/igjdocv6ryn5/konglish-vs-english-different/ (accessed 7 June 2020).

SBS Pop Asia HQ (2018), 'K-pop 101: 21 Words Every Fan Should Know', Available online: https://www.sbs.com.au/popasia/blog/2018/03/13/k-pop-101-21-words-every-fan-should-know (accessed 17 May 2020).

Schilling-Estes, N. (1998), 'Investigating "Self-Conscious" Speech: The Performance Register in Okracoke English', *Language in Society*, 27 (1): 53–83.

Schneider, E. (2007), *Postcolonial English: Varieties around the World*, Cambridge: Cambridge University Press.

Schneider, B. (2014), *Salsa, Language and Transnationalism*, Bristol: Multilingual Matters.

Scollon, R. and Scollon, S.W. (2003), *Discourses in Place: Language in the Material World*, London: Routledge.

Seargeant, P. and Tagg, C. (2011), 'English on the Internet and a "Post-Varieties" Approach to Language', *World Englishes*, 30 (4): 496–514.

Seemile Korean (2019), 'Do You Know 'Konglish'?', Available online: https://www.youtube.com/watch?v=__ed3KDXVoU (accessed 18 May 2020).

Seidlhofer, B. (2001), 'Towards Making 'Euro-English' a Linguistic Reality', *English Today*, 17: 14–16.

Seong, M.H. and Lee, K.Y. (2008), 'Syntactic Features of Korea English: Word Order, Ellipsis, Articles, Prepositions, Passive, and Miscellaneous', *Journal of Pan-Pacific Association of Applied Linguistics*, 12 (1): 81–95.

Seoul Homes (2020), Available online: https://seoulhomes.kr/property/large-lofty-type-officetel-near-gangnam-stn-short-term-available/ (accessed 5 June 2020).

Shim, R. (1994), 'Englishized Korean: Structure, Status, and Attitudes', *World Englishes*, 13 (2): 225–44.

Shim, R. (1999), 'Codified Korean English: Process, Characteristics and Consequence', *World Englishes*, 18 (2): 247–58.

Shim, R.J. and Baik, M.J. (2004), 'English Education in South Korea', in H.W. Kam and R.Y.L. Wong (eds.), *English Language Teaching in East Asia Today: Changing Policies and Practices*, 241–61, Singapore: Eastern Universities Press.

Shin, J., Eslami, Z and Chen, W.C. (2011), 'Presentation of Local and International Culture in Current International English-Language Teaching Textbooks', *Language, Culture and Curriculum*, 24 (3): 253–68.

Siqi, L. and Sewell, A. (2014), 'Phonological Features of China English', *Asian Englishes*, 15 (2): 80–101.

Smith, M. (2015), 'Is Harry Potter Fandom Real?—Literacy & Discourse', Available online: https://medium.com/literacy-discourse/is-harry-potter-fandom-real-21b5b407f3c8#.hz9khas7n (accessed 8 June 2020).

Snell, J. (2013), 'Dialect, Interaction and Class Positioning at School: From Deficit to Difference to Repertoire', *Language and Education*, 27 (2): 110–28.

Song, J.J. (1998), 'Forum. English in South Korea Revisited via Martin Jonghak Baik (1994, 1995) and Rosa Jinyoung Shim (1994)', *World Englishes*, 17 (2): 262–71.

Song, H. (2013), 'Deconstruction of Cultural Dominance in Korean EFL Textbooks', *Intercultural Education*, 24 (4): 382–90.

Song, J.J. (2016), 'A Rose by Any Other Name? Learner English and Variety-Status Labelling: The Case of English in South Korea', *English Today*, 32 (4): 56–62.
Speicher, B. and Bielanski, J. (2002), 'Critical Thoughts on Teaching Standard English', *Curriculum Inquiry*, 30 (2): 147–69.
Squires, L. (2010), 'Enregistering Internet Language', *Language in Society*, 39 (4): 457–92.
Stanlaw, J. (2004), *Japanese English: Language and Culture Contact*, Hong Kong: Hong Kong University Press.
Strother, J. (2015), 'What is Proper English? In South Korea it Starts with Sounding American', The World in Words. Public Radio International, Available online: http://www.pri.org/stories/2015-12-18/whats-proper-english-south-korea-it-starts-sounding-american (accessed 15 May 2020)
Takeshita, Y. (2012), 'East Asian Englishes: Japan and Korea', in A. Kirkpatrick (ed.), *The Routledge Handbook of World Englishes*, 265–81, Abingdon; New York: Routledge.
Thorkelson, T.S. (2005), 'Konglish in the Classroom: The Teachers' Backdoor', Presented at KOTESOL Daegu workshop on 4 June, 2005.
Touhami, B. and Al-Abed Al-Haq, F. (2017), 'The Influence of the Korean Wave on the Language of International Fans: Case Study of Algerian Fans', *Sino-US English Teaching*, 14 (10): 598–626.
Trudgill, P. (1995), *Sociolinguistics: An Introduction to Language and Society*, London: Penguin.
Turner, G. (1984), 'Australian English as a World Language', *English in the World*, 3: 153–5.
van der Walt, J. and van Rooy, B. (2002), 'Towards a Norm in South African Englishes', *World Englishes*, 21 (1): 113–28.
van Rooy, B. (2011), 'A Principled Distinction between Errors and Conventionalized Innovation in African Englishes', in J. Mukherjee and M Hundt (eds.), *Exploring Second-Language Varieties of English and Learner Englishes: Bridging a Paradigm Gap*, 189–207, Amsterdam: John Benjamins.
van Rooy, B. (2014), 'Progressive Aspect and Stative Verbs in Outer Circle Varieties', *World Englishes*, 33 (2): 157–72.
Wang, Y. and Zhang, R. (2016), 'From Local Standards to National Standards: A Milestone in Research on the Translation of Public Signs', *Chinese Translators Journal*, 37 (3): 64–70.
Warshauer, M., Black, R. and Chou, Y. (2010), 'Online Englishes', in A. Kirkpatrick (ed.), *The Routledge Handbook of World Englishes*, 490–505, London: Routledge.
Wee, L. (2002), 'When English is Not a Mother Tongue: Linguistic Ownership and the Eurasian Community in Singapore', *Journal of Multilingual and Multicultural Development*, 23 (4): 282–95.
Wei, l. (2020), 'Multilingual English Users' Linguistic Innovation', *World Englishes*, 39 (2): 236–48.
Westphal, M. (2021), 'Question Tags across New Englishes', *World Englishes*: 1–15.
Widdowson, H.G. (1994), 'The Ownership of English', *TESOL Quarterly*, 28: 377–89.

Wrenn, E. (2012), 'British Diplomats to India Must Learn 'Hinglish' as Mix of Hindi and English Becomes the Most Used Language', *Daily Mail*, 11 October 2012, Available online: British diplomats to India must learn 'Hinglish' as mix of Hindi and English becomes the most used language | Daily Mail Online (accessed 14 May 2021).

Wu, K. and Ke, C. (2009), 'Haunting Native Speakerism? Students' Perceptions Toward Native Speaking English Teachers', *English Language Teaching*, 2 (3): 44–52.

Xu, M. and Tian, C. (2018), '"Open Water Room" = "Hot Water Room"?: Language Reality and Normativity with Respect to the Use of English in China's Public Service Areas', *English Today*, 1–6.

Yano, Y. (2009), 'English as an International Lingua Franca: From Societal to Individual', *World Englishes*, 28 (2): 246–55.

Yoo, I.W. (2014), 'Nonnative Teachers in the Expanding Circle and the Ownership of English', *Applied Linguistics*, 35 (1): 82–6.

Young, J. and Walsh, S. (2010), 'Which English? Whose English? An Investigation of 'Non-Native' Teachers' Belief about Target Varieties', *Language, Culture and Curriculum*, 23 (2): 123–37.

Z (2020), 'Sydney to Seoul: A Self-Study Korean Language Blog', Available online: https://sydneytoseoul.wordpress.com/2013/08/02/lexical-borrowings-from-english-in-konglish/ (accessed 8 June 2020).

Zhang, Q. (2010), 'A Study of Chinese Learning of English Tag Questions', *Journal of Language Teaching and Research*, 1 (5): 578–82.

Zoghbor, W. (2018), 'Revisiting English as a Foreign Language (EFL) vs English Lingua Franca (ELF): The Case for Pronunciation', *Intellectual Discourse*, 26 (2): 829–58.

Index

Black South African English 41
British council 61–4, 188

China English 2–3, 26–7, 29, 34, 46, 48, 60, 69, 78–9, 96
Chinglish 2–3, 24, 26, 27, 46, 48, 86, 130
code-switching 85, 110, 111, 113, 155, 157, 159, 162, 165, 192
codification 18–21
  contextual 20, 73, 75, 84, 155–7, 159, 175
  societal 11–12, 18–21, 39, 42, 48, 55–81, 92, 104, 109, 125, 138, 156–76, 183, 185, 191, 193
  traditional 18–19, 20, 21, 29–30, 39, 42, 48, 55–7, 59, 60, 62, 68, 69, 94, 99, 109, 125, 128, 178, 183

dictionaries
  online 19, 56, 79–81, 92, 129–54
  traditional 19, 21, 56

Ebonics 13, 15, 161–2, 181
EFL teaching 177–90, 192
English as a lingua franca (ELF) 44, 66, 76, 110, 163, 167, 179, 182
English language complex 157
errors 9–12, 32–49, 104–5, 129–31, 136, 143, 153–4, 170–1, 173, 182, 188, 189
ethnolect 86
expanding circle 7, 17, 24–7, 29, 31, 35, 45, 47, 48, 52, 56, 58, 68, 69, 78, 79, 87, 92, 107, 109, 111, 147, 167

Global Englishes Language Teaching (GELT) 179

hallyu 17, 64, 66, 141, 159
Hinglish 7, 15

Indian English 7, 15, 112, 123, 171, 177, 187
informal digital learning of English (IDLE) 187
inner-circle English 7, 16, 18, 29, 31, 33, 34, 44, 59, 71–3, 77, 86, 96, 98–110, 119–20, 122–4, 126, 130, 131, 133, 135, 137, 142, 144, 147, 152, 154, 158, 161, 171–4, 177, 180, 181, 183, 186–8, 190–2. *See also* standard English
  dialects 10, 29, 31, 35, 36, 52, 95, 119, 148, 168, 172, 179, 185, 191
  standard 8–9, 13, 14, 32, 33, 35–7, 40, 46, 47, 60, 84, 90, 95, 156, 165–6, 168, 172, 177, 178, 184, 188, 191–2
innovations 9–12, 32–49, 129, 143, 166
internet linguistics 79

Japanese English 26, 46, 187

Konglish 2–3, 16, 24, 61, 63, 86–8, 91, 127–54, 170, 178, 188
Korean English 3–7, 17, 45, 52, 57, 59, 62–4, 67, 69, 77, 78, 83–154, 172, 173, 175, 178, 181, 182, 184, 186–9, 191–3
  grammar 88, 97–109, 124, 126, 182
  vocabulary 44, 46, 70–5, 77, 87, 88, 91, 95, 97, 123, 129–54, 172, 181
Korean media English 66, 75, 84, 155–76, 192–3
  advertisements 85, 95, 111, 158, 168–76
  internet 75–9, 111, 160, 187
  Korean drama 64, 65, 75, 84, 137, 162–6, 192
  K-POP 17, 19, 64–8, 75, 84, 111, 137, 159–62, 192
  newspapers 92, 121–3
  public media 45, 56, 57, 74–5, 92
  public signage 95, 103–4, 156, 174–5
  TV shows 141, 166–8

medialect 141, 142, 167, 168
multicultural London English
    (MLE) 30–1, 86

native speaker 12–16, 41, 49–53, 59, 76,
    89, 93, 110, 148, 170, 177, 179, 182,
    183, 191
Nigerian English 38, 39
non inner-circle Englishes (NICE) 8, 10,
    13–15, 18, 20, 25, 33, 37, 46–51,
    69, 95, 98, 105, 108, 113, 123,
    177, 179, 180, 185–7, 189, 191,
    192
non-native speaker 12–16, 33, 39, 44,
    49–53, 76, 93, 110, 161

outer circle 7, 26, 30, 35, 58, 86, 89, 188,
    190

Pakistani English 188
Philippine English 190
pragmalinguistic errors 63, 64, 114–20

repertoires 66

Singlish 7, 28, 113, 126
South African Indian English 114, 157
standard English 8–9, 13–14, 27, 29, 32,
    33, 35–7, 40, 46–9, 60, 61, 77, 84,
    90, 105, 126, 135, 137, 147, 148,
    156, 166, 177, 178, 181, 182, 184–6,
    191–2. *See also* inner-circle standard

Thai English 78

World Englishes 8–9, 19, 27, 68, 69, 78,
    95, 113, 179

www.ingramcontent.com/pod-product-compliance
Lightning Source LLC
Chambersburg PA
CBHW062225300426
44115CB00012BA/2226